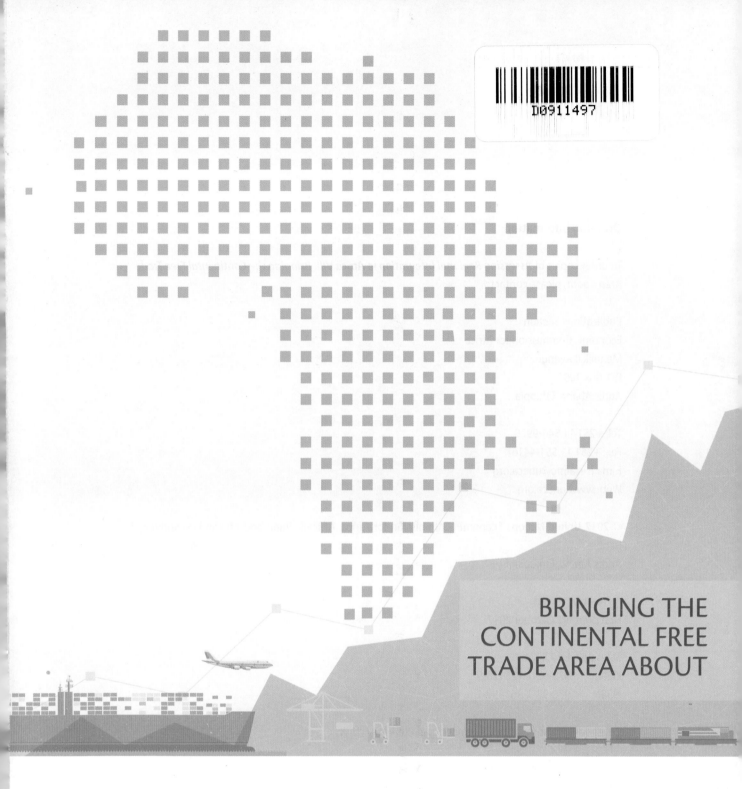

BRINGING THE
CONTINENTAL FREE
TRADE AREA ABOUT

ASSESSING REGIONAL
INTEGRATION IN AFRICA **VIII**

AFRICAN UNION

ECA

**AFRICAN DEVELOPMENT
BANK GROUP**

Ordering information

To order copies of *Assessing Regional Integration in Africa VIII: Bringing the Continental Free Trade Area About*, please contact:

Publications Section
Economic Commission for Africa
Menelik II Avenue
P.O. Box 3001
Addis Ababa, Ethiopia

Tel: +251 11 544-9900
Fax: +251 11 551-4416
E-mail: ecainfo@uneca.org
Web: www.uneca.org

Sales no.: E.17.II.K.4
ISBN: 978-92-1-125128-9
eISBN: 978-92-1-361559-1

Cover design and layout: ECA Printing and Publishing Unit

Printed in Addis Ababa by the ECA Printing and Publishing Unit. ISO 14001:2004 certified.
Printed on chlorine free paper.

Table of Contents

Acknowledgements

The eighth edition of Assessing Regional Integration in Africa (ARIA VIII) is a joint publication of the Economic Commission for Africa (ECA), the African Union Commission (AUC) and the African Development Bank (AfDB).

The report was prepared under the overall guidance of Abdallah Hamdok, ECA Deputy Executive Secretary and Chief Economist, with oversight by Stephen Karingi, Officer-in-Charge, Regional Integration and Trade Division.

The core team preparing the Report consisted of David Luke, Coordinator of ECA's African Trade Policy Centre (ATPC) and Jamie MacLeod, ATPC Trade Policy Fellow. William Davis, Associate Economic Affairs Officer at ECA supported the core team.

Background papers were provided by Mia Mikic (ESCAP), Elizabeth Gachuiri (UNCTAD), Joy Kategekwa (UNCTAD), Sebastián Hereros (ECLAC), Jan Vanheukelom (ECDPM), David Primack (ILEAP), James Gathii (Loyola University Chicago School of Law), Caroline Dommen (consutant), Kilara Suit (World Bank), Paul Brenton (World Bank), Frans Lammersen (OECD), Raffaela Muoio (OECD), Michael Roberts (WTO), Trudi Hartzenberg (TRALAC), Caroline Ncube (University of Cape Town), Jeremy de Beer (University of Ottawa) and Chidi Oguamanam (University of Ottawa); and Robert Tama Lisinge, Anthony Mehlwana and John Sloan (ECA).

The core team would like to acknowledge the support of ATPC colleagues, in particular, Senait Afework, Haimanot Assefa, Batanai Chikwene, Guillaume Gérout, Eden Lakew, Simon Mevel, Lily Sommer and Heini Suominen.

The core team is also grateful to the African Union Trade and Industry Commissioner Albert Muchanga for his encouragement to examine the issues in this report and to take the conclusions wherever they led. African Union Commission colleagues including Babajide Sodipo and Giles Landry Dossan provided valuable inputs to the report. Inye Nathan Briggs of the AfDB anchored the Bank's oversight of the report.

The following contributed to consultations on the report concept note and peer review of the draft report: Wafa Aidi, Judith Ameso, Patient Atcho, Joseph Atta-Mensah, Nassirou Ba, Beatrice Chaytor, Emmanuel Chinyama, Oswald Chinyamakobvu, Chiza Charles Chiumya, Adama Ekberg Coulibaly, Festus Fajana, Caroline Gomes Nogueira, Soteri Gatera, Kebour Ghenna, Grace Gondwe, Kiranne Guddoy, Million Habte, Khaled Hussein, Faizel Ismail, Phiri Israel, Susan Karungi, Aileen Kwa, Stephen Lande, Myranda Lutempo, Zodwa Florence Mabuza, Khauhelo Mawana, Mehdi Mehamha, Maximiliano Mendez-Parra, Neijwa Mohammed, Viola Morgan, Gimbi Moroda, Sanusha Naidu, Jane Nalunga, Ndiitah Ngipondoka-Robiati, Alou Niang, Halima Noor, Olawale Ogunkola, Christopher Onyango, Nassim Oulmane, Maharouf Oyolola, Laura Paez, Selsah Pasali, Guy Ranaivomanana, Prudence Sebahizi, Willie Shumba, Nozipho Simelane, Komi Tsowou and Sean Woolfrey.

A special mention goes to the Publications Section of ECA for ensuring the translation, design, printing and distribution of ARIA VIII.

Finally, ATPC would like to acknowledge the support of Global Affairs Canada to its work programme through a partnership that stretches back to 2004.

Foreword

The Continental Free Trade Area (CFTA) is the first flagship project of the African Union's Agenda 2063 and a key initiative in the industrialization and economic development of the continent. It has the potential to boost intra-African trade, stimulate investment and innovation, foster structural transformation, improve food security, enhance economic growth and export diversification, and rationalize the overlapping trade regimes of the main regional economic communities. Fundamentally, the CFTA aims to provide new impetus and dynamism to economic integration in Africa.

While Africa exports mainly commodities to the rest of the world, intra-African trade displays high concentrations of value-added products (and services). It is therefore of particular value to Africa's development. In recent years, intra-African trade has contributed to 57 per cent of the growth in Africa's exports of capital goods, 51 per cent of processed food and beverages, 46 per cent of consumer goods, 45 per cent of transport equipment and 44 per cent of processed industrial supplies. The CFTA provides a legal arrangement through which this promising trend can be extended to generate win-win gains for all participating African Union Member States.

Against this background, Assessing Regional Integration in Africa VIII is dedicated to "Bringing the CFTA About." After providing a status update of regional integration in Africa, the report considers how to ensure that the potential of the CFTA is fulfilled.

It has long been known that a major challenge in Africa is not a lack of good policies or strategies, but a lack of their effective implementation. Crucial to implementation is an understanding of the political economy underpinning economic integration in Africa. Conceptual issues in this area form the theoretical basis of the report. The insights from this perspective can help to frame the policy choices and institutional arrangements required for effective implementation. The report demonstrates that the CFTA potentially embodies a "win-win" approach to sharing its benefits, so that all countries in Africa benefit and the interests of vulnerable communities are carefully addressed. To this end, the CFTA will require "flanking policies" that governments can use to smooth the impact of the CFTA and a strong focus on achieving tangible outcomes from the Boosting Intra-African Trade Action Plan at national, regional and continental levels. Recommendations are made to assure mutual gains for all countries, irrespective of their current level of development.

These recommendations cannot be fulfilled without strategic investments and financing. The report considers methods of financing for bringing the CFTA about, including the role of domestic resource mobilization, non-traditional financial vehicles and regional Aid-for-Trade. Financing must, however, be buttressed with effective implementing institutions and an appropriate CFTA governance structure. The report emphasizes the need to ensure that CFTA institutional structures are based on practical approaches that work in Africa.

The context of this report is a changing world trade environment in which people's scepticism of trade agreements has become common. Africans are also frustrated by the lack of progress in the Doha Development Agenda at the World Trade Organization. These shifts call for a renewed vision of the role of trade in Africa's development trajectory. Bringing the CFTA about is part of that vision, in a way that benefits all African countries and leaves nobody behind, in line with the aspirations of Agenda 2063 and the Sustainable Development Goals. It is also a vision for trade policy coherence in Africa in the changing global environment.

These are crucial messages that should guide the design and implementation of the CFTA. We commend them to African policy makers, to stakeholders at all levels and to our development partners.

Moussa Faki Mahamat
Chairperson
African Union Commission

Vera Songwe
UN Under-Secretary-General and
Executive Secretary,
Economic Commission for Africa

Akinwumi Adesina
President
African Development
Bank Group

Report Structure, Key Messages and Policy Recommendations

Report Structure

- **Chapter 1—Introduction** brings thematic issues into focus and provides a general guide to the report.

- **Chapter 2—Status of Regional Integration in Africa** is a recurrent part of the report, and outlines trends in Africa's economic integration at national, regional and continental levels. It provides an update on the Africa Regional Integration Index.

- **Chapter 3—Conceptual Issues in the Political Economy of Integration and the CFTA** provides insights on political economy dimensions leading, or constraining, regional integration in Africa and the CFTA. These are framed across five "lenses" that help to unpack and explain the complexities of regional integration. Consideration of the political economy is crucial for "bringing the CFTA about" and the messages from this chapter are mainstreamed throughout those which follow it.

- **Chapter 4—Revisiting the Case for the CFTA** outlines the theoretical and empirical rationale for the CFTA, and provides some measures of potential trade gains. It also provides a progress update on the CFTA negotiations and its envisaged scope as a point of reference for subsequent chapters.

- **Chapter 5—A Win-Win Approach to the CFTA: Sharing the Benefits** focuses on distributional impacts of the CFTA across the broad range of African countries party to the CFTA negotiations, as well as the vulnerable communities whose interests must be carefully considered. It is vital that the CFTA be designed such that its benefits are shared in accordance with Sustainable Development Goal No. 1, that "no one will be left behind."

- **Chapter 6—A Win-Win Approach to the CFTA: Critical Policies** is a partner to Chapter 5 and offers policy recommendations to ensure that the interests of different stakeholders and vulnerable groups are met. It proposes approaches to the substantive content of the CFTA Agreement and to its accompanying policies.

- **Chapter 7—Financing for Bringing the CFTA About** sets out a framework for analysing and assessing the implementation costs associated with the CFTA, including structural adjustment costs accruing to the private sector, tariff revenue losses, implementation costs and flanking policy costs for the public sector. Resource mobilization and development assistance is discussed as a means of financing these costs.

- **Chapter 8—CFTA Governance** brings trade governance under the spotlight with recommendations on different institutional aspects of the CFTA, including the role of a CFTA Secretariat, and the national, regional and continental institutional structures that will be necessary for successful implementation. It also discusses the possible role of the regional economic communities (RECs) under a CFTA regime.

- **Chapter 9—The CFTA in a Changing Trade Landscape** reviews the evolving international trading environment, such as rising scepticism towards trade agreements, the implications of potential mega-regional trade agreements, growing trade ties with emerging economies, the period after the African Growth and Opportunity Act (AGOA) and Brexit. A key recommendation is that the CFTA should present a coherent trade policy response.

- **Chapter 10—Phase 2 Negotiations: Competition Policy, Intellectual Property Rights and E-commerce** outlines the main issues for negotiators in the second phase of the CFTA negotiations.

Key Messages and Policy Recommendations

Chapter 2: Status of Regional Integration in Africa

Key messages

Rapid conclusion of the CFTA is important to keep on track for achieving the African Economic Community (AEC) as foreseen in the Treaty Establishing the African Economic Community (commonly known as the Abuja Treaty). While progress towards achieving the AEC has been made, some RECs are far from achieving regional customs unions as building blocks for continental integration. The CFTA can help bridge this gap.

The level of integration in Africa varies highly across RECs. REC members also differ highly in their degree of integration within their respective RECs, as can be seen from the Africa Regional Integration Index.

African countries cooperate significantly on the coordination of mining policies, peace and security and public health. However, there is further scope for beneficial coordination. They are also liberalizing their visa regimes for other Africans and aim to achieve a protocol on free movement of persons, although for some African countries visa requirements are still restrictive for nationals of other African countries.

A vast range of projects is under way to upgrade Africa's infrastructure, but for now infrastructure deficits are holding back the continent's development and the expansion of intra-regional trade (and will need to be addressed for the CFTA to reach its full potential).

A lot of existing intra-African trade takes place within established REC free trade areas (FTAs) or customs unions. The value of the CFTA will be in bringing all African countries to this level of integration across the continent.

Africa has progressed on eliminating non-tariff barriers (NTBs) and facilitating trade, but there is still more to do, including implementing the World Trade Organization (WTO) Trade Facilitation Agreement.

Chapter 3: Conceptual Issues in the Political Economy of Integration and the CFTA

Key messages

The structural and historical foundations of Africa's political economy need to be understood and appreciated, but are not deterministic. Deliberate policy choices and action can change the status quo and overcome barriers, including entrenched national interests or economic configurations. However, this requires political leadership **to use the political economy windows of opportunity.**

Trade negotiators conducting the CFTA negotiations are driven by their experiences, expertise and capacities, but may well bring more caution to the CFTA than the ambitions expressed by their heads of state.

Historically, trade agreements in Africa have shown high levels of ambition and lower levels of implementation, mainly because they receive less political support as they relate to medium- to long-term gains, rather than short-term visible results.

Policy recommendations

As the CFTA faces the complexity of aligning interests across 55 very different African countries, flexibilities and variable geometry are needed, and compromise will be required. The CFTA should be designed (and supported with measures) to ensure that it benefits the interests of its wide range of stakeholders.

The CFTA institutions must be designed such that they serve their intended functions, rather than imitate unachievable or idealistic best practice examples.

The CFTA must be constructed to carefully balance the national interests of influential states and coalitions of smaller states, because if the gains are perceived as being captured by only a few countries, trade agreements are more likely to unravel. Effective implementation can be supported if influential states champion the CFTA through the application of their diplomatic, financial and technocratic resources.

The interests of private sector actors and civil society organizations engaging in the CFTA process must also be considered. Mechanisms for consultation must be attuned to small private sector and civil society actors, and to vulnerable groups.

Development assistance can be better used for narrowing the implementation gap if it avoids overemphasizing institutional forms or incentivizing empty "signalling."

Although the political economy of integration in Africa helps to explain "why things are the way they are," moving forward from there requires dedicated actions of developmental states, led by political leadership that is committed to national developmental goals and empowered by competent and professional bureaucracies.

Chapter 4: Revisiting the Case for the CFTA
Key messages
Studies imply positive gains for the CFTA with intra-African trade expanding by an estimated 50–200 per cent over the long run. Additional benefits include facilitating trade in food security products, improving the stability of fragile countries, enhancing firms' access to inputs and intermediate goods, and reducing the costs of innovation.

Since 2000, intra-African trade has contributed to a large share of the growth in Africa's industrial export sectors, and is therefore especially valuable for Africa's industrialization. By reducing the tariff and non-tariff barriers that constrain this trade, the CFTA seeks to contribute to Africa's industrialization and structural transformation.

While the Abuja Treaty envisages the integration process as culminating in the AEC, attention must first focus on the CFTA, including designing and implementing it. Later stages of the Abuja Treaty should be addressed sequentially.

The CFTA has garnered considerable support at the highest policy-making levels within Africa. Designing the CFTA at the technical level, and ensuring its effective implementation, is now the critical task at hand.

Policy recommendations
The CFTA should include complementary policies to maximize its gains but also to ensure that its benefits are shared more equally to produce a win-win outcome for all countries. Such policies include measures to improve

trade facilitation and reduce transaction costs, and the Boosting Intra-African Trade (BIAT) Action Plan—the "sister" initiative to the CFTA that provides a basis for addressing the trade barriers faced by African countries.

The African Union Commission (AUC) should be mandated to undertake a thorough review of the Abuja Treaty with a view towards modernizing it so as to address the challenges of early 21st century African economic integration.

Chapter 5: A Win-Win Approach to the CFTA: Sharing the Benefits

Key messages
Sharing the benefits of the CFTA is important not only for reasons of equity, but also to ensure that the agreement actually works for countries at different levels of development. Trade agreements that are not win-win tend to remain unimplemented or unravel because partner countries have little interest in their application.

Africa's countries span a diversity of economic configurations and are accordingly expected to be affected by the CFTA in divergent ways. Hence measures that support the particular needs of different types of country will be needed.

The CFTA will involve structural adjustment—indeed one of its goals is to contribute to Africa's industrial transformation. Implicit in this will be structural adjustment costs in the short run as labour and capital are reallocated to respond to trade opportunities and threats. However, structural adjustment costs are likely to be modest—given the low level of intra-African trade and the fact that much of this trade already flows through existing REC FTAs

The CFTA provides a liberalized market to drive agricultural productivity and agro-industry. Those countries with strong agricultural production and potential will be particularly well placed to tap into new opportunities provided in the agro-industry and agro-processing sectors, helping to satisfy Africa's food security requirements and reduce its food import bill to make the continent more food self-sufficient. The African market has already accounted for over 50 per cent of the growth in Africa's processed food and beverage exports since 2000.

The liberalized market will also drive value addition to natural resources. The majority of African countries are classified as resource rich. Tariffs on raw materials are already low and so the CFTA will do little to further promote these exports. However, by lowering intra-African tariffs on intermediates and final goods, the CFTA will create additional opportunities for adding value to natural resources. Perhaps most important for these countries, the CFTA will offer opportunities for export diversification into other industrialized export sectors, but this will require investment and new productive capacities.

The CFTA can enhance the connectivity of land-locked countries, but they require additional accompanying measures to improve transit, trade-related infrastructure and trade facilitation.

In the long run, the CFTA will be beneficial to vulnerable groups—notably smallholder farmers, informal cross-border traders, women and youth—by expanding agricultural trade opportunities, improving trade facilitation and creating jobs.

Policy recommendations
Although the CFTA provides all African countries—irrespective of current levels of industrial development—with opportunities, certain countries may require further support in realizing these opportunities. The BIAT Action Plan provides the framework that member states can use to prioritize the policy reforms required to derive the full benefits of the CFTA.

Tariff revenue losses due to the CFTA will be modest and can be more equitably balanced across countries by allowing for flexibilities, such as exclusion lists, but these must not be so pervasive as to undermine the gains from the CFTA.

To help firms—predominantly small- and medium-sized enterprises—engage in intra-African trade, investments must be made in trade information and facilitating access to trade finance. Factor market integration, including the improved movement of persons and cross-border investments, would be especially valuable in fostering regional value chains.

Special measures are required for vulnerable groups that could be hurt by trade liberalization under the CFTA. The CFTA and its accompanying measures should ensure

that these groups share the gains of the CFTA and are protected where necessary. However, as a second-best option, exclusion list provisions and safeguards can also be used to protect such groups where necessary. Here it will be important to ensure that the mechanism for adopting safeguards is sufficiently accessible for less-developed CFTA member countries. These groups will also require close monitoring and evaluation to track the impact of these measures.

Smallholder farmers (around 53 per cent of Africa's agricultural producers) can be supported by measures to promote their integration into larger value gains, simplified rules of origin requirements and help for them to meet sanitary and phyto-sanitary export standards. Such farmers may also require capital and reskilling to focus their production on export opportunities.

Tariffs will be reduced, helping to make it more affordable for informal cross-border traders to operate through formal channels. The CFTA can further support this group with trade facilitation and trade information measures, along the lines of the Simplified Trade Regime in the Common Market for Eastern and Southern Africa (COMESA), which simplifies clearing procedures and the requirements to qualify for the COMESA preferential duties for a common list of products.

Women can be supported by their explicit involvement in the design and processes of the CFTA, including through national consultations and by including more female negotiators. Women account for approximately 70 per cent of informal cross-border traders and can be supported here with improvements to storage facilities, illuminated border areas and hygiene facilities. Women can also benefit from initiatives to connect female agricultural workers to export food markets.

For youth, the CFTA will help to drive the structural transformation that is required to produce new jobs and absorb new entrants into the labour force and to move Africa from capital-intensive commodities towards labour-intensive sectors. Supporting Africa's youth will require improved access to credit and initiatives such as tech incubators and accelerators, as well as revamped policies in education and skills development.

Chapter 6: A Win-win Approach to the CFTA: Critical Policies

Key messages

The BIAT Action Plan is the framework for flanking policies to fully exploit the opportunities of the CFTA, targeting Africa's trade barriers in seven clusters: **trade policy, trade facilitation, productive capacity, trade-related infrastructure, trade finance, trade information and factor market integration**.

While improvements to physical infrastructure, such as roads and ports are important, these must be flanked by addressing the non-physical barriers to transport and trade. Strategic logistics management and the supply chain approach should be mainstreamed, not only in the continent's regional infrastructure initiatives, but also in management of trade corridors.

Facilitating intra-African investment is critical to allow the flow of much-needed resources for transforming Africa's agriculture and industry.

Services liberalization and regulation are increasingly important, both for facilitating trade in services and with services as an important component in traded goods. Services constitute roughly 70 per cent of global gross domestic product and 60 per cent of employment, and accounted for a quarter of world trade in 2014.

Policy recommendations

It is important to "get right" six key components of the CFTA—NTBs, rules of origin, investment and cross-border movement of persons, services liberalization and regulation, trade remedies, and monitoring and evaluation.

To get the NTBs right, a NTB mechanism should be included in the CFTA. Rather than duplicating the existing NTB mechanisms of the RECs this should build on their successes by expanding their operations across Africa to include trade between and within all RECs.

Getting rules of origin right will require balancing the desire of more-developed countries for product-specific rules with more accessible rules of origin favoured by less-developed countries. It is suggested to limit product-specific rules to only the most controversial or sensitive products and apply simple and liberal rules of origin as far as possible; to use simple rules of origin

over a transitionary five-year period; and to include preferential rules of origin to help make it easier for Africa's less-developed countries to satisfy rules of origin requirements.

In the investment component of investment and cross-border movement of persons, a fully fledged, standalone investment chapter in the CFTA Agreement is recommended (rather than being part of the services component of the negotiations). It would necessarily mean that all aspects related to supply of services through establishment of commercial presence would be looked at. For cross-border movement of persons, negotiators should design an approach that does not take away from African entrepreneurs what they already have in their RECs, while creating new opportunities for inter-REC movement.

Getting services right requires an approach that is ambitious but realistic, flexible, credible and inclusive, building on the existing REC achievements and challenges in services liberalization and regulatory cooperation. For liberalization, flexibility would entail sticking with what Member States already know. For regulatory cooperation, this involves deploying the most appropriate mechanism—formal or informal—based on sector-specific variables. It may entail harmonization in certain sectors, Mutual Recognition Agreements in others, treaties or more informal approaches.

Trade remedies are a crucial fail-safe for countries wary that competition could damage certain domestic industries. Getting them right in the CFTA will require regional investigating authorities, which will help extend remedies to small and less-developed African countries as well as set up a system that would enable these countries to protect themselves from more advanced international competitors.

Monitoring and evaluation is needed to oversee the compliance of each country with its obligations under the CFTA, to track progress with the BIAT Action Plan, and to ensure that the CFTA is contributing to Africa's development goals. A self-assessment monitoring and evaluation "scorecard" is recommended, as is the collection of data by gender and vulnerable group.

Overall, securing the BIAT Action Plan's benefits will require an implementing institutional structure, possibly combined with that of the CFTA to avoid institutional duplication; a continental framework for monitoring and evaluation, which can also be combined with the CFTA's; and resources for the BIAT initiatives.

Chapter 7: Financing for Bringing the CFTA About

Key messages

Financing is required to bring about the CFTA and meet its implementation costs. The private sector will require financing options to retrain labour and repurpose capital as structural adjustment takes place in response to new trade opportunities and challenges. In the public sector, support will be required to offset lower tariff revenues (though the impact of the CFTA is likely to be small); to finance the implementation of CFTA provisions and reforms; and to fund the BIAT Action Plan.

Financing in Africa has to be increasingly based on domestic public and private resources. This will help to overcome challenges with official development assistance (ODA), including risks with perpetuating donor-driven, rather than Africa-led initiatives, and fostering donor "signalling," where actions are taken superficially to satisfy donor obligations rather than drive development. Self-financing will help to improve ownership and responsibility for projects, and in turn drive implementation.

Aid-for-Trade, an initiative launched in 2006, will remain important for bringing the CFTA about, particularly for Africa's poorest countries with little access to private finance and low levels of domestic resources. It may also remain important for Africa's lower-middle-income countries over the short run as they mobilize their own domestic resources. Aid-for-Trade—and especially regional Aid-for-Trade—is the particular vehicle of choice for leveraging ODA towards the CFTA. Aid-for-Trade disbursements to Africa have recently risen strongly to $14 billion, more than twice the amount during the 2002–05 baseline period.

Policy recommendations

African governments must commit to enhancing domestic resource mobilization. Domestic revenue collection can be improved by making tax systems fairer, more transparent and effective, tackling corruption and weak institutional capacities, and addressing narrow tax bases and pervasive tax avoidance and evasion. Innovative approaches to self-financing are

also needed. Strategies include leveraging pension funds, insurance funds, private equity, the diaspora market, public–private partnerships, and stemming illicit financial flows. Even minor improvements in domestic resource mobilization can contribute to the costs associated with implementing the CFTA and its accompanying measures.

Self-financing can be pursued with the AU's proposed 0.2 per cent levy on imported goods into Africa. The proposed levy is an important tool for self-financing the AU's operations and projects of Agenda 2063, including the CFTA. WTO compatibility of the levy can be eased through the creation of the CFTA, which will allow African country members of the WTO to circumvent the normal WTO requirement of non-discrimination between WTO members.

Care should, however, be taken with sequencing—if the CFTA is not in place prior to the AU levy, there will be a period during which African countries would be breaking this rule. The levy could face further WTO compatibility challenges with WTO tariff binding schedules, though ad hoc measures could address the violation of the binding schedules. Against all these issues African countries may apply for a WTO waiver.

Care must also be taken with compatibility between the AU levy and Africa's other regional trade agreements (RTAs). Future agreements could be designed to allow for compatibility with the AU levy.

Regional Aid-for-Trade programmes should be improved in four ways: better mainstreaming regional initiatives within national planning; better aligning regional Aid-for-Trade projects with Africa policy frameworks, such as the BIAT; more closely involving the private sector in project design; and strengthening institutional mechanisms to ensure smooth in-country coordination for regional and subregional programmes.

Chapter 8: CFTA governance
Key messages

The current restructuring of the AU—as part of the AU reform—provides an opportunity to determine how the AU can be reformed so that flagship projects like the CFTA can be better institutionalized and implemented. However, designing an institutional framework for the CFTA will be challenging if the main aspects of the AU reform have not been finalized.

The links between the AU reform and the institutional framework for the CFTA might lead some Member States to consider establishing a totally independent institution for implementing the CFTA. This body could take several forms: a specialized agency of the AU or, in a more extreme approach, an "African WTO"—a new international and inter-governmental organization. Alternatively, CFTA institutions could be hosted within the AUC as a CFTA department, or even within the AUC Department of Trade and Industry.

The structure of the Abuja Treaty should be the platform on which to build an institutional framework for the implementation of the CFTA at the continental level. This ensures that the proposed CFTA institutional structure is consistent with the Treaty. Still, African continental integration should not "hide" behind the Treaty but reopen debate on how best to integrate the continent so as to achieve the principles and objectives elaborated in it, for today's world. It may be that the pathway to continental integration envisaged in the Abuja Treaty can be amended to take stock of Africa's achievements in the last 26 years and rerouted to bypass revealed challenges along this pathway. Whatever approach is adopted, the accumulated wide expertise in trade integration matters gained by the RECs must be incorporated into the CFTA institutional structure, especially as they are the building blocks of the CFTA.

The vision outlined in the Abuja Treaty suggests that as the CFTA is transformed into a continent-wide customs union and adopts "common policies," the RECs will gradually cease their major role in forming trade policy. The main authority for trade policy will graduate to the continental level as the CFTA works to consolidate Africa's overlapping "spaghetti bowl" of FTAs. Such consolidation will enable Africa to economize the resources now required to undertake these activities in each of the RECs. It is expected that the RECs will contribute to continental trade policy through their roles in the CFTA institutional architecture.

Policy recommendations
Five guiding principles are important in the formation of the CFTA's institutions: Use the Abuja Treaty as the backbone to the CFTA institutional form; use and empower existing structures of African integration where available; ensure that the institutions of the CFTA are accessible to the African people; support the joint implementation of the BIAT Action Plan alongside the

CFTA; and develop practical institutional forms, rather than those which are idealistic.

But first things first: Interim steps towards an ideal institutional structure are required. The most important first step in approaching a CFTA institutional structure will be the requirement of each CFTA partner state to designate or create a ministerial level agency that will be responsible for implementing and communicating on CFTA issues. This follows the successful approach used in EAC, in which lead agencies for each country were charged with coordinating implementation and application of EAC commitments at the national level.

The CFTA architecture should be buttressed with regional and national institutions. These can be based on those envisaged in the BIAT Action Plan, but should use existing regional and national structures, including the RECs and national ministries responsible for trade or regional integration.

Finally, the CFTA should draw on the positive experiences of COMESA and use non-litigious dispute settlement mechanisms to address CFTA-related disputes where possible. Its dispute settlement arrangements should be inter-governmental. And to ensure that the individuals' rights under the CFTA are fully implemented, national courts of the CFTA Member States will be important.

Chapter 9: CFTA in a Changing Trade Landscape

Key messages
Trade protectionism seems to be increasing in some developed countries while developing countries are increasingly applying trade defence measures against other developing countries.

Trade with the emerging market economies, including China, India, Brazil and Turkey, has diversified Africa's trade from an overdependence on traditional markets. However, this trade is concentrated in extractive industry exports and will not in itself adequately support African industrialization, which must instead leverage the opportunities of intra-African trade. Intra-African trade accounts for a far larger share of growth in Africa's value-added and industrialized exports than does Africa's trade with any other market.

Policy recommendations

African countries should use the apparent slowdown in the build-up of mega-regional trade agreements as breathing space in which to establish a strong and unified CFTA with which to better tackle future trading issues.

The CFTA should present itself as a platform for solidifying Africa's position on the new trade issues, such as e-commerce; micro, small and medium-sized enterprises; domestic regulation of services; and investment facilitation.

Africa should push for the UK's post-Brexit trade policy and trade-related development assistance to reinforce Africa's continental integration agenda, including the CFTA. Relatedly, it should consider using Brexit to reopen EPA discussions for better achieving the trade interests of Africa.

African leaders should heed the caution of integration presented by Brexit and ensure that integration projects in Africa, including the CFTA, are cognizant of the potential pitfalls of integration and responsive to their root causes, including people's perceptions of sovereignty loss.

They should also conclude the CFTA and press forward with continental integration so that Africa can address the post-AGOA agenda in the United States as a single entity. This will ensure that individual FTAs with "can-do" countries, as in the current United States strategy, do not pick apart the African integration agenda.

Chapter 10: Phase 2 Negotiations— Competition and Intellectual Property Rights and E-commerce

Key findings

Competition and intellectual property will be part of phase 2 of the CFTA negotiations and there is scope for also introducing issues of e-commerce and the digital economy. Negotiations in these policy areas are expected to be launched after the conclusion of the negotiations in goods and services.

As African countries are affected in different ways by anti-competitive practices, a regional approach is needed for dealing with cross-border cartels, mergers, acquisitions and abuse. National competition laws operate on a "territorial" basis and are incapable of addressing cross-border anti-competitive practices. The CFTA can be used as a vehicle to address such cross-border competition issues. In doing so it can draw on the successes of COMESA approach to cross-border competition challenges.

Procedural and substantive failures around intellectual property (IP) issues have contributed to a backlash against trade agreements, notably the WTO's Agreement on Trade-related Aspects of Intellectual Property (TRIPS) and EAC's early experience.

Innovation in Africa is different, occurring mostly in the informal sector and in the absence of strong intellectual property institutions: an intellectual property framework in the CFTA must reflect this. Traditional, formal IP protections cannot exist in the absence of strong IP institutions and may be ill-suited to the African context in which industries operate successfully without IP.

E-commerce and the rise of the digital economy is causing a shift in traditional economic sectors and the emergence of new digital products and services. The scale of this process is considerable and this will alter Africa's trade and industrialization pathway.

Policy recommendations

A competition framework should be designed to implement any decision to develop competition law and policy in the CFTA negotiations. Existing competition policy and legislation at national and regional levels must be taken into account.

The CFTA provides an opportunity to close gaps and strengthen existing competition law frameworks both domestically and regionally. The CFTA should help countries with no competition laws to enact some in conformity to an agreed approach as envisaged in a continental competition framework.

CFTA Member States need to tackle the following specific and immediate priorities:

- Agree on a common objective for the CFTA competition framework.

- Identify and understand the provisions of the present competition law frameworks, identify gaps in each of the approaches, and devise a means of rationalizing all systems within the framework of any CFTA competition law.

- Establish other parameters/areas of law that need to support implementation of the CFTA competition framework and formulate key features of these laws, synchronizing them with the preferred approach so as to allow for seamless implementation.

- Secure the cooperation of the various Member States and their agencies.

- Rationalize key public international law, regional law and domestic law issues that may impact on the legality of a CFTA competition framework.

- Pay attention to consumer protection issues, how to delineate them from competition and how to deal with diversity in legislative and institutional arrangements in this context.

A CFTA Enforcement Cooperation Protocol on Competition Law and Policy should be developed to help implement competition provisions.

An agreement regarding intellectual property in the CFTA must seek to overcome several hurdles. They include overlapping subregional IP organizations, the proliferation of IP matters in RECs, and misalignment with the continent's overall development goals. The agreement should also consider the backlash against the inclusion of IP in free trade agreements. This can be done by addressing the particular demands of African innovation with appropriate procedural and substantive principles.

On procedure, a CFTA intellectual property agreement should be negotiated, while on substance, a CFTA intellectual property agreement should address the particular challenges of the African context.

An African digital industrial strategy is recommended to address the opportunities and disruptive challenges entailed by the digital economy. The CFTA should provide a platform for consolidating a common stance on e-commerce rules and for establishing an integrated market for Africa's own digital businesses.

Chapter 1
Introduction

The establishment of the Continental Free Trade Area (CFTA) is a major milestone in the long march of African integration. As foreseen in the Treaty Establishing the African Economic Community (commonly known as the Abuja Treaty), which entered into force in 1994, the integration process is to culminate in the African Economic Community. A review of the current status of Africa's economic integration is the subject of Chapter 2.

The CFTA aspires to liberalize trade between African countries across the continent and to build on the considerable successes already achieved within Africa's regional economic communities (RECs). By doing so, the CFTA is set to facilitate intra-African trade; foster regional value chains that can facilitate integration into the global economy; and energize industrialization, competitiveness and innovation—and thereby contribute to African economic and social progress and development. These issues have been the focus of several earlier editions of the *Assessing Regional Integration in Africa (ARIA)* series, notably *ARIA V*, which made the case for a CFTA.

The CFTA's developmental approach is solidly grounded in Africa's political economy realities and development challenges. Any trade agreement embodies a confluence of broad political economy considerations underpinned by such principles as variable geometry, flexibility, and special and differential treatment. These are typically seen through such modalities as exceptions and exclusions, the time frame for implementation of commitments, and trade remedies, etc.

An ambitious initiative for the world's second-largest continent, the CFTA comprises the 55 member states of the African Union (AU) and 8 AU-recognized RECs with varying trade liberalization legal frameworks, plus a tripartite trade integration initiative for 3 of those regions. Matching ambition with implementation will be a critical challenge. To quote Nkosazana Dlamini-Zuma, former Chairperson of the African Union Commission (AUC), speaking at an event on 6 October 2014, "I don't think Africa is short of policies. We have to implement. That is where the problem is." Realism requires an astute appreciation of the political economy of integration and the implications of implementing trade reforms. Chapter 3 looks at the political economy of the CTFA and offers a conceptual approach to understanding it.

The CFTA will be more than a traditional free trade agreement and will contain several elements of a single market. The scope of the CFTA Agreement (discussed in Chapter 4) covers trade in goods and services, investment, intellectual property rights and competition policy; whereas a traditional free trade agreement would often require only the elimination of tariffs and quotas on trade in goods. Norms and regulations related to services, for example, are typically harmonized when a single market is set up. The inclusion of services for negotiation alongside trade in goods recognizes that for 21st century value chains, services are critical inputs into the production of trade in goods. The services sector already contributes a substantial share to the output of most African economies.

The CFTA is also the first flagship project of the AU's Agenda 2063 and a keystone initiative that can help leverage Africa's progress towards attaining several Sustainable Development Goals, including targets for no poverty (Goal 1), food security (Goal 2), gender equality (Goal 5), affordable and clean energy (Goal 7), decent work and economic growth (Goal 8), industry, innovation and infrastructure (Goal 9), reduced inequalities (Goal 10), responsible consumption and production (Goal 12), climate action (Goal 13), peace, justice and strong institutions (Goal 16) and partnerships for the goals (Goal 17). The international community must focus on Goal 1 by keeping the pledge that "no one will be left behind... starting with the furthest behind first."

Chapter 5 looks into this pledge and highlights the CFTA as a means of eradicating poverty. It considers how different countries with different economic configurations can benefit from the CFTA and its distributional impacts at the subnational level and across vulnerable groups. It is essential that the benefits of the CFTA be shared equitably across the continent (a win-win approach).

The CFTA is being rolled out in parallel with the Boosting Intra-African Trade (BIAT) Action Plan, which aims to address the constraints and challenges of intra-African trade relative to seven priority policy clusters: trade policy reform, trade facilitation, productive capacity, trade-related infrastructure, trade finance, trade information and factor market integration. Effective implementation of the BIAT Action Plan will be crucial for minimizing the challenges and maximizing the gains of tariff and services liberalization, and for ensuring that African economic operators and countries can take advantage of the CFTA. It is also important that the substantive content of the CFTA—including provisions on non-tariff barriers (NTBs), services, investment, and free movement of persons, trade remedies and monitoring and evaluation—be addressed. Both the BIAT flanking policies and the substantive content of the CFTA are examined in Chapter 6, which considers critical policies for ensuring a win-win CFTA.

Financing the CFTA is the subject of Chapter 7. A framework is presented for analyzing the implementation costs, including the structural adjustment costs, to both the private and public sectors. Domestic resource mobilization and development assistance are also discussed as options for financing the initiative.

At the heart of the CFTA is a developmental approach that recognizes the need for trade liberalization to proceed, and at the same time, address supply capacities and promote structural transformation. This approach is not only unconventional but also sidesteps many aspects of the carefully defined schedule of the Abuja Treaty's progression towards the African Economic Community. One option for the legal contextualization of the CFTA Agreement is as an amendment to the Abuja Treaty, which would bring the Abuja Treaty up to date and refocus its operationalization for the task at hand—implementing the CFTA. These issues are discussed in Chapter 8, which looks into questions of trade governance, including the role of RECs at the regional level, and strategic public–private partnerships at the national level.

Chapter 9 situates the CFTA in a changing world. While Africa has placed "developmental regionalism" at the centre of its strategy for growth and structural transformation, current global trends show a growing scepticism towards regional integration and trade agreements. It is therefore critical that Africa not backtrack on its commitments to continental trade liberalization and related structural reforms through the CFTA. Trade remains a key driver of productivity, growth and welfare gains. It is also an important means of implementation and financing of the Africa development agenda. However, current concerns about the unequal distributive impact of trade require efforts to ensure a progressive pro-poor CFTA (as discussed in Chapters 5 and 6). This is important in a world marked both by recent tectonic changes in the outlook of several major international trading partners and a stagnation at the multilateral trade negotiating fora.

Finally, Chapter 10 looks ahead to the second phase of the CFTA negotiations and addresses key issues for achieving a development-friendly outcome for competition policy and intellectual property rights. A case is made for including electronic commerce in the second phase of the negotiations in light of the rapid digitilization of modern economies.

Chapter 2
Status of Regional Integration in Africa

This chapter provides the economic context for the Continental Free Trade Area (CFTA), with a focus on the major shifts in African regional integration since *ARIA VII*, published in April 2016. The chapter summarizes integration by country, and developments in mining, agriculture, health, peace and security, financial integration, free movement of persons, infrastructure integration, trade integration and trade trends.

During the period under review, Africa continued to take steps towards further integration, with national and regional policies in a range of areas.

Economic context[1]

Africa's gross domestic product (GDP) growth in 2016 was estimated at 1.7 per cent (ECA, 2017a), with economic performance among countries diverging: Côte d'Ivoire grew by 8 per cent, the United Republic of Tanzania by 7 per cent, Kenya and Senegal by 6 per cent, Cameroon by 5.3 per cent, Central African Republic by 5.1 per cent, Mozambique by 4.2 per cent, Ghana by 3.8 per cent, Mauritius by 3.6 per cent, Gabon by 3.2 per cent, Morocco by 1.7 per cent, Chad by 1.1 per cent and South Africa by 0.6 per cent. The oil-dependent Nigerian economy contracted by 1.6 per cent while that of Equatorial Guinea contracted by 4.5 per cent.

Over the last two years, inflation generally continued to decline in Africa, reflecting prudent monetary policies, decreasing global prices for oil and other commodities and good harvests, although some countries experienced a sharp rise due to currency depreciation, and they responded with tighter monetary policy.

Inflation in 2016 was 10 per cent and is expected to remain at around that rate in 2017. Inflation was 2.3 per cent in Central Africa in 2016, 5.3 per cent in East Africa, 8.7 per cent in North Africa, 11.4 per cent in Southern Africa and 13 per cent in West Africa.

North Africa has the largest fiscal deficit of Africa's subregions, although it declined slightly due to a narrowing fiscal deficit in Egypt. Central Africa's fiscal deficit increased from 5.1 per cent of GDP in 2015 to 5.8 per cent in 2016. This was mainly due to expansionary fiscal policies in the context of lower oil revenues in these countries: Cameroon (public expenditure on transport and power infrastructure), Equatorial Guinea (increased public investment in infrastructure) and Republic of the Congo (spending on public sector wages).

East Africa's fiscal deficit increased from 4.0 per cent of GDP to 4.6 per cent in 2016, owing to expansionary fiscal policies, mainly in Ethiopia (investment in infrastructure), Kenya (investment in a new railway line, sharply increased government salaries and transfers to new counties) and Uganda (investment in hydropower projects).

West Africa's fiscal deficit rose from 1.8 per cent to 2.8 per cent of GDP in 2016, largely reflecting increased public spending in Nigeria (especially on security), an increased minimum wage and higher spending on security and infrastructure in Côte d'Ivoire, and election-related expenses and greater spending on public sector wages in Ghana.

Southern Africa's fiscal deficit remained unchanged at 4.4 per cent of GDP. Though South Africa's deficit increased because of slow growth in revenue and heavier spending, this increase was counterbalanced at the regional level by declines in the fiscal deficits of Mozambique (which enacted capital spending cuts), Namibia and Zambia (which improved tax enforcement and postponed spending on large investment projects).

Figure 2.1. shows recent trends in Africa's current account deficits by country groupings. The decline in commodity prices has reduced the continent's export earnings, resulting in a much wider current account deficit.

African currencies continued to depreciate in 2016. Angola, Ethiopia and Nigeria devalued their currencies. The CFA franc is expected to depreciate gradually. Egypt floated its currency in 2016, a year in which the South African rand was volatile. The Ghanaian cedi was stable

Figure 2.1.
Africa's current account deficit

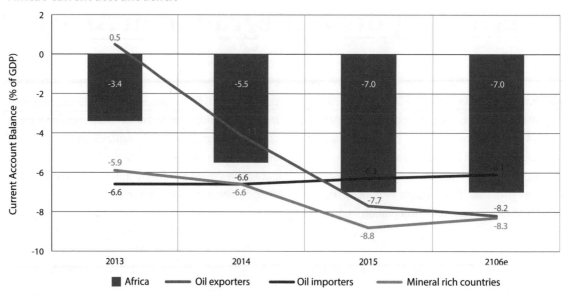

Note: "e" stands for estimates.
Source: ECA (2017a).

in 2016, after considerable volatility in recent years, though gradual depreciation is expected.

A sharper slowdown than anticipated in China could pose problems for African countries, as could geopolitical tensions, the policies of the new administration in the United States and the impact of the departure of the United Kingdom from the European Union (EU), especially as the EU is Africa's main trading partner. (Further details on these issues, and their implications for the CFTA, are in Chapter 9.)

Overall integration

While Africa has many policy initiatives that express commitments to continental integration, the framework that provides both legitimacy and inspiration is the Treaty Establishing the African Economic Community (the Abuja Treaty), which entered into force in 1994. The following subsection reviews the progress towards realizing the commitments of that Treaty. Roadmap towards an African Economic Community shows the stages of integration to which African countries committed themselves under the Treaty.

According to the Economic Commission for Africa (ECA) (2016),

The first stage has now been completed, with eight RECs formally recognized by the African

Union. These are the Arab Maghreb Union (AMU), Economic Community of West African States (ECOWAS), East African Community (EAC), Intergovernmental Authority on Development (IGAD), Southern African Development Community (SADC), Common Market for Eastern and Southern Africa (COMESA), Economic Community of Central African States (ECCAS) and the Community of Sahel-Saharan States (CEN-SAD). The second stage has not been fully completed because progress by the RECs and by members within the RECs has been uneven. The third stage is under way in a number of RECs but not all. Only three of the eight recognized RECs have both a FTA and Customs Union (ECOWAS, EAC and COMESA), although with varying degrees of implementation. While a continental free trade area (CFTA) does not feature explicitly in the AU roadmap, in accordance with the sequential stages of regional economic integration, it is a stepping stone to the creation of a continental Customs Union.

Status of regional economic integration by REC summarizes the status of regional economic integration in each of the eight African Union (AU)-recognized RECs (Figure 2.3). The RECs are progressing at different speeds across the various components of the Abuja Treaty. The EAC has made the most progress across the board.

Figure 2.2.

Roadmap towards an African Economic Community

| **Stage 1:** Strengthen existing RECs and establish new RECs in regions where they do not exist (by 1999) |

| **Stage 2:** Ensure consolidation within each REC (gradual removal of tariff and non-tariff barriers) and harmonization between the RECs (by 2007) |

| **Stage 3:** Establish FTAs and Customs Unions (CUs) in each REC (by 2017) |

| **Stage 4:** Coordinate and harmonize tariff and non-tariff systems among the RECs with a view to creating a continental CU (by 2019) |

| **Stage 5:** Create an African Common Market (ACM) by 2023 |

| **Stage 6:** Establish an AEC, including an African Monetary Union and a Pan-African Parliament (by 2028) |

Source: ECA (2016).

Table 2.1.

Status of regional economic integration by REC

REC	Free Trade Area	Customs Union	Single Market	Countries having implemented freedom of movement protocol	Economic and Monetary Union
EAC	✔	✔	✔	3 out of 5	✘
COMESA	✔	✘	✘	Only Burundi has ratified; Rwanda's ratification is in progress	✘
ECOWAS	✔	✔	✘	All 15	✘
SADC	✔	✘	✘	7 out of 15	✘
ECCAS	✔	✘	✘	4 out of 11	✔[2]
CEN-SAD	✘	✘	✘	Unclear	✘
IGAD	✘	✘	✘	No protocol	✘
AMU	✘	✘	✘	3 out of 5	✘

Source: ECA (2016).

The following extract from ECA (2016) shows how the CFTA fits into the achievement of the African Economic Community:

> The scope of the CFTA Agreement covers trade in goods, trade in services, investment, intellectual property rights and competition policy. This wide scope moves beyond the requirements of a traditional FTA, which requires only the elimination of tariffs and quotas on trade in goods. Therefore, similar to other trading bloc arrangements, it is difficult to neatly place the CFTA under one of the five stages of regional economic integration. The wide coverage of the CFTA is expected to ease

the subsequent process of further regional economic integration in Africa.

> The harmonization of norms and regulations related to services typically takes place with the establishment of a [single market]. It is however important that trade in services is negotiated alongside trade in goods, since services are inputs into the production of trade in goods and the sector contributes a substantial share to the output of most African economies. The CFTA Agreement will therefore include a sub-agreement on trade in services on the basis of progressive liberalization,

Figure 2.3

Map of Africa and REC memberships

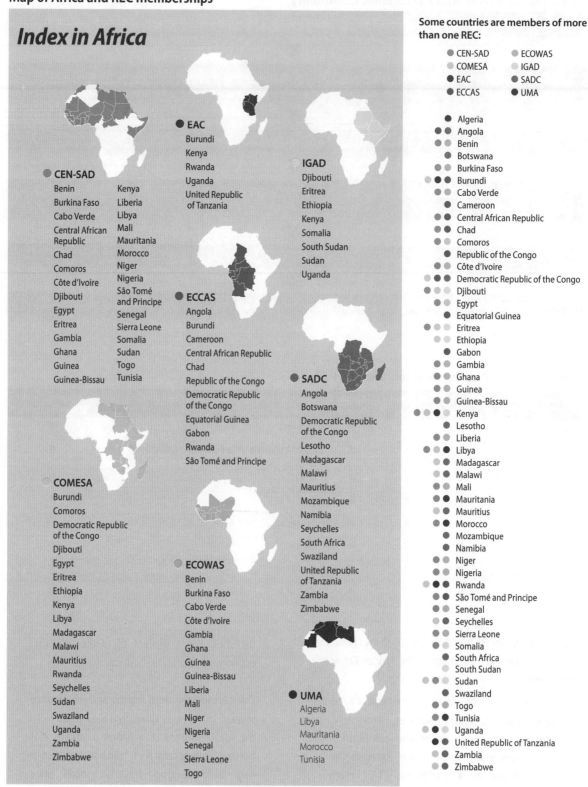

Index in Africa

CEN-SAD

Benin	Kenya
Burkina Faso	Liberia
Cabo Verde	Libya
Central African Republic	Mali
	Mauritania
Chad	Morocco
Comoros	Niger
Côte d'Ivoire	Nigeria
Djibouti	São Tomé and Principe
Egypt	Senegal
Eritrea	Sierra Leone
Gambia	Somalia
Ghana	Sudan
Guinea	Togo
Guinea-Bissau	Tunisia

COMESA

Burundi
Comoros
Democratic Republic of the Congo
Djibouti
Egypt
Eritrea
Ethiopia
Kenya
Libya
Madagascar
Malawi
Mauritius
Rwanda
Seychelles
Sudan
Swaziland
Uganda
Zambia
Zimbabwe

EAC

Burundi
Kenya
Rwanda
Uganda
United Republic of Tanzania

ECCAS

Angola
Burundi
Cameroon
Central African Republic
Chad
Republic of the Congo
Democratic Republic of the Congo
Equatorial Guinea
Gabon
Rwanda
São Tomé and Principe

ECOWAS

Benin
Burkina Faso
Cabo Verde
Côte d'Ivoire
Gambia
Ghana
Guinea
Guinea-Bissau
Liberia
Mali
Niger
Nigeria
Senegal
Sierra Leone
Togo

IGAD

Djibouti
Eritrea
Ethiopia
Kenya
Somalia
South Sudan
Sudan
Uganda

SADC

Angola
Botswana
Democratic Republic of the Congo
Lesotho
Madagascar
Malawi
Mauritius
Mozambique
Namibia
Seychelles
South Africa
Swaziland
United Republic of Tanzania
Zambia
Zimbabwe

UMA

Algeria
Libya
Mauritania
Morocco
Tunisia

Some countries are members of more than one REC:

- CEN-SAD
- COMESA
- EAC
- ECCAS
- ECOWAS
- IGAD
- SADC
- UMA

Algeria
Angola
Benin
Botswana
Burkina Faso
Burundi
Cabo Verde
Cameroon
Central African Republic
Chad
Comoros
Republic of the Congo
Côte d'Ivoire
Democratic Republic of the Congo
Djibouti
Egypt
Equatorial Guinea
Eritrea
Ethiopia
Gabon
Gambia
Ghana
Guinea
Guinea-Bissau
Kenya
Lesotho
Liberia
Libya
Madagascar
Malawi
Mali
Mauritania
Mauritius
Morocco
Mozambique
Namibia
Niger
Nigeria
Rwanda
São Tomé and Principe
Senegal
Seychelles
Sierra Leone
Somalia
South Africa
South Sudan
Sudan
Swaziland
Togo
Tunisia
Uganda
United Republic of Tanzania
Zambia
Zimbabwe

Source: http://www.uneca.org/sites/default/files/PublicationFiles/arii-report2016_en_web.pdf.

consolidating and building on the RECs' achievements.

Some common investment rules are typically covered under the free movement of capital required by a [single market], whereas an [economic union] would usually contain a fully-fledged common investment policy. Investment issues are rarely covered in free trade areas (FTAs). The CFTA Agreement however is expected to include a sub-agreement on investment that is broad in scope, covering both goods and services. The provision of common rules for state parties in introducing incentives would help to encourage investment into African countries to accelerate development, and would also help to avoid any race to the bottom. A continent-wide dispute settlement system for investment disputes to be settled among state parties will also be key.

Intellectual property and competition policy would typically only be required under an [economic union], the fifth and final stage of regional economic integration. Since few African countries have the institutional capacities and expertise to utilize trade remedy instruments such as anti-dumping, safeguards and countervailing measures, the scope of the CFTA however also covers these areas. Competition policy is a particularly important instrument for regulating unfair trade practices and providing clarity to businesses. Inclusion of a mechanism for regulating competition and facilitating dispute settlement early on will also help to build confidence in the CFTA.

The CFTA Agreement is also expected to include an appendix on the movement of natural persons involved in services and investment, an area of cooperation that is usually not covered until the establishment of a [single market]. This is needed to transform the opportunities provided through the liberalization of trade in goods, services and investment.

Finally, the CFTA project is being rolled out in parallel with the implementation of the Action Plan for Boosting Intra-African Trade (BIAT), which was adopted by the AU Heads of State in January 2012. This initiative goes significantly beyond the requirements of a traditional FTA and is aimed at addressing the constraints and challenges of intra-African trade which are organized under the clusters of trade policy, trade facilitation, productive capacity, trade-related infrastructure, trade finance, trade information and factor market integration. Effective implementation of the BIAT initiative will be crucial to minimizing the challenges and maximizing the gains of tariff liberalization, and ensuring that all African firms and countries are able to take advantage of the CFTA.

In April 2016, the African Development Bank (AfDB), African Union Commission (AUC) and ECA unveiled the Africa Regional Integration Index. The Index seeks to track African countries' progress in implementing their regional integration commitments to one another in the framework of the RECs. It measures each country's integration across five dimensions, which have a total of 16 indicators. The following tables capture, for each of the eight AU-recognized RECs, how its members integrate with the rest of the membership, in terms of the country's overall score and each of its dimensions.

Data updates, not available in AfDB, AUC and ECA (2016), include the most recent data from the African Development Bank's African Infrastructure Development Index (published in 2016). These data show the average scores for 2011–13 (rather than 2010–12). Work is under way on the second edition of the Index, which will include a sixth dimension on social integration and on gender and will, in addition to measuring within-REC integration, compare how all African countries integrate with the rest of the continent.

Table 2.2

Integration among Common Market for Eastern and Southern Africa members

COMESA						
	Overall rank	Trade integration	Regional infrastructure	Productive integration	Free movement of persons	Financial and macroeconomic integration
Country	Rank	Rank	Rank	Rank	Rank	Rank
Zambia	1	1	8	3	4	12
Uganda	2	5	15	2	2	6
Kenya	3	4	13	6	4	10
Egypt	4	2	7	1	18	11
Seychelles	5	17	2	10	1	1
Mauritius	6	11	14	12	3	4
Madagascar	7	12	4	4	10	8
Zimbabwe	8	7	10	15	6	9
Rwanda	9	9	16	9	8	5
Democratic Republic of the Congo	10	3	9	14	14	13
Swaziland	11	15	1	7	7	19
Comoros	12	14	6	17	10	2
Burundi	13	13	12	8	13	14
Malawi	14	10	11	11	9	17
Libya	15	6	3	19	19	7
Djibouti	16	19	17	5	12	3
Sudan	17	8	5	18	17	16
Eritrea	18	16	19	13	15	15
Ethiopia	19	18	18	16	16	18

Table 2.3

Integration among Southern African Development Community members

SADC						
	Overall rank	Trade integration	Regional infrastructure	Productive integration	Free movement of persons	Financial and macroeconomic integration
Country	Rank	Rank	Rank	Rank	Rank	Rank
South Africa	1	1	4	2	6	1
Namibia	2	3	1	12	6	2
Botswana	3	4	2	14	8	3
Swaziland	4	5	5	5	1	8
Zambia	5	2	8	3	3	11
Zimbabwe	6	15	7	1	5	5
Seychelles	7	14	6	9	1	4
Mozambique	8	7	11	4	11	9
Lesotho	9	6	3	15	8	7
Mauritius	10	8	14	11	4	6
United Republic of Tanzania	11	13	15	6	12	13
Madagascar	12	9	13	8	13	10
Malawi	13	10	12	13	8	15
Democratic Republic of the Congo	14	11	9	7	14	12
Angola	15	12	10	10	15	14

Table 2.4
Integration among East African Community members

EAC						
	Overall rank	Trade integration	Regional infrastructure	Productive integration	Free movement of persons	Financial and macroeconomic integration
Country	Rank	Rank	Rank	Rank	Rank	Rank
Rwanda	1	4	1	4	1	1
Kenya	2	1	3	3	1	2
Uganda	3	2	5	1	3	3
Burundi	4	5	2	5	3	4
United Republic of Tanzania	5	3	4	2	5	5

Table 2.5
Integration among Community of Sahel-Saharan States members

CEN-SAD						
	Overall rank	Trade integration	Regional infrastructure	Productive integration	Free movement of persons	Financial and macroeconomic integration
Country	Rank	Rank	Rank	Rank	Rank	Rank
Côte d'Ivoire	1	1	12	14	1	8
Benin	2	14	16	4	7	9
Togo	3	15	4	9	6	7
Senegal	4	4	15	10	11	3
Niger	5	10	13	15	2	1
Mali	6	6	17	18	2	6
Burkina Faso	7	11	8	20	5	2
Tunisia	8	3	18	7	15	15
Ghana	9	12	3	8	13	20
Morocco	10	17	1	3	18	11
Gambia	11	19	6	5	7	16
Guinea-Bissau	12	26	9	25	9	5
Nigeria	13	8	11	22	10	23
Egypt	14	2	14	6	29	22
Kenya	15	21	19	1	17	21
Central African Republic	16	20	27		22	10
Djibouti	17	22	23	2	21	14
Guinea	18	18	7	19	2	27
Libya	19	13	2	21	27	18
Mauritania	20	16	21	23	16	17
Chad	21	24	29	17	19	4
Liberia	22	28	20	11	13	19
Comoros	23	9	28		23	13
Sierra Leone	24	23	24	13	12	26
Cabo Verde	25	27	5		28	12
Eritrea	26	7	26	16	26	25
Sudan	27	5	10	24	25	28
São Tomé and Príncipe	28	29	25	12	24	24
Somalia		25	22	26	20	

Table 2.6

Integration among Economic Community of West African States members

ECOWAS						
	Overall rank	Trade integration	Regional infrastructure	Productive integration	Free movement of persons	Financial and macroeconomic integration
Country	Rank	Rank	Rank	Rank	Rank	Rank
Côte d'Ivoire	1	2	12	7	1	7
Togo	2	7	3	2	1	6
Senegal	3	3	13	4	1	3
Niger	4	8	8	9	1	1
Ghana	5	4	2	3	1	12
Burkina Faso	6	9	6	14	1	2
Benin	7	11	14	8	1	8
Mali	8	6	15	12	1	5
Nigeria	9	1	7	10	1	13
Guinea-Bissau	10	10	9	15	1	4
Gambia	11	14	4	1	1	10
Cabo Verde	12	12	1	13	1	9
Sierra Leone	13	5	11	6	1	14
Liberia	14	15	10	5	1	11
Guinea	15	13	5	11	1	15

Table 2.7

Integration among Economic Community of Central African States members

ECCAS						
	Overall rank	Trade integration	Regional infrastructure	Productive integration	Free movement of persons	Financial and macroeconomic integration
Country	Rank	Rank	Rank	Rank	Rank	Rank
Cameroon	1	1	4	3	4	3
Gabon	2	3	3	4	7	1
Republic of th	3	8	2	5	3	5
Central African Republic	4	6	5	9	2	4
Chad	5	4	11	6	4	2
Rwanda	6	5	8	2	6	7
Equatorial Guinea	7	7	7	10	7	6
Angola	8	2	1	11	11	11
Burundi	9	10	10	1	9	9
São Tomé and Príncipe	10	11	9	7	1	10
Democratic Republic of the Congo	11	9	6	8	9	8

Table 2.8

Integration among Arab Maghreb Union members

AMU						
	Overall rank	Trade integration	Regional infrastructure	Productive integration	Free movement of persons	Financial and macroeconomic integration
Country	Rank	Rank	Rank	Rank	Rank	Rank
Morocco	1	2	2	2	4	1
Tunisia	2	1	5	1	3	2
Algeria	3	4	4	4	1	3
Libya	4	3	1	3	5	5
Mauritania	5	5	3	5	2	4

Table 2.9

Integration among Intergovernmental Authority on Development members

IGAD						
	Overall rank	Trade integration	Regional infrastructure	Productive integration	Free movement of persons	Financial and macroeconomic integration
Country	Rank	Rank	Rank	Rank	Rank	Rank
Kenya	1	2	2	1	2	2
Uganda	2	1	8	2	1	3
Djibouti	3	5	1	3	5	1
Ethiopia	4	6	5	4	4	5
Eritrea	5	4	7	5	3	4
Sudan	6	3	6	6	8	7
South Sudan			3		7	6
Somalia		7	4	7	5	

Other areas of regional cooperation: Mining, health and peace and security

Mining

The Africa Mining Vision, adopted by African Heads of State in 2009, provides a framework for a diversified, inclusive and integrated African economy built around the responsible use of natural resources. Its seven pillars outline the fundamental and institutional shifts needed to realize mineral-based industrialization and job creation, which will lessen the continent's exposure to harmful boom- bust commodity cycles. Indeed, the large mineral rents accruing in the 2000s, followed by dramatic falls in prices and returns, make clear the imperative to develop value-added activities along regional mineral value chains. An institutional arrangement with mineral-based transformation at its centre is needed.

The African Minerals Development Centre (AMDC)— an AUC and ECA centre of excellence—was set up in 2013 as the custodian of the Africa Mining Vision. Their mandate is to assist African Member States with implementation and mainstreaming of the Vision in national frameworks.

Achieving the Vision's ambitious goals is contingent on stronger regional integration in Africa. Regional value chains (RVCs) for minerals are instrumental in both upstream and downstream mineral activities at the subregional and regional levels. Research by the AMDC is identifying potential in mineral RVCs throughout the SADC region, where established mining economies, new entrants to the sector, and countries with strong sectors in agriculture, transport and other areas all have a role in a regional approach to mineral-based industrialization.

Because the national demand for mineral sector inputs, and the critical mass of producers of those inputs, may be too small to reach efficiency and economies of scale, regional markets can pool production and demand to reach that threshold. Mineral RVCs also draw on comparative advantages in skills, mineral endowments, connectivity and existing industrial linkages, which are spread across subregions.

AMDC is also researching the potential of pooled markets for mining supplies and input products in ECOWAS. Regional infrastructure development—particularly for harnessing cross-border energy endowments and transport corridors—is crucial for these RVCs, as activities at the nexus of mining and manufacturing are inherently energy intensive and strain the already overburdened national power supplies. Regional cooperation can also help spread skills and best practices in mineral-based industrial sectors.

Another area of integration vital to building mineral linkages involves regional approaches to illicit financial flows. Of the more than $50 billion in such flows that exit the continent annually,[3] more than half are driven by the extractives industry. Several factors contribute to these outflows, including issues of transparency and tax administration capabilities. However, the features of the fiscal regime governing the mineral sector, and the poor extent of harmonization of fiscal regimes across countries, also has a deleterious effect. For example, many African countries continue to employ contractual approaches to mineral taxes, and so tax measures can vary from contract to contract.[4] Licensing systems should be pursued in which tax and royalty laws are consistently applied.

Fiscal regimes across countries remain incoherent and inconsistent, allowing external actors and multinational corporations to exploit these disparities. This situation triggers a race to the bottom of overly compensatory agreements and contracts. Fiscal harmonization, particularly through alignment and streamlining of policies, allows countries to coordinate their tax activities while recognizing the specificities of their own fiscal regimes, which might be glossed over by a uniform system.

There has been significant buy-in at the regional level of the need to develop an African framework for addressing illicit financial flows in the extractives sector through closer cooperation and greater harmonization of fiscal regimes; global frameworks and guidelines alone may not help in addressing very specific issues that occur along the mineral value chain across Africa, such as transfer mispricing, and the fact

that regional fragmentation allows such conditions to persist. Coordinated training and capacity-building programmes are being implemented to ensure that authorities in various jurisdictions are "on the same page" in addressing and reversing these illicit flows.

Comprehensive mineral frameworks have recently been established at the subregional level, which seek to promote and harmonize policies conducive to mineral-based transformation. For example, ECOWAS has adopted a directive on harmonizing guiding principles and policies in the mining sector that would create a common mining code for West Africa, and support priorities such as value addition through linkages and beneficiation, environmental protection, good governance and respect for human rights.[5]

Adopting a regional approach to "onboarding" the Africa Mining Vision—particularly over policies for mineral-based transformation—will help African countries overcome the limitations and hurdles of unilateral economic policy making, contract negotiation, infrastructure development and other steps that are burdensome without cooperation. In isolation, mineral producers compete in a race to the bottom rather than pooling markets for value addition and increasing bargaining power in contract negotiations.

Implementation remains the most difficult part of mineral policy and governance; well-prepared policies exist and are being developed, but there is little enforcement, especially for regional and cross-border policies. To rectify this, AMDC support to Member States in writing "country mining visions"—the actionable, national forms of the Africa Mining Vision—is increasingly addressing the importance of RVCs, harmonization aspects and other regional approaches. AMDC is also beginning to embrace the fact that regional mining visions can boost opportunities for linkages (between the mining sector and the rest of the economy) and for new economic opportunities.

In addition, the development of the African Minerals Governance Framework, the Country Mining Vision Handbook, training, and policy and law reviews offer avenues to address a range of development issues in Africa's mining sector and to preclude the sector from exacerbating the existing imbalances and inequalities. Going forward, it will be important to consider the needs of those working in the informal mining sector (often considered illegal; see the section below on informal trade) and also the gender-disaggregated impacts of mining policy.

Public health

Following the Ebola crisis in West Africa in 2014–15, African countries are cooperating in the prevention and management of public health crises. The African Centre for Disease Control and Prevention launched a five-year strategic plan in March 2017. This plan and its accompanying roadmap set priorities for prevention, disease control and the response to public health threats and emergencies on the continent (AU, 2017a; AU, 2017b).

Peace and security

In this area, African countries have established extensive cooperation:

- ECOWAS Member States prevailed on the outgoing president of Gambia to leave office, following his defeat in the country's recent election, even though he refused to do so. Subsequently, regional military forces supported the incoming president by securing his passage into the country and providing protection during his initial period in office in 2017.

- African countries contribute 38,071 personnel across the nine United Nations peacekeeping missions in Africa (of which one, UNAMID, is a joint operation with the AU) (ECA calculations based on UN, 2017a, 2017b); this is fewer personnel than in June 2016 (as reported in the last edition of *ARIA*), although the number of peacekeeping missions has remained the same.

- The AU has its own military mission in Somalia to destroy Al-Shabaab strongholds in central Somalia and to cut its supply routes. As part of these operations, the mission liberated the town of Adan Yabal in the Shabelle Dhexe region and Galcad in the Galguduud region (ECA, 2017f).

- Multinational action against Boko Haram continued in West Africa (ECA, 2017e).

- Women have played an important role in peace-building across Africa, including in peace negotiations in Burundi, Democratic Republic of the Congo, the Mano River Women's Peace Network and Somalia.

Financial integration

Table 2.10. shows intra-African outward direct investment. A negative value shows that a country has reduced the value of its total direct investment position, either because the investments have declined in value or because investors from that country have withdrawn investments. The volume of investments in Mauritius, despite its small economy, suggests that a lot of foreign investments to Africa may be routed through that country to take advantage of its favourable tax regime and its status as an offshore financial centre.

Table 2.10.

Intra-African outward direct investment positions, 2015 ($ million)

Benin	-5
Botswana	1,386
Burkina Faso	362
Cabo Verde	87
Guinea-Bissau	70
Mali	502
Mauritius	21,380
Morocco	222
Mozambique	5,856
Niger	490
Nigeria	5,284
Rwanda	877
Seychelles	367
South Africa	3,341
Togo	1,251
Uganda	1,466
Zambia	1,988

Source: ECA calculations, based on IMF (2017).

Some regional groupings have partial-payment systems integration; for example, EAC, SADC (which has payment systems integration) and West and Central Africa (Karingi and Davis, 2017). The COMESA payment and settlement system is being operated in 9 of its member states (COMESA, 2017). In addition, EAC Partner States recently agreed on direct convertibility of their currencies.

In North Africa, ECA is working with Arab Maghreb Union to increase trade finance. ECOWAS is pursuing efforts to pave the way for a single currency, and it has six convergence criteria for Member States (West African Monetary Agency, cited in ECA, 2017b).

Free movement of persons and the right of establishment

In 2016, the African Development Bank and McKinsey launched the Africa Visa Openness Report, which analyses visa openness in African countries. The report showed that there is still considerable room for African countries to liberalize their visa regimes.

Figure 2.4. summarizes countries' openness across three dimensions.

The following entities have taken steps to support the free movement of persons:

• Rwanda has begun the process of ratifying the Common Market for Eastern and Southern Africa (COMESA) Protocol on Free Movement of Persons.

Figure 2.4.

Degree of visa openness to other African countries

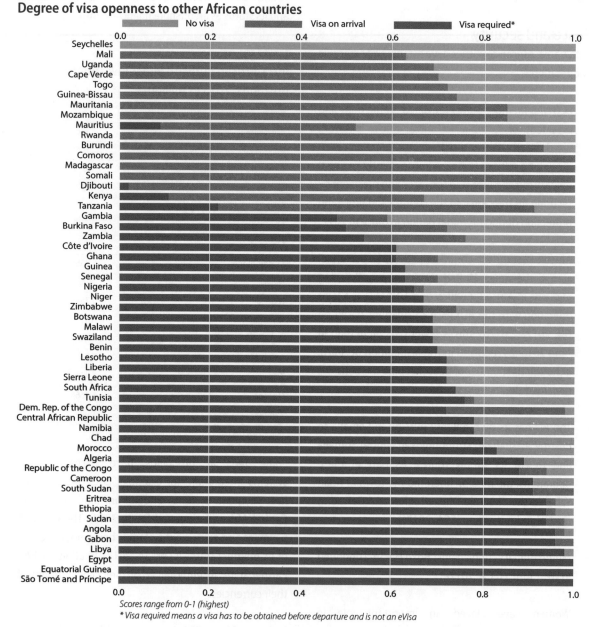

Scores range from 0-1 (highest)
* Visa required means a visa has to be obtained before departure and is not an eVisa

Source: Based on AfDB (2016).

- Benin, Ghana, Nigeria and Zimbabwe have all taken steps towards liberalizing their visa regimes for nationals of other African countries.

- Namibia and Rwanda plan to abolish visas for all Africans (Geingob, cited in *The Citizen*, 2016; *The East African*, 2017).

- The CFTA is expected to include an agreement on the movement of economic operators involved in trade and investment.

- The AU Assembly requested a draft protocol on the free movement of persons in Africa for consideration at its meeting in January 2018.

Infrastructure integration

Infrastructure remains one of the key factors for ensuring sustainable and inclusive development in Africa. It is also an important enabler of intra-African trade, particularly the development of RVCs within the continent. Improving the continent's infrastructure is essential to make the most of the potential of the CFTA (ECOSOC, 2017). The AU's Programme for Infrastructure

Figure 2.5

Quality of railway and port infrastructure, 2016

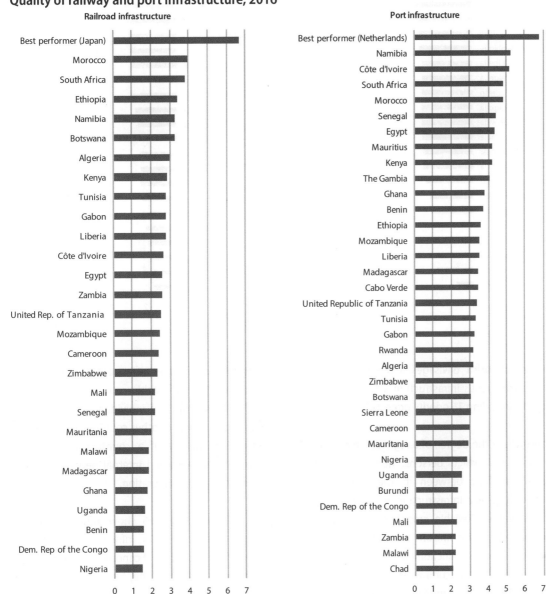

Note: Data were only available for a selection of African countries; the best performer of the dataset is included to show the distance to the global frontier. Ratings in the various categories of infrastructure quality are based on surveys of businesspeople.

Source: WEF (2016).

Figure 2.6

Quality of air transport and electricity supply infrastructure, 2016

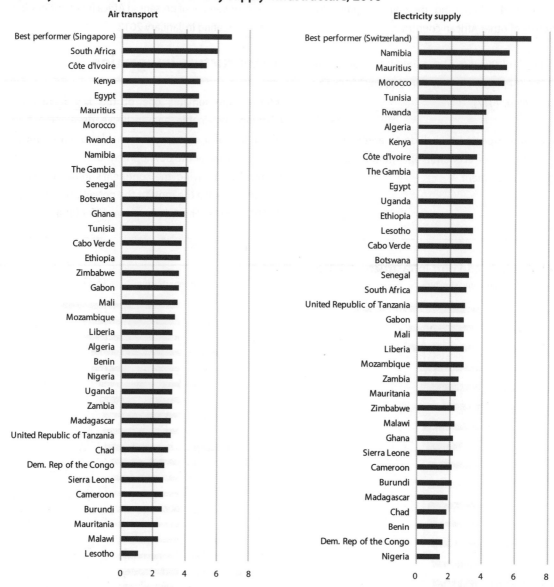

Source: WEF (2016).

Development in Africa envisages a broad effort to improve the continent's infrastructure, which consists of 51 projects, including 16 priority projects.[6]

If one conceives of the degree of a region's integration as the ease with which persons, goods, services and capital can flow between its members, it is clear that high-quality infrastructure is essential for regional integration. Reliable cross-border transport infrastructure reduces the time and cost of transporting goods across borders. A functioning communications infrastructure facilitates communication within a region, across the continent and beyond. And a well-run energy infrastructure is essential for both transport and communications infrastructure.

It is not only cross-border infrastructure that supports regional integration; within-country infrastructure networks allow firms and individuals to more easily penetrate the interior of other countries in the region. Therefore, the quality of a country's infrastructure (international linkages and internal networks) is vital for boosting regional integration.

Figure 2.6 and Figure 2.6 show African countries' performance on quality of infrastructure indicators compiled for the World Economic Forum's Global Competitiveness Index. They reveal that African countries still have a way to go to meet the "global frontier," although some countries appear to be performing well (WEF, 2016).

Most African countries are upgrading their infrastructure.[7] The sections below give details on achievements recorded since the last edition of *ARIA*. World Bank (2017c) has a more complete list of projects with private participation in infrastructure. (That dataset has many projects not listed here, because there have been no updates to their status during the period under review.)

Energy

Many African countries continue to struggle with their energy infrastructure. Ghana, for example, has experienced load-shedding power outages that are thwarting the country's economic prospects (ECA, 2017c).

Still, a number of countries are upgrading their energy infrastructure. For instance, Angola has raised funds for investment in the 2,070 megawatt (MW) Lauca hydropower project, located on a section of the Kwanza River between the Cambambe and Capanda complexes and the Caculo Cabaça hydro facility. The Organization of the Petroleum Exporting Countries (OPEC) Fund for International Development has allocated funds to mini-grid projects in Benin, Cabo Verde, Senegal and Sierra Leone, and more than 4,250 people in 850 households will reportedly directly benefit, as well as 123 commercial clients and small enterprises and 57 public buildings and services. Benin has raised funds for a 120 MW thermal power plant at Maria Gleta. Burundi, Côte d'Ivoire, Ghana and Guinea-Bissau have raised funds for rural electricity projects, and Côte d'Ivoire has worked on rehabilitating its electricity grid. Democratic Republic of Congo has mobilized funds for a distribution facility in Bandundu province and a transmission and distribution project in Kasai province (ICA, 2016). Djibouti increased its electricity production by 10.3 per cent from 2014 to 2015 (ECA, 2017g).

Egypt has mobilized substantial funds for its 1,800 MW combined-cycle gas turbine Damanhour power plant, alongside the 650 MW Cairo West Power project. The first of these projects will be supplied by the Egyptian Natural Gas Company and will be connected to the 500 kilovolt national grid via two new transmission lines: a 14 km connection to the existing Abu Qir/Kafr El-Zayat 500kV line, and a 60 km double-circuit 500kV line to connect Damanhour with the Abo El-Matamir 500/220kV substation. A project is also under way to create an interconnection between Egypt and Saudi Arabia's electricity grids, enabling an energy exchange between the two grids "during normal operating times, especially at peak time and during emergency conditions. The project also aims to reduce operating costs and reinforce the stability of both grids" (ICA, 2016). Also in Egypt, the construction of a wind farm at Gabal el Zeit was completed, with a capacity of 200 MW (World Bank, 2017a).

Ethiopia has opened the Gibe III hydroelectric dam, which has the capacity to double the country's energy output, and it is expected to produce 15,000 MW of electricity over the next five years (*The Economist*, 2016; Meseret, 2016). The country plans to raise the power output of hydropower, wind and geothermal sources to 17,436 MW (from the current 2,200 MW) under the 2015–2020 development plan (Maasho, 2016). In Ghana, gas from Sankofa is being developed for domestic energy production, so that 1,000 MW can be addeded to Ghana's capacity of 3,215 MW (ICA, 2016).

Kenya mobilized funds for a wind farm project at Lake Turkana. The Kenya Tea Development Agency raised funds to invest in hydropower for several of its tea factories, and for the country's Last Mile Connectivity Project to promote electricity access. Lesotho opened its Metolong dam, which "brings Lesotho's installed power generation capacity up to a level that should meet demand until 2025" and will electrify "75 villages previously without electricity," in addition to increasing its water supply. Morocco has mobilized funds for investing in rural electrification and a substantial investment in its solar power sector, as well as rehabilitating hydropower plants and dams and creating a 120 MW wind farm near Tangiers. In Mozambique, the Moamba-Major hydroelectric dam project is in progress and is expected to produce 15 MW of electricity to add to the national energy grid by 2019. Construction of this dam is also "expected to involve restoration of railways and new road building" (ICA, 2016).

Nigeria established a transitional power market in 2015 and achieved financial closure for investment in the construction of a 450 MW gas-fired power plant at Azura (World Bank, 2017a). Senegal has mobilized funds for investment in a power plant at Tobene and brownfield investment in the 135 MW oil-fired power plant in Rufisque. South Africa is upgrading its utility distribution network and power generation, including at least 1.5 gigawatts of new generation capacity through wind and solar power projects, such as the 40 MW Linde Solar Photovoltaic Plant, a 100 MW concentrated solar power plant in the Northern Cape, the 100 MW Karoshek Solar One project and a 138.9 MW wind farm in De Aar. Tunisia has raised funds for a 600 MW gas-fired power plant in Mornaguia (ICA, 2016; World Bank, 2017a). Uganda is continuing to invest in hydropower generation, including the 5.5 MW power plant in Paidha, the 5.6 MW Rwimi river small hydropower project and the 5 MW Siti Small Hydro Power Plant. Uganda also has a 10 MW solar power plant project under way in Soroti (ECA, 2017a; ICA, 2016; World Bank, 2017a). Zimbabwe is renovating its Bulawayo thermal power plant and has mobilized investment for the Gawanda solar project and the Hwange thermal power station (ICA, 2016).

In addition to the importance of upgrading national infrastructure, it is important to support the interconnection of national electricity grids. Cross-border interconnections "Allow countries to take advantage of significant hydroelectric potential in neighbouring countries, while also allowing the exporting of more expensive forms of generation to balance system costs" (ICA, 2016).

Some cross-border energy projects have continued during the period under review. These include the Central African power interconnection; the second Democratic Republic of the Congo–Zambia Interconnector; the Kenya–United Republic of Tanzania power interconnection; and the Ruzizi III hydropower project in Burundi and Rwanda. The last two projects raised additional funds in 2015. This transmission network is expected to be functioning in 2019. Côte d'Ivoire and Mali have planned an electricity interconnection project, while Mozambique, South Africa and Zimbabwe have raised funds for an energy interconnection project between the three countries.

The Côte d'Ivoire–Liberia–Sierra Leone–Guinea transmission programme (OMVG) (which is a priority West African Power Pool project), along with other projects under way, will see an extensive network of connections among the countries of West Africa, plus it will connect with the existing Côte d'Ivoire–Benin–Togo–Nigeria interconnection, the West African Power Pool Coastal Transmission Backbone, the Senegal River Basin Organization transmission grid and the above OMVG programme. Funding for the project is coming

from participating governments and international donors. Feasibility studies have been carried out with technical assistance provided for preparation studies and environmental and social impact assessments. A 500 kilovolt interconnection line between Ethiopia and Kenya is progressing, with a critical substation expected to come online in December 2017. The Inga III dam project, which could eventually generate 50 gigawatts, remains under development (ICA, 2016).

Source: ICA (2016). shows existing energy generation plants in Africa, superimposed with selected new projects that received financial closure in 2015.

Communications

At the national level, Angola has a project to roll out high speed data transmission for corporate markets and individual customers; the cities of Lubango, Cabinda, Huambo and Soyo are expected to benefit. Benin is working to convert all of its television stations from analogue to digital and has raised funds to develop its broadband network. Cameroon has raised funds for the second phase of its National Telecommunications Broadband Network project (in country) and is planning to link Kribi, Cameroon with Fortaleza, Brazil by a submarine communications cable. International data traffic from Africa to the Americas "is currently routed via Western Europe... before going to America." This cable project will provide Brazil, Cameroon and neighbouring countries with improved communications, and add to Cameroon's other submarine cables, which link South Africa and France, Portugal, Spain and the United Kingdom (ICA, 2016).

Chad, Republic of the Congo, Democratic Republic of the Congo and the United Republic of Tanzania have investments committed for upgrading or constructing new telecommunications towers. An Egyptian telecoms provider signed a deal in 2015 that is likely to cut costs, and additional investments were agreed to for Uganda's telecoms sector. In Kenya, an ongoing project will provide 1,600 kilometres (km) of fibre optic cable (plus an additional 500 km for military use) and link to the existing 4,300 km of cable. Niger has mobilized further investment in its telecoms sector as well as funds for building a fibre optic backbone. Telecommunications towers are being built in Nigeria to improve coverage; Niger's telecoms sector provides an estimated 80 million people with internet access, including broadband, and there are almost 150 million active mobile phone

Figure 2.7.
Africa's energy sector, 2015

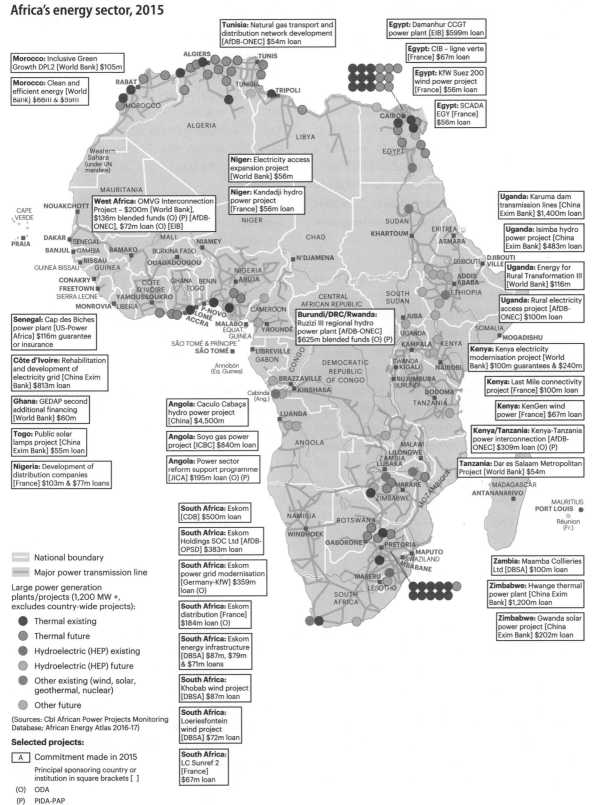

Tunisia: Natural gas transport and distribution network development [AfDB-ONEC] $54m loan

Egypt: Damanhur CCGT power plant [EIB] $599m loan

Egypt: CIB – ligne verte [France] $67m loan

Morocco: Inclusive Green Growth DPL2 [World Bank] $105m

Egypt: KfW Suez 200 wind power project [France] $56m loan

Morocco: Clean and efficient energy [World Bank] $66m & $59m

Egypt: SCADA EGY [France] $56m loan

Niger: Electricity access expansion project [World Bank] $56m

Uganda: Karuma dam transmission lines [China Exim Bank] $1,400m loan

West Africa: OMVG Interconnection Project – $200m [World Bank], $136m blended funds (O) (P) [AfDB-ONEC], $72m loan (O) [EIB]

Niger: Kandadji hydro power project [France] $56m loan

Uganda: Isimba hydro power project [China Exim Bank] $483m loan

Uganda: Energy for Rural Transformation III [World Bank] $116m

Uganda: Rural electricity access project [AfDB-ONEC] $100m loan

Senegal: Cap des Biches power plant [US-Power Africa] $116m guarantee or insurance

Burundi/DRC/Rwanda: Ruzizi III regional hydro power plant [AfDB-ONEC] $625m blended funds (O) (P)

Kenya: Kenya electricity modernisation project [World Bank] $100m guarantees & $240m

Côte d'Ivoire: Rehabilitation and development of electricity grid [China Exim Bank] $813m loan

Kenya: Last Mile connectivity project [France] $100m loan

Ghana: GEDAP second additional financing [World Bank] $60m

Kenya: KenGen wind power [France] $67m loan

Togo: Public solar lamps project [China Exim Bank] $55m loan

Angola: Caculo Cabaça hydro power project [China] $4,500m

Kenya/Tanzania: Kenya-Tanzania power interconnection [AfDB-ONEC] $309m loan (O) (P)

Nigeria: Development of distribution companies [France] $103m & $77m loans

Angola: Soyo gas power project [ICBC] $840m loan

Tanzania: Dar es Salaam Metropolitan Project [World Bank] $54m

Angola: Power sector reform support programme [JICA] $195m loan (O) (P)

South Africa: Eskom [CDB] $500m loan

Zambia: Maamba Collieries Ltd [DBSA] $100m loan

South Africa: Eskom Holdings SOC Ltd [AfDB-OPSD] $383m loan

Zimbabwe: Hwange thermal power plant [China Exim Bank] $1,200m loan

South Africa: Eskom power grid modernisation [Germany-KfW] $359m loan (O)

Zimbabwe: Gwanda solar power project [China Exim Bank] $202m loan

National boundary

Major power transmission line

Large power generation plants/projects (1,200 MW +, excludes country-wide projects):

- Thermal existing
- Thermal future
- Hydroelectric (HEP) existing
- Hydroelectric (HEP) future
- Other existing (wind, solar, geothermal, nuclear)
- Other future

South Africa: Eskom distribution [France] $184m loan (O)

South Africa: Eskom energy infrastructure [DBSA] $87m, $79m & $71m loans

(Sources: CbI African Power Projects Monitoring Database; African Energy Atlas 2016-17)

South Africa: Khobab wind project [DBSA] $87m loan

Selected projects:

A Commitment made in 2015

Principal sponsoring country or institution in square brackets [ ]

South Africa: Loeriesfontein wind project [DBSA] $72m loan

(O) ODA
(P) PIDA-PAP

South Africa: LC Sunref 2 [France] $67m loan

Source: ICA (2016).

subscriptions in the country. The Nigerian government plans to boost the information and communications technology sector and enable it to contribute more to the economy through reforming the sector's tax and regulatory framework (ICA, 2016).

In Zambia, investments in the telecommunications towers will improve accessibility and reliability of coverage. The government of Togo has awarded a contract to connect over 500 of its public buildings to fibre optic cable. In Zimbabwe's telecommunications sector, investors have been funding market consolidation, new services and network modernization (ICA, 2016).

At the subregional level, broadband infrastructure is being upgraded with the Djibouti Africa Regional Express submarine broadband cable, which will extend to Djibouti, Kenya, Somalia and the United Republic of Tanzania (World Bank, 2017a). The Economic Community of Central African States (ECCAS) is taking steps to implement a one-area network, similar to that in East Africa, that would reduce or eliminate roaming charges. A number of Economic Community of West African States (ECOWAS) member states have moved towards launching a similar one-area network. In addition, the private sector and international donors are setting aside further funds for investment in telecommunications across Africa (ICA, 2016).

Transport

Figure 2.8 shows a map of Africa's transport networks.

Railways
African countries are revamping their railway networks, including those with a regional dimension. For instance, the Addis Ababa light rail system and the Djibouti–Ethiopia railway have entered into service, with plans to expand this network to connect to Burundi, Djibouti, Kenya Rwanda, South Sudan, Sudan and Uganda (Appiah, 2015; Morylln-Yron, Scott, Kwok and Darvenzia, 2017). Gabon is rehabilitating the Transgabonais railway (World Bank, 2017a). Egypt has mobilized funds for investment in new rail stock (ICA, 2016).

Kenya is planning to build an underground rail system in Nairobi, and it will extend the Mombasa–Nairobi railway line to Naivasha (Parke, 2016).

Mozambique has a project to invest in railways in Nacala, which will also have its port and airport upgraded (ICA, 2016). Nigeria has completed a rail link between Abuja and Kaduna; it also signed a new memorandum of understanding in 2016 with a contractor for building a 1,400 km coastal railway between Calabar and Lagos, which will include an urban transit system for Lagos; and it has begun light rail projects for the Abuja and Kano metropolitan area (Barrow, 2016; Jacobs, 2017; Rogers, 2016; *Railways Africa*, 2016; Lu and Lau, 2016).

Malawi and Zambia together have launched a railway construction project that would connect with existing rail links to provide connections between the two countries and Mozambique (*Railway Gazette*, cited in Morylln-Yron et al., 2017). Senegal has raised funds for the Dakar–Kidira rail project. South Africa has secured funding to acquire new locomotive stock for its state-owned transport and logistics company, Transnet (ICA, 2016).

Railways planned, under construction or already completed in Eastern Africa shows additional railways in selected countries in Eastern Africa that are planned, under construction or already completed.

Air transport
Cabo Verde and Senegal have signed an agreement on air transport links between them (ECA, 2017d). Air Djibouti, a public–private partnership, has launched cargo operations to capture a share of the regional market for such services. It has also resumed passenger flights to neighbouring countries (ECA, 2017g). The terminal expansion project for Ethiopia's Bole International Airport in Addis Ababa continues, and Nairobi's Jomo Kenyatta International Airport has also been upgraded in the period under review. Additional funds have been allocated for capital investment in Ghana's airports, including the construction of a new terminal at Kotoka International Airport in Accra and rehabilitation of other airports. With assistance from China, a new airport is under construction in Sierra Leone near Freetown. Mozambique has an ongoing project under review to rehabilitate Nacala airport. The Sharm el-Sheikh international airport in Egypt raised new investment funds (ICA, 2016).

Maritime and waterway transport
Additional funds have been mobilized for investment in Côte d'Ivoire's Abidjan port. Kenya continues to

Figure 2.8
Africa's transport networks, 2015

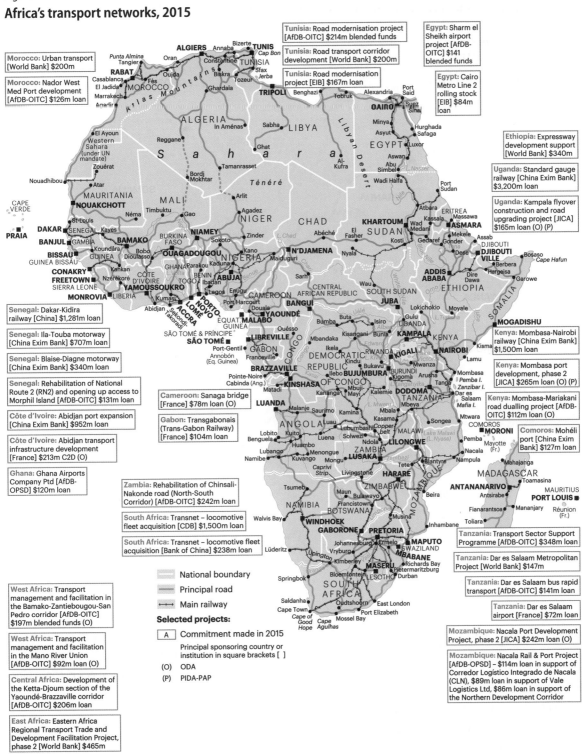

Morocco: Urban transport [World Bank] $200m

Morocco: Nador West Med Port development [AfDB-OITC] $126m loan

Tunisia: Road modernisation project [AfDB-OITC] $214m blended funds

Tunisia: Road transport corridor development [World Bank] $200m

Tunisia: Road modernisation project [EIB] $167m loan

Egypt: Sharm el Sheikh airport project [AfDB-OITC] $141 blended funds

Egypt: Cairo Metro Line 2 rolling stock [EIB] $84m loan

Ethiopia: Expressway development support [World Bank] $340m

Uganda: Standard gauge railway [China Exim Bank] $3,200m loan

Uganda: Kampala flyover construction and road upgrading project [JICA] $165m loan (O) (P)

Senegal: Dakar-Kidira railway [China] $1,281m loan

Senegal: Ila-Touba motorway [China Exim Bank] $707m loan

Senegal: Blaise-Diagne motorway [China Exim Bank] $340m loan

Senegal: Rehabilitation of National Route 2 (RN2) and opening up access to Morphil Island [AfDB-OITC] $131m loan

Côte d'Ivoire: Abidjan port expansion [China Exim Bank] $952m loan

Côte d'Ivoire: Abidjan transport infrastructure development [France] $213m C2D (O)

Ghana: Ghana Airports Company Ptd [AfDB-OPSD] $120m loan

Cameroon: Sanaga bridge [France] $78m loan (O)

Gabon: Transgabonais (Trans-Gabon Railway) [France] $104m loan

Kenya: Mombasa-Nairobi railway [China Exim Bank] $1,500m loan

Kenya: Mombasa port development, phase 2 [JICA] $265m loan (O) (P)

Kenya: Mombasa-Mariakani road dualling project [AfDB-OITC] $112m loan (O)

Comoros: Mohéli port [China Exim Bank] $127m loan

Zambia: Rehabilitation of Chinsali-Nakonde road (North-South Corridor) [AfDB-OITC] $242m loan

South Africa: Transnet – locomotive fleet acquisition [CDB] $1,500m loan

South Africa: Transnet – locomotive fleet acquisition [Bank of China] $238m loan

Tanzania: Transport Sector Support Programme [AfDB-OITC] $348m loan

Tanzania: Dar es Salaam Metropolitan Project [World Bank] $147m

Tanzania: Dar es Salaam bus rapid transport [AfDB-OITC] $141m loan

Tanzania: Dar es Salaam airport [France] $72m loan

Mozambique: Nacala Port Development Project, phase 2 [JICA] $242m loan (O)

Mozambique: Nacala Rail & Port Project [AfDB-OPSD] – $114m loan in support of Corredor Logístico Integrado de Nacala (CLN), $89m loan in support of Vale Logistics Ltd, $86m loan in support of the Northern Development Corridor

West Africa: Transport management and facilitation in the Bamako-Zantiebougou-San Pedro corridor [AfDB-OITC] $197m blended funds (O)

West Africa: Transport management and facilitation in the Mano River Union [AfDB-OITC] $92m loan (O)

Central Africa: Development of the Ketta-Djoum section of the Yaoundé-Brazzaville corridor [AfDB-OITC] $206m loan

East Africa: Eastern Africa Regional Transport Trade and Development Facilitation Project, phase 2 [World Bank] $465m

Legend:
- National boundary
- Principal road
- Main railway

Selected projects:

[A] Commitment made in 2015

Principal sponsoring country or institution in square brackets [ ]

(O) ODA

(P) PIDA-PAP

Source: ICA (2016).

mobilize resources for its Mombasa Port Development Phase 2 project, which is part of the Programme for Infrastructure Development in Africa's Priority Action Plan. Morocco has secured funds for its Nador West port, while Mozambique continues working towards developing Nacala port in combination with a rail project for that city: The Nacala port has a natural depth of 14 metres, the best natural harbour in southeastern Africa with very high potential. Senegal completed the final phase of its Maritime Infrastructure Establishment Project II, thereby opening the Ndakhonga harbour terminal. This creates a harbour that connects the central Ndakhonga region to the sea via the river, which

Figure 2.9

Railways planned, under construction or already completed in Eastern Africa

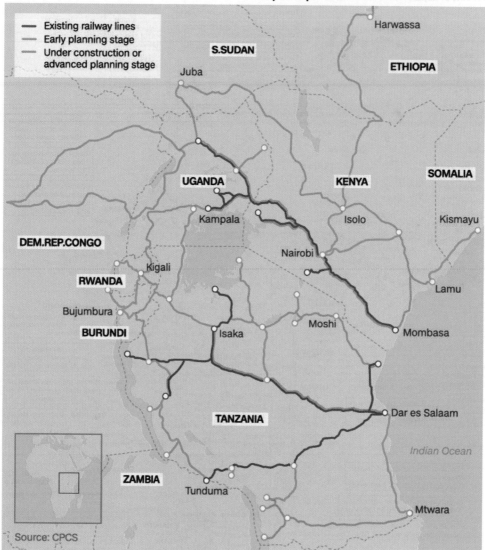

Source: Based on CPCS, cited in Morylln-Yron et al. (2017).

is a critical improvement. Togo mobilized investment for constructing the Lomé Container Terminal (ICA, 2016).

Among cross-border projects, Cabo Verde and Senegal have signed an agreement for a direct maritime link between Dakar and Praia (ECA, 2017d). Countries forming a line from Egypt to Lake Victoria are working on a feasibility study for a project to achieve waterway connectivity between the lake and the Mediterranean Sea (the VICMED project). African countries also concluded the Lomé Charter on Maritime Security during the period under review.

Multimodal transport
A multimodal Praia–Dakar–Abidjan corridor is planned under the Programme for Infrastructure Development in Africa. The Northern Multimodal Corridor has sought

funding, and the Northern Corridor Trade and Transit Coordination Authority is working on a revised strategic plan with support from ECA's African Trade Policy Centre. The Lamu Port Gateway Project is continuing (ICA, 2016).

Pipelines
A project is planned to extend the Lake Victoria pipeline to Tabora, Igunga and Nzega in the United Republic of Tanzania. The extension is expected to benefit 89 villages in a 12 km radius of the pipeline.

Road transport
African countries are raising and committing funds for upgrading road infrastructure across the continent. Cameroon, for example, raised and committed funds for the Lena–Tibati road segment of the Batchenga–Lena–

Tibati–N'Gaoundere Corridor (which will also make trade between Cameroon, the Central African Republic and Chad easier) and the Sanaga Bridge. Côte d'Ivoire raised funds to construct an interchange in Abidjan on Boulevard Valery Giscard d'Estaing. Gambia plans to expand its road network to connect previously isolated areas of the country and to facilitate tourism; this expansion will include the installation of weighbridges. Ghana has a project to improve the N2 Eastern Corridor Road. Morocco has raised funds for the El Jadida–Safi Motorway project. Niger has assigned a new project for its dry port, and Senegal is planning to invest in two motorways (Aéroport International Blaise Diagne to Thiès and Ila to Touba) and has raised the financing for them. Togo has plans to construct a 60 km road from Katchamba to Sadori. In Uganda, the Kampala Flyover Construction and Road Upgrading Project has secured funds, while Zambia has done likewise for road improvements between Chirundu and Lusaka, and for the New Kafue Weighbridge (ICA, 2016).

At the regional level, work on the Abidjan–Lagos Corridor, the most heavily travelled West African corridor, is progressing. The 1,028 km road in the corridor (under construction) links West Africa's largest cities of Abidjan, Accra, Lomé, Cotonou and Lagos, which between them account for 75% of trade in the ECOWAS region. The corridor will link seaports to land-locked countries, facilitating intra- and inter-African trade. In 2014, the presidents of Benin, Côte d'Ivoire, Ghana, Nigeria and Togo approved the project, each pledging $50 million for preparatory activities. One-stop border posts are also being introduced. In addition to the impacts on trade and on the broader economy, travel corridors also help to develop rural and border areas (ICA, 2016).

Infrastructure financing

Public–private partnerships, and private finance more broadly, are important for financing infrastructure investments in Africa. The World Bank's Private Participation in Infrastructure Database listed 528 "active" (or "distressed") projects using private financing in transport, energy or communications infrastructure across 52 African countries (World Bank, 2017a). The projects involve a variety of different operating models, from those where the private contractor builds, owns and operates the project, to those where the facility is owned by the government. African countries are also using a range of financing vehicles to supplement state resources (Source: Based on World Bank (2015).).

Public–private partnerships help African countries to upgrade their infrastructure faster than would otherwise be possible, particularly for renewable energy projects. For example, 64 renewable energy projects reached financial closure over two years (to April 2016), committing $13.8 billion in private funding to construct nearly 4,000 MW of power-generating capacity. This is more than the total generating capacity of most African countries (ECA, 2016).

Private finance is also listed as being used for nine active multi-country infrastructure projects in Africa: the Abidjan–Ouagadougou Railway, the Beitbridge Border Post (between South Africa and Zimbabwe), the Dakar–Bamako Railway, the DARE submarine broadband cable (Djibouti, Kenya, Somalia and the United Republic of Tanzania), the Maghreb Gas Pipeline (Algeria and Morocco), Moov (Etisalat) (Central African Republic and Togo), the Mozambique–South Africa Gas Pipeline, the N4 Toll Road linking Mozambique and South Africa, and the West African Gas Pipeline (Benin, Ghana, Nigeria and Togo). In addition, "blended finance" and development funds are increasingly being used to

Figure 2.10.

Sources of financing for public–private partnership investments, end-2015

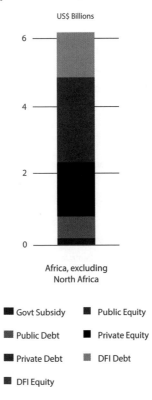

US$ Billions

Africa, excluding North Africa

- ■ Govt Subsidy
- ■ Public Debt
- ■ Private Debt
- ■ DFI Equity
- ■ Public Equity
- ■ Private Equity
- ■ DFI Debt

Source: Based on World Bank (2015).

Table 2.11.

New investment commitments in Africa's infrastructure by end-2015 by economic sector

Economic sector	Transport	Water	Energy	Information and communications technology	Multi-sector investments	Unallocated investments
Amount ($ billion)	34.7	8.1	34.7	2.5	2.2	1.2
Share of total commitments (per cent)	41.6	9.7	41.6	3.0	2.7	1.4

Source: ICA (2016).

Table 2.12.

New investment commitments in Africa's infrastructure in 2015 by funder

Funder	Amount committed in 2015 ($)
44 African governments[8]	28.402 billion
China	20.868 billion
Private sector	7.442 billion
ECOWAS Bank for Investment and Development	7 million
World Bank Group	6.039 billion
East Africa Development Bank	5 million
AfDB	4.166 billion
France	2.455 billion
Islamic Development Bank	2.166 billion
Japan	1.768 billion
European Investment Bank	1.414 billion
Germany	1.139 billion
Arab Fund for Economic and Social Development	984 million
Development Bank of Southern Africa	929 million
European Union bodies	897 million
Other European funders	876 million
India	524 million
Brazil	500 million
Saudi Fund for Development	392 million
Banque Ouest Africaine de Développement	352 million
Kuwait Fund for Arab Economic Development	342 million
OPEC Fund for International Development	312 million
United States	307 million
United Kingdom	287 million
International Finance Corporation	246 million
Canada	195 million
Arab Bank for Economic Development in Africa	135 million
Republic of Korea	88 million
Abu Dhabi Fund for Development	81 million
Banque des États de l'Afrique Centrale	55 million

Source: ICA (2016).

finance infrastructure investment projects in Africa (ICA, 2016).

Sectorally, infrastructure financing in Africa in 2015 is delineated by sector in Table 2.11.

New commitments in 2015 to funding African infrastructure are listed by funder in Table 2.12., which shows that African governments' own resources (together) comprise the largest source of funding, followed by China, and multilateral development banks (combined).

Trade integration

This section examines trends in formal trade followed by a review of intra-African trade data and progress on liberalizing tariffs, facilitating trade, and removing non-tariff barriers (NTBs).

Currently there are four functioning free trade areas by AU recognized RECs: COMESA, ECOWAS, EAC and SADC. Further intra-African trade is liberalized through mechanisms beyond the AU-recognized RECs, including the Pan-Arab free trade area, the Central African Economic and Monetary Community (CEMAC) and the Southern African Customs Union (SACU). The Tripartite Free Trade Area (TFTA) will liberalize more intra-African trade. This is also the expectation for the CFTA.

Most intra-African trade occurs between African countries that are members of the same regional grouping. For instance, the average country in the EAC sources 86 per cent of its African imports from other EAC countries. For ECOWAS, the comparable figure is 64 per cent, for SADC 90 per cent, and for COMESA 78 per cent.

Figure 2.11 to Figure 2.15 show the makeup of intra-African imports by country, with a breakdown of imports that are already traded under FTAs, those that would be covered by the TFTA, and those from other African countries that would be additionally covered by the CFTA. Though imports are covered by these REC free trade areas, several REC free trade areas exclude certain products. Free trade area utilization rates are also less than 100 per cent: For instance, the ECOWAS Trade Liberalization Scheme is cumbersome for traders, meaning that many still pay tariffs (OECD, 2010; Bossuyt, 2016). The figures therefore do not show the level of liberalization, but merely reflect REC free trade area coverage.

EAC countries already have considerable coverage through their EAC single market and the COMESA FTA. Including the TFTA, the EAC countries would on average cover 99 per cent of their intra-African trade.

As ECOWAS coverage is much lower, the CFTA would add considerable value. It could also help to solidify free trade in ECOWAS given the reported constraints to traders regarding the ECOWAS Trade Liberalization Scheme.

The TFTA will be especially important for the COMESA countries that are not in the EAC and are not operating the SADC FTA, as well as for several countries that are not yet implementing other REC FTAs, including Angola, Djibouti, Eritrea and Ethiopia. It will also be valuable for Sudan, which has only a small amount of its intra-African trade captured by the Pan-Arab FTA. For the remaining African countries that are not party to an operating REC FTA, the CFTA is expected to contribute to a large amount of intra-African trade liberalization.

These characteristics of intra-African trade are relevant for the CFTA for two reasons: They show that the tariff revenue losses expected of the CFTA are low, because for many countries a large proportion of intra-African trade is already covered through REC FTAs; and the CFTA will help cover intra-African trade for those countries that do not have operating FTAs within their RECs.

They also suggest that the immediate effects of the CFTA—positive and negative—are unlikely to be dramatic in many countries. The CFTA amounts to a step, rather than a leap, forward for African integration, which will help advance all countries to an improved level of trade integration. (As Chapter 5 highlights, the incremental approach can reduce the structural adjustment costs associated with trade liberalization, and still lead to the trade gains identified in Chapter 4, including improved conditions for forming RVCs, permitting better economies of scale, diversifying exports and facilitating the trade growth forecast by numerous trade models.)

Figure 2.11

Share of EAC Member States' intra-African imports that enter under FTAs, 2015

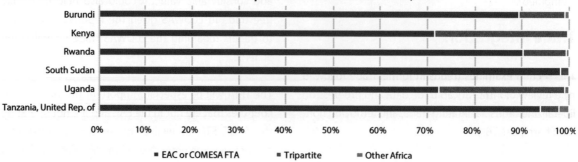

Source: ECA calculations.

Figure 2.12

Share of ECOWAS Member States' intra-African imports that enter under FTAs, 2015

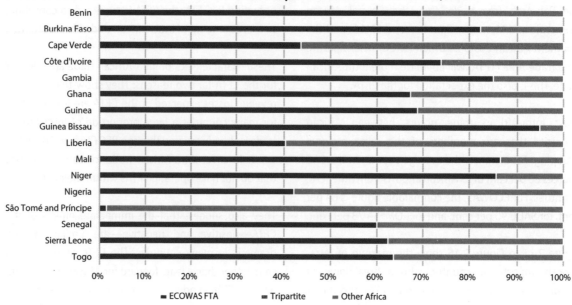

Source: ECA calculations.

Figure 2.13

Share of SADC Member States' intra-African imports that enter under FTAs, 2015

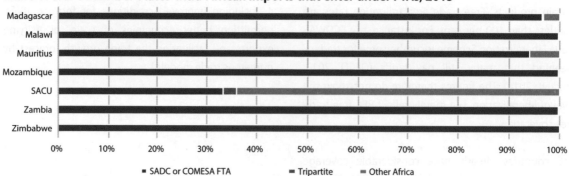

Note: Angola, Democratic Republic of the Congo and the Seychelles have not yet implemented the SADC FTA.

Source: ECA calculations.

Figure 2.14

Share of remaining COMESA (those not operating SADC or EAC FTAs) Member States' intra-African imports that enter under FTAs, 2015

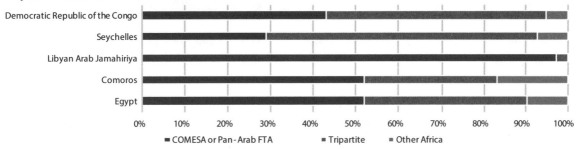

Source: ECA calculations.

Figure 2.15

Share of Other African countries' intra-African imports that enter under FTAs, 2015

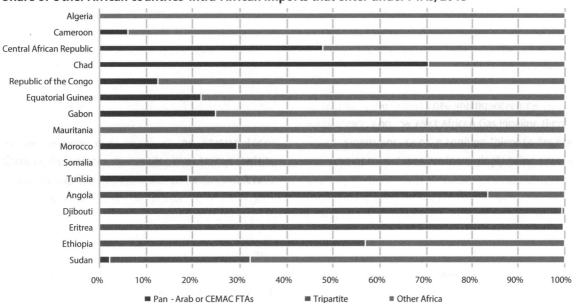

Note: Djibouti, Eritrea, Ethiopia, Sudan and Swaziland have yet to fully implement the COMESA FTA.
Source: ECA calculations.

Formal trade arrangements

Since *ARIA VII*, Africa's RECs have made further advances in liberalizing trade.

COMESA

Democratic Republic of the Congo joined the COMESA free trade area in 2016 through an Act of Parliament, taking the total number of countries to 16. The country will reduce tariffs on imports from other COMESA members over a three-year period, with a 40 per cent reduction on duties in 2016 followed by a 30 per cent reduction in 2017 and another 30 per cent in 2018 (COMESA, 2016).

EAC

South Sudan has completed its accession to the EAC, having received approval from the EAC Heads of State in March 2016 and having signed the accession treaty in April 2016.

ECOWAS

The ECOWAS customs union, which came into force in January 2015, applies a common external tariff at the following rates:

* Zero per cent on essential social goods, covering 85 tariff lines.

- 5 per cent on goods of primary necessity, raw materials, capital goods and specific inputs, covering around 2,100 tariff lines.

- 10 per cent on intermediate goods, covering around 1,400 tariff lines.

- 20 per cent on final consumer goods and goods not specified elsewhere, covering 2,200 tariff lines.

- 35 per cent on specific goods for economic development, covering 130 tariff lines (ECOWAS Commission, 2015a, cited in ECA, AUC and AfDB, 2016).

ECOWAS has created the following mechanisms to ensure that their member states implement the common external tariff:

- A customs valuation mechanism, to ensure that all member states apply the same system of customs valuation.

- Regulations to ensure that inputs for the manufacture of zero-rated products do not face tariffs significantly above those placed on the final product.

- Safeguard, trade, defense and anti-dumping measures: These include supplementary protection measures allowing member states to deviate from the common external tariff for a maximum of 3 per cent of the tariff lines identified in it.

The ECOWAS Common External Tariff came into force on 1 January 2015. Ten out of 15 ECOWAS members were implementing it by 2016 (Obideyi, cited in *Daily Post*, 2016; Ghana Revenue Authority, 2016). In 2017, ECOWAS member countries authorized the ECOWAS Commission to coordinate members' negotiating positions in the discussions for the CFTA.

Tripartite Free Trade Area (TFTA)
The following developments took place in the negotiations of the TFTA since *ARIA VII* was written:

- Eighteen of 26 TFTA member states have signed the Agreement, with a 19th due to sign by 10 June 2017, and one (Egypt) has ratified it.

- Rules of origin for product types covering more than 60 of the 96 Harmonized System chapters had already been agreed on by end-May 2017.

- Annexes on trade remedies, dispute settlement and rules of origin have been finalized.

- The start of the second phase of negotiations has been delayed from its original date.

- TFTA member states are discussing whether to drop separate TFTA-level negotiations on trade in services and simply to focus on CFTA negotiations on services trade.

Continental Free Trade Area
The CFTA negotiations continued during 2016 and 2017, including the first meeting of technical working groups and discussions on modalities. (A more detailed review is in Chapter 4.) As shown in ARIA V, and supported by a more recent study by UNCTAD, the CFTA is expected to bring significant economic benefits to Africa via deeper regional integration and higher incomes and GDP (ECA, AUC and AfDB, 2012; UNCTAD, 2017a).

Intra-African trade in goods
Such benefits are needed, as intra-African exports fell steeply in absolute value from $85 billion in 2014 to $69 billion in 2015 (UNCTAD, 2017b). Intra-African trade as a share of the continent's GDP also declined, from around 3.4 per cent to around 2.9 per cent over the period (Figure 2.16).

As a share of Africa's total imports, intra-African imports stood at 14 per cent in 2015 (UNCTAD, 2017c). As a share of Africa's total exports, intra-African exports stood at 18 per cent in 2015 (UNCTAD, 2017c).

Intra-REC trade
Figure 2.17 shows the share of intra-regional trade in GDP among 25 selected regional trade agreements

Figure 2.16

Growth in share of intra-African trade in Africa's GDP, 1995–2015

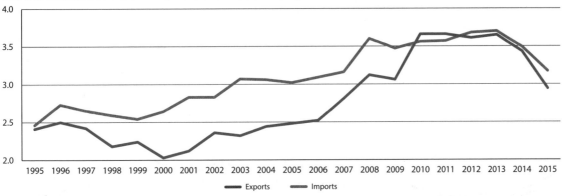

Source: ECA calculations based on UNCTAD (2017b and 2017c).

Figure 2.17

Intra-regional exports as a share of regional GDP plotted against GDP, 2015 ($ billion)

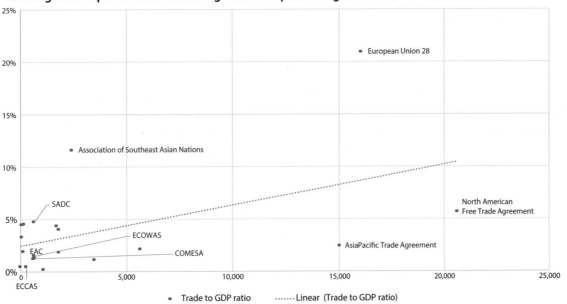

Source: ECA calculations based on UNCTAD (2017c) and WTO (2017a).

in force worldwide and reported to the World Trade Organization (WTO), relative to the total GDP of the bloc (since economic blocs with larger GDP may have greater economic diversity within them, creating greater potential gains from trade and therefore a higher share of intra-regional trade in GDP). Based on this comparison, Africa's RECs that have regional trade agreements (that is, COMESA, EAC, ECCAS, ECOWAS and SADC), tend to underperform in terms of the share of intra-regional trade in GDP (except for SADC).

Among the eight AU-recognized RECs, SADC consistently has the highest share on this metric (Figure 2.18), even though it does not have the lowest intra-regional economic community average–applied tariffs. Other factors, such as trade complementarity, may explain the pattern of trade within SADC.

Non-tariff barriers and trade facilitation

Africa remains far behind the world on its efficiency of document and border processing requirements for

Figure 2.18

Intra-regional economic community exports as a share of GDP, 1996–2015

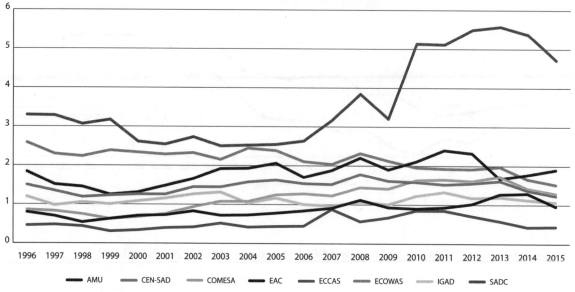

Source: ECA calculations based on UNCTAD (2017c).

trading across borders (ECA, AUC and AfDB, 2016; World Bank, 2017a), despite significant recent progress. The following figures show the time and cost of importing and exporting for various African countries. For both document and border processing requirements, the best-performing countries and territories in the global dataset achieved a cost of less than one U.S. dollar and a processing time of one hour or less (World Bank, 2017b and 2017c).[9]

For the TFTA, great effort has been put into eliminating NTBs. A mechanism for reporting, monitoring and eliminating them was developed to address eight categories: government participation in trade and restrictive practices tolerated by governments; customs and administrative entry procedures; technical barriers to trade; sanitary and phyto-sanitary measures; specific limitations; charges on imports; other procedural problems; and transport, clearing and forwarding. As of June 2017, 527 complaints have been resolved and 57 remain active.[10]

On 22 February 2017, the World Trade Organization's (WTO's) Trade Facilitation Agreement (TFA) entered into force. It commits members to taking measures to reduce the cost of international trade by simplifying, modernizing or harmonizing the country's rules and procedures for exporting or importing. While the Agreement obliges developed countries to implement all measures from the date at which it takes effect, developing and least-developed countries will have longer. Each developing or least-developed country will apply an individual list of measures from countries from the date at which the Agreement takes effect, to be decided by the country in question; these are called "category A" measures. A second individual, nationally determined list of measures ("category B") will be implemented after a transition period (which can be different from measure to measure), to be decided by the country in question. A third individual, nationally determined list of measures ("category C") will be implemented by the country after a transition period to be determined by the country (which again can be different from measure to measure) and only once it receives capacity building support to do so. Each developing or least-developed country must notify each measure included in the Agreement in one of these three categories (WTO, 2017b, 2017c, 2017d).

Figure 2.19

Time and cost to export for African countries, 1 June, 2016

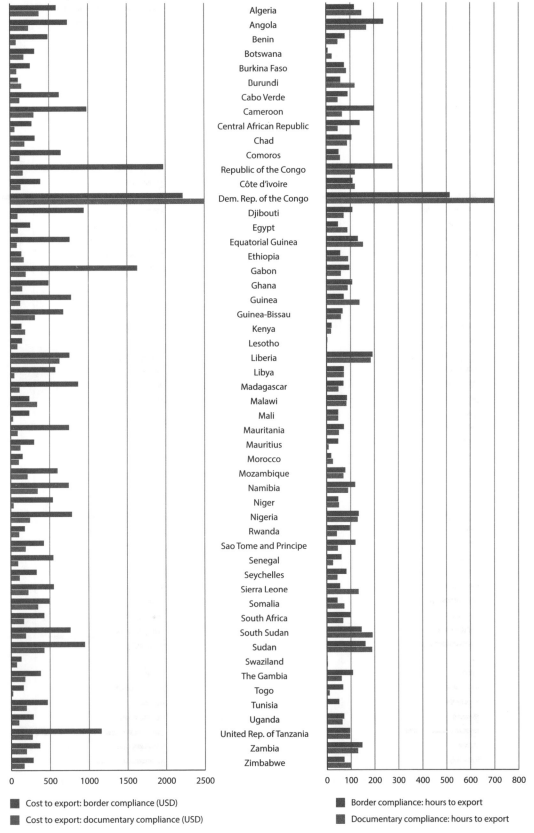

Cost to export: border compliance (USD)
Cost to export: documentary compliance (USD)

Border compliance: hours to export
Documentary compliance: hours to export

Source: World Bank (2017b).

Figure 2.20

Time and cost to import for African countries, 1 June, 2016

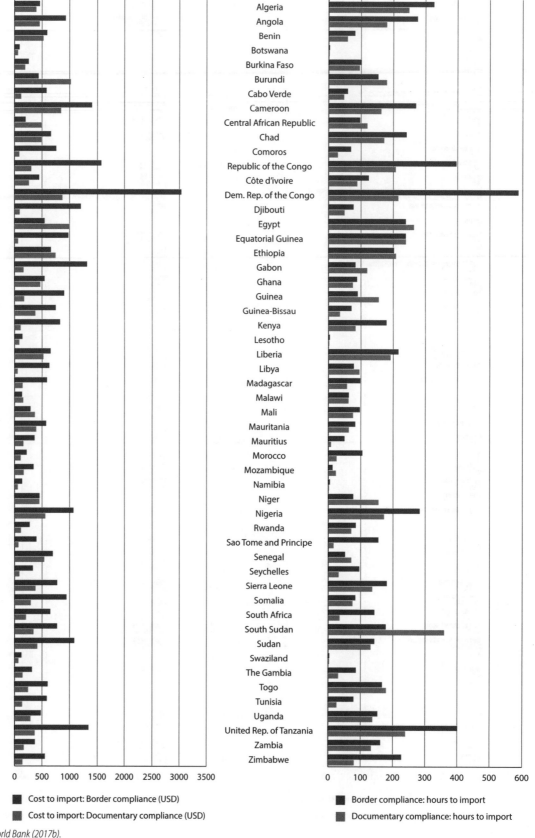

Source: World Bank (2017b).

As African countries start to implement the TFA, trade is expected to be facilitated and boosted, not only among African WTO members likely to become parties to the Agreement, but also between African countries party to the Agreement and non-party African countries. This is because traders from any country (whether party to the Agreement or not) should be able to benefit when trading with a country that is party to the Agreement from measures taken to simplify or modernize export/import rules and procedures.

As of 20 April 2017, of 44 African WTO members party to the TFA, 19 had ratified it (WTO, 2017e). By the same date, 27 had submitted at least some notifications as to which measures will fall into which categories. However, only five (Chad, Malawi, Mauritius, Mozambique and Zambia) had already notified for all of the measures under the Agreement (WTO, 2017f).

The African Corridor Management Alliance, which will promote information and experience sharing and joint projects among Africa's corridor management agencies, was inaugurated in February 2017. This inaugural meeting included discussion of the Alliance's work plan and related issues. ECA has provided funding and substantive support for start-up activities.

Trade in services

Data on services trade are notoriously weak, with woefully poor coverage on both what is being traded and with whom, and questionable reliability of the meagre data that are available. Moreover, drawing on balance-of-payments data, services trade data essentially ignores investment flows. Notwithstanding improvements in the collection of services trade data over the past 15 years, the macro- and micro- level services data needed for meaningful economic analysis simply do not exist—a challenge exacerbated in Africa (Primack, 2016).

One technique commonly used for filling (services) trade flow gaps is to make use of "mirror data," i.e. look at what, for example, the United Kingdom reports as

services imports from Ethiopia as a proxy for what services Ethiopia exports to the UK. While helpful to fill certain gaps, the technique is biased towards understanding North–South trade (as it relies on better reporting from countries in the North). But no public bilateral mirror data exist on intra-African services trade flows, so the oft-cited African share of trade with itself (14% of imports or 18% of exports) does not account for services trade in any way. Case study literature (e.g. AUC, 2015) and experience from African services firms strongly suggest that the majority of business for most African micro, small and medium-sized enterprises (MSMEs) is intra-African.

For barriers to services trade—found "behind the border" in the form of regulatory measures—the World Bank's Services Trade Restrictiveness Index offers a unique snapshot of prevailing discriminatory restrictions in a subset of 27 African countries, sectors and modes.[11] While there is significant diversity among countries, in aggregate the continent scores relatively well relative to high-income Organisation for Economic Co-operation and Development (OECD) countries, with an average overall index score of 33 compared with 19 for the latter. By mode, Africa scores reasonably well, at 31–21 in mode 1, 31–18.6 in mode 3, and 60.7–58.4 in mode 4 (World Bank, 2017d).[12] This aggregation masks significant diversity at the country and sector levels, notably where African countries maintain fairly restrictive regimes, for example in professional, retail and transport services.

This seemingly good performance contrasts with broader narratives about the restrictiveness of African economies, as well as with anecdotal evidence that suggests that services barriers and regulations in African countries still heavily impede services trade opportunities for firms. Data issues notwithstanding, this highlights the fact that non-discriminatory barriers (which are not captured in the Services Trade Restrictiveness Index) are no doubt significant. As increased trade and integration take place between African services markets, this emphasizes the importance of looking at the role of discriminatory barriers and non-discriminatory regulations in intra-African services trade.

Informal trade

Much trade between African countries is not recorded in official statistics because it is informal. For example, an estimated 20 per cent of Benin's GDP is based on informal trade with Nigeria alone (World Bank, cited in Banque de France, 2016). However, data on informal trade are, by its very definition, very limited.

The following graphs show informal and formal trade in some agricultural commodities in Eastern Africa.

The lack of information on informal trade in Africa makes it difficult to evaluate the impact of policies on informal traders and their livelihoods. And while some policies or economic challenges are known to harm informal traders (e.g. cumbersome customs procedures), it can be hard to estimate their economic impact and the importance of changing these policies without accurate data on the extent of informal trade. If these policies are worsening the livelihoods of informal traders, they may also worsen gender exclusion, since women are known to make up 70 per cent of informal cross-border traders. All of this underlines the need to collect and produce better information on informal cross-border trade in Africa, extending to understanding which products and services are being traded informally, and who (men or women) is trading in them.

Economic Partnership Agreements

After negotiating for 12 years, African countries have recently made progress towards signing Economic Partnership Agreements with the EU, though only a handful have started provisionally applying them. Such agreements with Côte d'Ivoire, Ghana and SACU have entered into provisional application since the publication of *ARIA VII*. Kenya and Rwanda have also signed them with the EU since then, but they have not yet entered into provisional application (EU, 2017).

Figure 2.21

Sum of formal and informal cross-border trade in maize grain in selected trade corridors in Eastern Africa (metric tonnes)

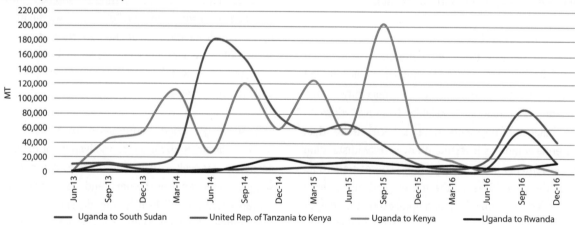

Source: FEWS NET and EAGC, cited in FSNWG (2017).

Figure 2.22

Sum of formal and informal cross-border trade in sorghum grain in selected trade corridors in Eastern Africa (metric tonnes)

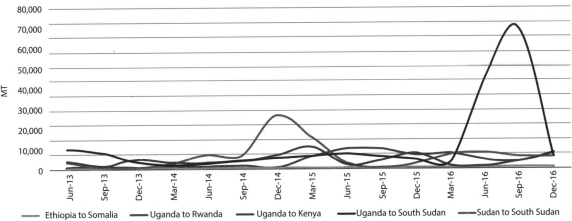

Source: FEWS NET and EAGC, cited in FSNWG (2017).

Figure 2.23

Sum of formal and informal cross-border trade in rice grain in selected trade corridors in Eastern Africa (metric tonnes)

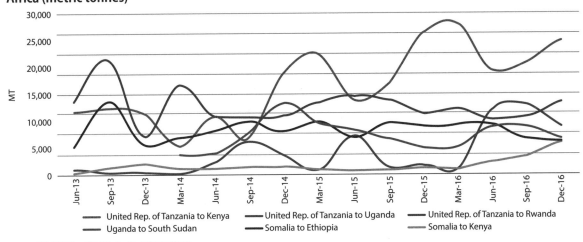

Source: FEWS NET and EAGC, cited in FSNWG (2017).

Figure 2.24.

Sum of formal and informal cross-border trade in dry beans in selected trade corridors in Eastern Africa (metric tonnes)

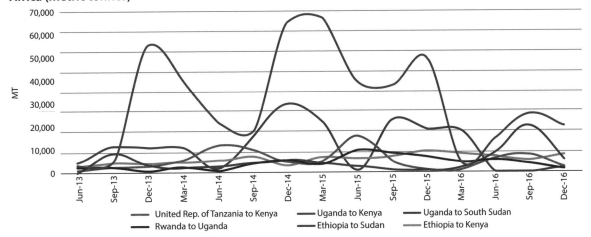

Source: FEWS NET and EAGC, cited in FSNWG (2017).

References

AfDB (African Development Bank). 2016. *Visa Openness Report*. Abidjan.

AMDC (African Minerals Development Centre). 2016. *Optimizing Domestic Revenue Mobilization and Value Addition of Africa's Minerals: Towards Harmonizing Fiscal Regimes in the Mineral Sector*. Addis Ababa: Economic Commission for Africa (ECA).

———. 2017. *Impact of Illicit Financial Flows on Domestic Resource Mobilization: Optimizing Revenues from the Mineral Sector in Africa*. Addis Ababa: ECA

Appiah, L.-A. 2015. "Ethiopia gets the first metro system in sub-Saharan Africa." *Cable News Network,* 14 October. http://edition.cnn.com/2015/10/14/tech/addis-ababa-light-rail-metro/.

AU (African Union). 2017a. "Africa CDC Centres for Disease Control and Prevention: Safeguarding Africa's Health." https://www.au.int/en/africacdc.

———. 2017b. "Africa Centres for Disease Control and Prevention's Regional Collaborating Centres in Africa agree on a strategic plan and roadmap for disease prevention and response in Africa." https://www.au.int/web/en/pressreleases/20170320/africa-centres-disease-control-and-prevention's-regional-collaborating.

AUC (African Union Commission). 2015. *Services Exports For Growth And Development: Case Studies from Africa*. Addis Ababa.

Banque de France. 2016. *La lettre de la zone Franc*, No. 7, Décembre. Paris. https://publications.banque-france.fr/sites/default/files/medias/documents/la-lettre-de-la-zone-franc-07_2016-12.pdf.

Barrow, K. 2016. "Nigeria inaugurates Abuja-Kaduna railway." *International Railway Journal*, 26 July. http://www.railjournal.com/index.php/africa/nigeria-inaugurates-abuja-kabuna-railway.html?channel=000.

Bossuyt, J. 2016. *The Political Economy of Regional Integration in Africa: The Economic Community of West African States (ECOWAS)*. Maastricht: European Centre for Development Policy.

Citizen, The. 2016. "Namibia to abolish visa requirements for Africans." *The Citizen*, 26 July. http://citizen.co.za/news/news-world/1221471/namibia-to-abolish-visa-requirements-for-all-africans/.

COMESA (Common Market for Eastern and Southern Africa). 2016. "Sixteen countries now in Free Trade Area." http://www.comesa.int/sixteen-countries-now-in-free-trade-area/.

———. 2017. "Bank's Governors push for Regional Payment and Settlement System." http://www.comesa.int/banks-governors-push-for-regional-payment-and-settlement-system/.

Daily Post. 2016. "10 countries implement ECOWAS Common External Tariff." *Daily Post*, 8 September. http://dailypost.ng/2016/09/08/10-countries-implement-ecowas-common-external-tariff/.

ECA (Economic Commission for Africa). 2012. *Assessing Regional Integration in Africa: Towards an African Continental Free Trade Area*. Addis Ababa.

———. 2016. Brief for the Office of the Executive Secretary on Regional Integration and the Continental Free Trade Area, prepared by the African Trade Policy Centre. Addis Ababa.

———. 2017a. *Economic Report on Africa 2017: Urbanization and Industrialization for Africa's Transformation*. Addis Ababa.

———. 2017b. *Nigeria Country Profile 2016*. Addis Ababa.

———. 2017c. *Ghana Country Profile 2016*. Addis Ababa.

———. 2017d. *Cabo Verde Country Profile 2016*. Addis Ababa.

———. 2017e. *Chad Country Profile 2016*. Addis Ababa.

———. 2017f. *Somalia Country Profile 2016*. Addis Ababa.

———. 2017g. *Djibouti Country Profile 2016*. Addis Ababa.

ECA, AUC and AfDB. 2016. *Assessing Regional Integration in Africa VII: Innovation, Competitiveness and Regional Integration*. Addis Ababa: ECA.

Economist, The. 2016. "Ethiopia opens Africa's tallest and most controversial dam." *The Economist*, 21 December. http://www.economist.com/news/21712281-gibe-iii-dam-has-capacity-double-countrys-electricity-output.

ECOSOC (United Nations Economic and Social Council). 2017. *Regional meeting on "Innovations for infrastructure development and sustainable industrialization."* New York. https://www.un.org/ecosoc/sites/www.un.org.ecosoc/files/files/en/2017doc/summary_dakar_meeting.pdf.

European Union. 2017. "Overview of Economic Partnership Agreements." http://trade.ec.europa.eu/doclib/docs/2009/september/tradoc_144912.pdf.

FSNWG (Food Security and Nutrition Working Group). 2017. *East Africa Crossborder Trade Bulletin*, Vol. 16. Nairobi: FEWS NET/FAO/WFP Joint Cross Border Market and Trade Monitoring Initiative.

Ghana Revenue Authority. 2016. "ECOWAS Regional Common External Tariff comes into effect on 1st February, 2016." http://www.gra.gov.gh/index.php/category/item/488-ecowas-regional-common-external-tariff-comes-into-effect-on-1st-february-2016.

ICA (Infrastructure Consortium for Africa). 2016. *Infrastructure Financing Trends in Africa – 2015*. Abidjan: Infrastructure Consortium for Africa Secretariat c/o African Development Bank. https://www.icafrica.org/fileadmin/documents/Annual_Reports/ICA_2015_annual_report.pdf.

International Monetary Fund. 2017. *Coordinated Direct Investment Survey*. Washington, DC. http://data.imf.org/?sk=40313609-F037-48C1-84B1-E1F1CE54D6D5&sId=1390030341854.

Jacobs, A. 2017. "Joyous Africans take to the rails, with China's help." *The New York Times*, 7 February. https://www.nytimes.com/2017/02/07/world/africa/africa-china-train.html?_r=0.

Karingi, S., and W. Davis. 2017. Mimeo. "Towards a transformative African integration process: Rethinking the conventional approaches." Submitted to the *Journal of Africa Economies*, pending decision.

Maasho, A. 2016. "Ethiopia plans new 2,000 MW dam: PM." *Reuters*, 10 March. http://www.reuters.com/article/us-ethiopia-hydro-idUSKCN0WC1P4.

Mabuza, Z., and D. Luke. 2016. Mimeo. "State of Play in the Tripartite Free Trade Area Negotiations."

Meseret, E. 2016. "Ethiopia opens massive Gibe 3 hydroelectric dam on Omo River." *US News & World Report*, 17 December. https://www.usnews.com/news/business/articles/2016-12-17/ethiopia-opens-massive-gibe-3-hydroelectric-dam-on-omo-river.

Moody's Investors Service. 2016. "Moody's: China Railway Construction's winning bid on Nigeria light rail project is credit positive." Press release, 1 September. https://www.moodys.com/research/Moodys-China-Railway-Constructions-winning-bid-on-Nigeria-light-rail--PR_354493.

Morylln-Yron, S., K. Scott, J. Kwok and A. Darvenzia. 2017. "All aboard! The Chinese-funded railways linking East Africa." *Cable News Network*, 17 January. http://edition.cnn.com/2016/11/21/africa/chinese-funded-railways-in-africa/.

Mugisha, I. R. 2017. "Rwanda to scrap visas for Africans by 2018." *The East African*, 28 May. http://www.theeastafrican.co.ke/news/Rwanda-to-scrap-visas-for-Africans-by-2018-/2558-3222744-view-printVersion-c8310cz/index.html.

OECD (Organisation for Economic Co-operation and Development). 2010. *Gap Analysis of the ECOWAS Trade Liberalization Scheme (ETLS)*. Aid-for-trade: Case Story—ECOWAS. Paris.

Parke, P. 2016. "Kenya's $13 billion railway project is taking shape." *Cable News Network*, 15 May. http://edition.cnn.com/2016/05/15/africa/kenya-railway-east-africa/.

Primack, D. 2016. "Services trade data: A fundamental roadblock to negotiations and policy-making to support structural transformation." London: Overseas Development Institute. http://set.odi.org/david-primack-services-trade-data-fundamental-roadblock-negotiations-policy-making/. Accessed 10 March 2017.

Railways Africa. 2016. "Nigeria To Start Construction On Light Rail Projects For Urban Mobility." *Railways Africa,* 14 October. http://www.railwaysafrica.com/news/nigeria-to-start-construction-on-light-rail-projects-for-urban-mobility.

Rogers, D. 2016. "China, Nigeria agree new deal for $12bn coastal railway." *Global Construction Review,* 7 July. http://www.globalconstructionreview.com/news/china-nigeria-agree-ne7w-dea7l-12bn-coas7tal/.

UN (United Nations). 2017a. *UN Mission's Summary detailed by country.* New York. http://www.un.org/en/peacekeeping/contributors/2017/feb17_3.pdf.

———. 2017b. "Peacekeeping Fact Sheet." http://www.un.org/en/peacekeeping/resources/statistics/factsheet.shtml.

UNCTAD (United Nations Conference on Trade and Development). 2017a. Presentation made by Christian Knebel at the capacity building workshop immediately preceding the fifth Continental Free Trade Area Negotiating Forum, Addis Ababa, 27–28 February.

———. 2017b. "Mapping of intra-Africa trade in goods, flows and destinations." Paper presented to the fifth Continental Free Trade Area Negotiating Forum, Addis Ababa, 1–4 March.

———. 2017c. UNCTADStat database. http://unctadstat.unctad.org/EN/.

WEF (World Economic Forum). 2016. Global Competitiveness Index Historical Dataset.

World Bank. 2015. *Sources of Financing for Public-Private Partnership Investments in 2015.* Washington, DC.

———. 2017a. Private Participation in Infrastructure Database. https://ppi.worldbank.org/data.

———. 2017b. Doing Business database. http://www.doingbusiness.org/data.

———. 2017c. *Doing Business 2017.* Washington, DC. http://www.doingbusiness.org/reports/global-reports/doing-business-2017.

———. 2017d. Services Trade Restrictiveness Index. http://data.worldbank.org/data-catalog/services-trade-restrictions.

WTO (World Trade Organization). 2017a. "List of all RTAs." http://rtais.wto.org/UI/PublicAllRTAList.aspx./WDSP/IB/2015/04/20/000442464_20150420122912/Rendered/PDF/ACS125280REVIS0itive0Private0Sector.pdf.

———. 2017b. "Trade Facilitation." https://www.wto.org/english/tratop_e/tradfa_e/tradfa_e.htm.

———. 2017c. *Trade Facilitation Agreement: Easing the flow of trade across borders.* Geneva. https://www.wto.org/english/thewto_e/20y_e/wto_tradefacilitation_e.pdf.

———. 2017d. "How to notify." http://www.tfafacility.org/how-present-notifications.

———. 2017e. "Ratifications." https://www.tfadatabase.org/ratifications.

———. 2017f. "Notifications List." https://www.tfadatabase.org/notifications/list.

Endnotes

1   This section draws on the *Economic Report on Africa 2017* (ECA, 2017).

2   Only six members (i.e. the Economic and Monetary Community of Central Africa, CEMAC) of the 11 members of ECCAS are members of the EMU.

3   According to the Mbeki High Level Panel on Illicit Financial Flows.

4   AMDC (2017). Impact of Illicit Financial Flows on Domestic Resource Mobilization: Optimizing Revenues from the Mineral Sector in Africa.

5   AMDC (2016). Optimizing Domestic Revenue Mobilization and Value Addition of Africa's Minerals – Towards Harmonizing Fiscal Regimes in the Mineral Sector.

6   The Ruzizi II hydropower project; Dar es Salaam port expansion; Serenge-Nakonde road (T2); Nigeria-Algeria gas pipeline; modernization of the Dakar-Bamako rail line; the Sambagalou hydropower project; the Abidjan-Lagos coastal corridor; the Lusaka-Lilongwe ICT terrestrial fibre optic; the Zambia-Tanzania-Kenya transmission project; the North African transmission corridor; the Abidjan-Ouagadougou road-rail link between Côte d'Ivoire and Burkina Faso; the Douala Bangui Ndjamena corridor road-rail link between Cameroon, Central African Republic and Chad; Kampala-Jinja road upgrades between Kampala and Jinja in Uganda; Juba-Torit-Kapoeta Nadapal-Eldoret road between Uganda and Kenya; the Batoka Gorge hydropower project on the border between Zambia and Zimbabwe; and the Brazzaville Kinshasa road–rail bridge between the Republic of the Congo and the Democratic Republic of the Congo and the Kinshasa Ilebo railways.

7   For just two examples, see Djibouti (ECA, 2017f) and Côte d'Ivoire's investments in transport (ICA, 2016).

8   Data were available for 2015 for 44 African governments only.

9   These countries and territories include a range of EU member states, plus Belarus, Hong Kong SAR, Kazakhstan, Norway, the Republic of Korea, San Marino and the State of Palestine.

10   http://www.tradebarriers.org/about.

11   The data are mostly circa 2009–2010, covering five sectors (financial, transport, retail, telecoms and professional services) and modes 1, 3 and 4, and scored out of 100 (being the most restrictive). The data are highly aggregated and biased to some extent in emphasizing those barriers most easily identifiable (i.e. investment related).

12   In services trade Mode 1 is cross-border trade, which is defined as delivery of a service from the territory of one country into the territory of another country; Mode 2 is consumption abroad, which covers supply of a service of one country to the service consumer of any other country; Mode 3 is commercial presence, which covers services provided by a service supplier of one country in the territory of any other country; and Mode 4 is presence of natural persons, which covers services provided by a service supplier of one country through the presence of natural persons in the territory of another country.

Chapter 3
Conceptual Issues in the Political Economy of Integration and the CFTA

This chapter reviews the political economy of the Continental Free Trade Area (CFTA). It seeks to understand why there is a gap between continental and regional policies and programmes and their implementation. Despite past and current efforts to accelerate the dynamism of intra-African trade, implementation remains a challenge.

The discussion draws on the "five-lens" analytical tool developed by the European Centre for Development Policy Management (ECDPM) (Byiers et al., 2015). The value of this tool is that it unpacks and explains the complexities and challenges of regional integration. It does this by identifying the actors and factors that have had a significant impact on regional integration processes, which helps to explain "why things are as they are."

However, the way things are need not be deterministic. The chapter concludes by drawing on Economic Commission for Africa (ECA)'s research on institutional

capacities and sustaining policy reform in the context of the developmental state and structural economic change (ECA, 2011, 2012, and 2014). It shows that a developmental state, guided by leadership committed to national developmental goals and empowered by competent bureaucracies, is needed to steer the CFTA process and to ensure the outcome is an implemented CFTA conducive to African development.

A conceptual approach to the political economy of the CFTA

The 10 key findings from the assessment are framed across the five lenses (Table 3.1).

Foundational factors

Foundational factors—the first of the lenses—come in two forms: the structural and the historical. The former refers to the geographic or economic structure of a country, the latter to its historical legacies. What they have in common is that they are either impossible, or

Table 3.1

A conceptual approach to the political economy of the CFTA—five lenses and 10 findings

Lens		Finding
FOUNDATIONAL FACTORS structural and historical		1. Foundational factors include Africa's structural and historical foundations. These shape but do not determine the environment in which the CFTA will be negotiated and implemented.
INSTITUTIONS form and function		2. The CFTA institutional forms must be designed such that they serve the stated functions, rather than imitate best practice examples that will not work in the CFTA context.
ACTORS interests and incentives		3. Member states may signal support for the CFTA even when implementation is not a political priority.
		4. Implementation of the CFTA will take place when in line with key national interests as defined by national decision makers.
		5. Influential states are in a strong position to drive the CFTA agenda and its implementation but small countries can adopt a variety of strategies to promote their interests.
		6. Individual personalities, leaders, negotiators and the choices they make will tend to shape—and can be decisive for—the negotiation and implementation of the CFTA.
		7. Engaging the diversity of private sector actors and civil society organizations in the CFTA is essential for recognizing the wide array of interests involved.
SECTOR-SPECIFIC dimensions		8. Trade agreements generally demonstrate high levels of ambition with low levels of implementation.
EXTERNAL FACTORS donors and critical junctures		9. The quantity and quality of donor support to the CFTA present opportunities and challenges for reducing the implementation gap.
		10. Critical junctures such as rising emerging market trade with Africa, the post-AGOA agenda, Brexit and the stagnation of the EPAs can trigger progress but also block dynamics conducive to the CFTA.

Note: EPA is the Economic Partnership Agreement; AGOA is the African Growth and Opportunity Act.

Source: Byiers et al. (2015).

at least very difficult, to change in the short to medium term. These structural and historical foundations frame the political economy interests of a country, but they need not be deterministic.

Structural foundations: Geography and economy

Africa's countries have a breadth of geographic and economic configurations. There are 15 land-locked countries and six Small Island Developing Economies in Africa (ECA, 2017). Africa's economies range from $337 million GDP in São Tomé and Príncipe to $568 billion GDP in Nigeria. GDP per capita extends from $130 in Somalia to $20,381 in Equatorial Guinea (UNDESA, 2017). Many of these countries are dependent on extractive resources, with 73 per cent of Africa's exports to the rest of the world comprising such resources.[1]

Regional integration is especially attractive to land-locked countries. It helps them establish transit corridors for port access and regional investments in transport infrastructure, all of which assist land-locked countries in trading with the outside world. Some examples: Successful integration in the East African Community (EAC) is eased by the strong desire of its land-locked countries for port access (Byiers, 2016). In West Africa, the Economic Community of West African States (ECOWAS) helps smooth the transit of goods from the ports of its coastal countries to the markets of its interior land-locked countries. The win-win benefits of linking land-locked and coastal economies can drive integration. The CFTA can be especially beneficial to land-locked countries if it improves the ease with which they can transit goods. (This is discussed further in Chapter 5.)

Discrepancies in size and relative strengths of economies create tensions over the perceived distribution of regional integration benefits. Competition from economically more sophisticated and powerful neighbours can intimidate economically weaker states. The collapse of the predecessor to the EAC in 1977 stemmed largely from the belief that the benefits accrued disproportionately to Kenya, which was more industrialized (Mathieson, 2016).

What does this mean for the CFTA? The breadth of economic forms across African countries has two implications. First, the industrial powerhouses, such as Egypt, Kenya, Nigeria and South Africa, may be perceived as having more to gain from the CFTA. As seen with the failed Free Trade Area of the Americas (FTAA) in Lessons learned from the Free Trade Area of the Americas (as well as the earlier phase of the EAC), such perceptions can unravel negotiations and cause trade agreements to fail. It is crucial that the CFTA be designed through a win-win approach that shares its benefits both across and within Africa's countries. (This is the topic of Chapters 5 and 6.)

Second, the larger and more influential countries are critical to bringing the CFTA about. Most successful regional arrangements around the world have been underpinned by one or more regional powers championing the arrangement. The attitude and behaviour of these champions towards the CFTA will be crucial. On the one hand, larger economies may be ably placed to tap into the gains from trade liberalization. On the other, they may fear opening up their own "backyards"—their immediate RECs—to competition from large economies in other subregions. For instance, Nigerian businesses might conceivably fear South African competitors in ECOWAS (see "Actors: interests and incentives" below).

Box 3.1

Lessons learned from the Free Trade Area of the Americas

The FTAA initiative was launched in December 1994 at the First Summit of the Americas, in Miami, US. The goal of this US-led project was to create, by 2005, the world's largest free trade area comprising 34 economies of the Western Hemisphere (only Cuba was excluded, on political grounds). Most of the actual negotiations took place between 2000 and 2003, coinciding with the first years of the Doha Round at the World Trade Organization (WTO). After repeatedly failing to reach an agreement, the FTAA process was terminated in November 2005.

From the start, the negotiations were complicated by huge disparities in development levels, institutional capacities and size (economic, demographic and geographic) among the 34 countries. At one end was the

Box 3.1

Lessons learned from the Free Trade Area of the Americas (continued)

world's largest economy and third-most populous country, the United States, while at the other were the English-speaking Caribbean countries, nearly all of which have populations below 1 million. Compared with the $18 trillion US economy, only Brazil, Canada and Mexico can be considered large economies (with a GDP above $1 trillion in 2015). Argentina, Chile, Colombia, Peru and Venezuela are mid-sized economies, with GDP in the $200–700 billion range, while all other Western Hemisphere countries are small economies. Per capita GDP of the United States exceeded $56,000 in 2015, while that of Haiti (the only least-developed country in the Western Hemisphere) was less than $1,000.

Yet the negotiations were conceived as a single undertaking, with the general principles agreed to in March 1998, that "the rights and obligations of the FTAA will be shared by all countries." With the exception of different phase-out schedules, this left limited scope for flexibility, special and differential treatment, and variable geometry.

The substance of liberalization proposed was ambitiously deep, and it was seen to be mainly of interest to the United States. It included elimination of almost all tariffs on goods, opening-up of government procurement, liberalization of trade in services and investment on a negative list basis,[2] investor-state dispute settlement, and TRIPs-Plus intellectual property rights protections.[3] It notably included weak or no substantive commitments on issues sensitive to the United States, such as antidumping and other trade remedies, trade-distorting domestic support to agriculture, or easing border restrictions to foreign individuals providing services.

Towards the end of the negotiations in 2004, alternative integration regimes were gaining traction with different political or integration objectives. This included the Bolivarian Alliance for the Peoples of Our America and the Community of South American Nations (which in 2007 became the Union of South American Nations, UNASUR). As the FTAA stalled, the United States readjusted its approach, expanding its network of alternative bilateral free trade areas with "can do" countries, starting with a Chilean free trade area in June 2003.

Today the United States has FTAs in force with 11 Latin American countries, effectively splitting Latin America between those countries that are more closely integrated with the United States, which lie mostly on the Western side of Latin America, and those on the Eastern side that are not. The effect is a fragmented Latin America of two main blocks: the US-friendly Pacific Alliance, and Mercosur. Intra-regional trade remains low, at just 16 per cent of exports in 2015.

The experience of the FTAA offers some important lessons for any large-scale regional integration project, including the CFTA:

- Leadership is essential, but the main driver of the negotiations cannot be seen as one country seeking to concentrate most benefits for itself.

- Differences among participants in terms of size, development levels and expectations make a "one size fits all" agreement politically impossible. Therefore, it is preferable to proceed incrementally, leaving enough space for poorer countries to assume more demanding commitments at their own pace. This would be especially important for the CFTA, given the large number of African least-developed countries.

- It would be advantageous if African countries formulated common positions for the CFTA within their RECs rather than negotiate individually. This would expedite the process; otherwise it is a negotiation with 55 participants.

- North–South negotiations are particularly difficult, since the demands of developed country participants in areas like intellectual property and investment tend to be resisted by developing countries fearing the loss of policy space. To that extent, reaching agreements within the CFTA could prove easier than in the FTAA, since it would be a purely African negotiation.

Many African countries have struggled to shrug off economic histories of natural resource extraction and the export of basic commodities. There is both similarity and limited complementarity between the trade profiles of most countries: Ghana need not import cocoa from Côte d'Ivoire, nor Kenya tea from Uganda, other than to re-export. Conversely, this lack of economic complementarity motivates a lot of the political support behind the CFTA: African leaders are keen to *change* the economic status quo and understand the CFTA as a means of promoting industrialization (Sommer and Luke, 2017).[4] Economic circumstances need not be deterministic.

Historical foundations: Colonial and liberation legacies

Shared experiences with decolonization and liberation struggles drive integration in Africa. These underpin a common identity and a sense of solidarity that in turn form the pan-African ideology. This is well encapsulated by the stated purpose of the Organisation of African Unity (OAU), the precursor to the African Union (AU), which brought together African countries for unity, solidarity and "eradicat[ing] all forms of colonialism from Africa" (OAU, 1963).

Alternative colonial legacies have, however, fostered very different administrative, religious and bureaucratic traditions. Africa's francophone countries are consolidated by a shared language, the civil law legal system, and in many cases monetary union. Likewise, Africa's arabophone countries to the north share language and Islamic law, and are covered by similar REC and FTA memberships. Continuing geopolitical tensions in the Horn of Africa can be traced back to the legacy of Italian occupation of the area (Plaut, 2016).

The legacy of these histories is that African countries approach the CFTA from a variety of legal systems (Figure 3.1), languages and geopolitics. On a practical note, negotiating in four languages[5] is cumbersome, and translation and interpretation add to negotiation expenses. On the other hand, these histories have helped coalesce countries into a number of regional free trade areas and customs unions that form useful building blocks for the CFTA. These histories have also fostered the shared pan-African spirit that underpins the grander pan-African vision, to which the CFTA contributes. (The regional economic communities [RECs] in the CFTA, CFTA institutions in the AU, and the Abuja Treaty as a framework for the CFTA, are discussed in Chapter 8.)

Figure 3.1
Legal systems of Africa

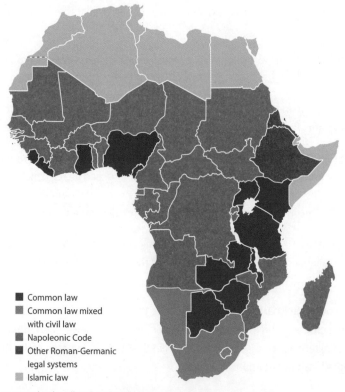

- ■ Common law
- ■ Common law mixed with civil law
- ■ Napoleonic Code
- ■ Other Roman-Germanic legal systems
- ■ Islamic law

Source: http://www.notarius-international.uinl.org/DataBase/2009/Notarius_2009_01_02_worldmaps.pdf.

Institutions: Form and function

The formal institutions to implement the CFTA are being constructed, and lessons can be drawn from the political economy of Africa's existing formal and informal regional institutions. (These ideas are incorporated in the institutional options outlined in Chapter 8.)

Africa has a well-developed architecture of formal institutions to support regional integration. Nevertheless, these institutional forms—often look-alikes of best-practice models—do not always match their stated functions. The *forms* that regional public institutions have—the budget and accountability rules and processes, the organizational structures, the apex decision-making bodies, regional parliaments and courts, etc.—may easily be mistaken for the stated institutional *functions* such as budget management accountability and transparency, conflict mediation and arbitration, or the delivery of regional public goods or services. In other words, what you see is *not* always what you get. This state of affairs helps explain the widely criticised gap between policy decisions and implementation.

Tensions between form and function apply to Africa's regional trade policies and agreements. Market integration and related policies of industrialization and of regional and continental infrastructure development all enjoy near unanimous support from the apex bodies. Multiple formal institutions and programmes have been put in place to implement these aspirations through the RECs, including arbitration or compliance institutions, such as courts or tribunals. Yet free trade policies are frequently circumvented or undone by a combination of the slow or incomplete transposition of regional commitments to national regulatory and legal texts; uneven or incomplete application of regional agreements; and other practices such as (legitimate and illegitimate) non-tariff measures that create de facto barriers to integration.

For instance, many RECs have free trade areas, yet in practice, trade between member states is restricted by a variety of non-tariff barriers (NTBs), internal taxes and lists of "sensitive" goods (Bilal et al., 2015). Prevailing norms against the use of formal dispute settlement procedures against other African states mean that those institutions that have been established to ensure compliance with regional agreements, such as the Common Market for Eastern and Southern Africa (COMESA) Court of Justice, the Southern African Development Community (SADC) Tribunal or the East African Court of Justice, are underused and do not effectively fulfil their functions, despite efforts to strengthen some of them.

The CFTA will be a set of formal institutions created to monitor, resolve conflicts, facilitate implementation, arbitrate and nudge stakeholders to implementation. It is crucial that the institutions for the CFTA be designed so that they can fulfil their intended functions. Depending on prevailing formal and informal norms and practices, the most effective institutional designs may not be those adhering to global best practices but could include, for example, dispute settlement procedures that adopt non-litigious methods as a first approach before resorting to formal procedures.

Actors: Interests and incentives

Regional integration is driven by groups and coalitions of actors. Important elements are the incentives driving the main groups and how these interact with the formal and informal institutions. This section identifies five groups critical for the CFTA.

National decision makers and national interests

Implementation of regional initiatives takes place when in line with key national interests as perceived and defined by national decision makers and in accord with domestic political pressures.

It is easy for leaders to express support for integration, but it is far harder to ensure the commitment of national decision makers operating on the basis of national interests. It would be a mistake to underestimate the resolve of negotiating delegations to promote national interests. As stated by Rob Davies, the South African Minister of Trade and Industry, "Trade negotiations have to be recognised now more than ever as being what they have always been, a process of giving and taking driven by competing interests" (Davies, 2017).

Influential states

Countries can be influential in different areas, depending on their ability to muster diplomatic, economic, military and political influence, and their capacity to compensate losers, unblock stalemates and overcome coordination failures in regional collective action. The considerable weight and leadership that some states can wield will be crucial in bringing the CFTA about.

Across Africa's regions, individual states wield more or less influence. Some, for instance, may fear that the CFTA would open up their economic sphere of influence to trade with other influential states from other regions. Others may pursue the CFTA as a means of articulating perceived trade interests. If these interests are not balanced, influential states may exercise their weight against the CFTA and threaten its implementation. However, there is reason for optimism. As it approaches conclusion, the Tripartite Free Trade Area (TFTA) is setting a precedent for how the sometimes-conflicting interests of influential states across regions can be balanced for a mutually beneficial trade agreement (Lessons learned from the Tripartite Free Trade Area).

Box 3.2

Lessons learned from the Tripartite Free Trade Area

The TFTA concerns 26 countries from the EAC, SADC and COMESA. Phase 1 of the negotiations (covering trade in goods) started in 2011 and is almost complete with a signed text and several annexes. Negotiations on issues outstanding at the TFTA's launch in 2015—trade remedies, dispute settlement and tariff negotiations—have been completed or have greatly advanced.

Like the CFTA, the TFTA aims to adopt better legal frameworks for promoting intra-African trade in the 21st century. It seeks to address similar challenges, such as the difficulties caused by overlapping membership in RECs, bottlenecks in movements of goods and services, trade facilitation issues, and more generally to establish a predictable and transparent trade environment. The TFTA concerns a diverse range of African countries with different incentives and foundational factors, and at different levels of economic and industrial development. The aims, modalities and major challenges and successes of the TFTA offer lessons for the CFTA.

Reconciling the preservation of RECs with the desire to rationalize overlapping REC membership

When negotiations started, the TFTA was expected to reconcile "the challenges of multiple [REC] membership and expedite the regional and continental integration processes."[6] It was resolved that the three RECs "should immediately start working towards a merger into a single REC."[7] This did not happen. The TFTA evolved to represent, in at least the short to medium term, a new layer of FTAs over the three RECs, rather than a consolidation. Why did this happen? The TFTA Negotiating Principles included "building on the REC acquis," which was not reconciled with the objective of consolidating the RECs.[8] Hence in the CFTA, considerable care must be taken to balance the desire to retain the existing RECs with the objective of rationalizing the REC FTAs into a consolidated trading area. If mishandled, the CFTA may merely add an FTA layer and miss an opportunity for rationalizing and simplifying trade in Africa.

Signing partially complete or "framework" agreements

The Agreement Establishing the TFTA was signed in June 2015 with transitional arrangements for the outstanding components (rules of origin, tariff offers and trade remedies). TFTA member states were to conclude the outstanding annexes by June 2016, but missed the deadline. Care should be taken with the CFTA to ensure that deadlines are provided and adhered to for any outstanding issues left when it is signed.

Resolving pan-African ideals with national interests

Though the TFTA was launched under the banner of pan-Africanism and African solidarity, the negotiations amounted to typical offensive and defensive exchanges. When concluding binding trade agreements, including the CFTA, national interests, such as dealing with unemployment at home, national development and industrialization plans, will prevail.

Funding large-scale negotiations in Africa

The TFTA negotiations involved three RECs and 26 Member/Partner States and four languages. Negotiations at this scale require financial, logistical, secretarial and technical support. The funding was based on donor support, which can be unpredictable—at one stage it looked like it would stall the TFTA negotiations. The funding of the CFTA should endeavour to be less donor reliant.

Influential states may drive regional dynamics. They could resource their participation in negotiations, for instance by funding large negotiating delegations with a broader range of expertise than smaller states. These experts are better able to steer negotiations, but there can be risks if they manipulate the process for their own gain.

In bringing the CFTA about, it is crucial that its benefits are shared across African countries for a win-win outcome. Trade agreements that are not win-win can remain unimplemented, as partner countries have little interest in their application (Jones, 2013). If the gains are perceived as being captured by only a few countries, trade agreements may unravel, as with the former EAC and the FTAA. (Policies to ensure the equitability of the CFTA are discussed in Chapters 5 and 6.)

Though there are undeniably some influential states in the CFTA, other countries can also exercise influence, through coalitions for example. By stitching together groups with similar views, smaller countries can effectively promote their interests. In the case of the CFTA, one such coalition involves the non-WTO states that form a diverse group of similar interests.

Political leaders
Individual personalities and the strength of exceptional leaders can define, drive and create momentum for regional integration initiatives. For example, the eminence of presidents Thabo Mbeki and Olusegun Obasanjo helped establish the AU.

Leadership and vision are required for designing and pursing policies to move Africa from its heavy dependence on primary commodity exports and low intra-African trade (ECA, 2011). Powerful leadership is an important resource for ensuring that political economy forces do not become deterministic. Leaders can drive scenarios that break with the status quo and achieve better outcomes. For the CFTA, such leadership will be required to overcome many of the political economy challenges seen in this chapter, and to use the political economy windows of opportunity.

Trade negotiators
The actors who most directly filter national interests, steer negotiations and pen the negotiated texts are the chief negotiators of member states. They channel their particular experience, expertise and capacity.

Trade negotiators tend to have more experience with the trade in goods and revenue interests of negotiations, rather than the "new" issues that populate the most comprehensive agreements. The expertise required to progress discussions on trade in services, investment and competition, for instance, is instead held by regulators and institutions that usually sit beyond traditional trade ministries. This arrangement can enable negotiations on goods to progress while causing a stumbling block for other areas of negotiations, which can be deferred to "phase 2" negotiations.

Trade technocrats devote more attention to the finer details of trade agreements than can be afforded by the heads of state who agree to "grander visions" which can be tempered by the risk aversion and analysis required of technocrats. The final communiqué adopted by the Heads of State and Government of the COMESA-EAC-SADC Tripartite Summit, for instance, envisaged the three RECs "working towards a merger into a single REC" (COMESA, EAC and SADC, 2008), but as the first phase of the negotiations draws to a close, it is clear that the negotiated outcome instead represents another FTA, rather than the envisaged and highly ambitious consolidation of RECs.

Africa's trade negotiators are influenced by their prevailing negotiating norms. Most African countries have been involved, for the last 14 years, in highly defensive negotiations with the European Union (EU)—the Economic Partnership Agreements (EPAs)—in which the goal for many African negotiators was to minimize and delay their market opening, limit restrictions to their policy space, and deal with a considerably better resourced and experienced negotiating partner. These negotiations offered little offensive interest to African negotiators, with most countries already enjoying duty-free access to the EU market. Consequently, African negotiators may be prone to approaching regional trade agreements with the defensiveness developed during the EU negotiations, and therefore reach for larger exclusion lists of sensitive products and longer liberalization timeframes.

The private sector and civil society
Private sector actors and civil society groups have the potential to influence regional agreements and initiatives by emphasizing the interests of those whom they represent. Regional institutions often include formal mechanisms for consultation with private sector

apex bodies and civil society organizations. However, Bilal et al. (2016) found little evidence of the impact of such groups on formal processes, agenda-setting or policy implementation within regional institutions.

The private sector often prioritizes working with national governments on regional issues, assuming it is more effective than engaging regional organizations directly. For instance, Kenyan and Tanzanian transport operators lobby at the national level to defend their interests and represent them as national interests when they engage in the EAC (Bilal et al., 2016). There is a perception that regional organizations can be dysfunctional "talking shops." By contrast, the COMESA Business Council has effectively informed COMESA's agenda on illicit trade, though this reportedly relies somewhat on the strength of the well-resourced tobacco business lobby.

It is also important to differentiate between different types of private sector actors and their ability to lobby. Incumbents who already trade across borders through informal channels have little incentive to adjust pre-existing regimes that may see their business advantage eroded; private sector actors can profit from the status quo. On the other hand, small cross-border traders, small and medium-sized enterprises and small civil society organizations may lack the means to lobby and raise their voices as effectively as larger private sector actors. (The considerations of these vulnerable groups form the subject of Chapter 5.)

Engaging private sector actors and civil society organizations in the CFTA must recognize the wide array of interests involved, including those of firms seeking to benefit from the status quo. Likewise, mechanisms for consultation must be cognizant of small private sector and civil society actors to ensure that their voices are heard.

Sector-specific dimensions

Particular technical and political characteristics are relevant to different sector or policy areas of regional integration. National interests vary greatly by sector, and they affect the choice of policy and of implementation arrangements. For instance, those concerning peace and security tend to be well resourced by donors and of special interest to countries in conflict-prone regions, while those involving infrastructure can be particularly important to land-locked countries.

Subject areas that concern immediate financial or human costs, such as peace and security, tend also to attract greater urgency. Trade relates to aspirations of future benefits, which lack such obvious immediacy.

However, the CFTA is taking place in an evolving world trade environment, and the AU readily highlights the risks and costs if the CFTA does not come to fruition. Here it is important to frame the timeliness and importance of the CFTA.

Trade covers a wide range of subsectors and issues, and it is important to prioritize them with political buy-in or the potential for political coalition building. An important sectoral factor facing the CFTA is the "spaghetti bowl" of regional FTAs that it will have to build on, as well as the yet-to-be concluded TFTA. A stated aim of the CFTA is to rationalize overlapping membership challenges and not to add another layer or complication. This must include effectively redefining the role of the RECs in trade, requiring the CFTA to outline that role and how the RECs will interact with new CFTA institutions.

External factors: Donors and critical junctures

External factors that can shape Africa's continental and regional agendas, including the CFTA, include donor support and changes to the international trade landscape.

The quality and quantity of donor support presents opportunities and challenges. Donor support can help finance negotiations, critical studies and analyses, and the participation of less well-resourced countries and groups. There is a risk, however, that donors move from supporting regional processes to driving them. For instance, they may be more willing to finance initiatives that address their own priorities for aid and other policies, which can be a concern if these policies are not aligned with Africa's. Most regional organizations, ECOWAS aside, are also heavily dependent on donor funding, giving donors an important say in their direction. (Chapter 8 expands on this topic by looking at resourcing the CFTA, and the particular role of Aid-for-Trade.)

Changes to the international trading landscape present another source of external factors that can hinder or help drive the CFTA process. These include the trade policy strategies of important trading partners, and developments in the multilateral trading system in general, as well as changes in trade patterns. For instance, concerned about rising protectionism, the South African Minister of Trade and industry, Rob Davies, stated, "what is emerging in the developed world is a backlash with the potential to propel us […] into a new era of outright mercantilism" (Davies, 2017).

Another change will come through the African Growth and Opportunity Act (AGOA), which offers duty-free access to the US for many African products, when it is replaced with reciprocal arrangements when the current legislation expires in 2025. Turmoil within Africa's traditional EU trading partners, and in particular Brexit, has stalled the conclusion and deployment of EPAs with African countries. Meanwhile, emerging market economies, in particular China and India, have evolved into key trading partners for many African countries. This may help African countries increase their policy space and prioritize more of their own development goals, but it also tends to boost Africa's natural resource exports rather than its industrialization (Chapter 9).

Addressing Africa's political economy challenges and opportunities: The developmental state

The political economy lens of integration in Africa and the CFTA helps to explain "why things are the way they are." Moving forward from that position requires the dedicated action of developmental states, led by political leadership committed to national developmental goals and empowered by competent and professional bureaucracies (ECA, 2011).

A developmental state can be defined as one that has "the capacity to deploy its authority, credibility and legitimacy in a binding manner to design and implement development policies and programmes for promoting transformation and growth, as well as expanding human capabilities" (ECA, 2011). One of the most critical challenges for African development is forming developmental states. Doing so requires a "democratic socio-political environment that endows the state with legitimacy and authority" (ECA, 2011). It also requires political leadership and a capacitated bureaucracy.

The political economy issues detailed in this chapter form the bedrock on which the developmental state must inevitably operate in approaching the CFTA. These issues concern factors that need to be taken as given, at least in the short to medium term. They must be considered by the developmental state as it takes responsibility for designing and implementing the CFTA.

For instance, the interests of various actors and their influence on the CFTA must be considered so that they do not capture the gains of the CFTA and reduce its developmental potential. Policy makers must be vigilant so that the interests of vulnerable groups are not drowned out by the voice of well-resourced lobbyists. Similarly, changes in the international trading landscape can threaten the benefits of integration, requiring action to be taken more urgently to conclude the CFTA.

Yet elements of the political economy can provide windows of opportunity through which development states can take action. For instance, the shared historical legacies can help coalesce African countries into building blocks for more easily negotiating the CFTA. Used correctly, development assistance can support the CFTA. Developmental leaders can also be aware that the CFTA relates to *aspirations* for realizing future benefits, which could result in its being otherwise under-supported relative to short-term and visible political goals. Such leaders can also instramentalize influential states to champion the CFTA.

The political economy of integration in Africa need not be deterministic. The developmental state provides a means to take hold of the rudder and direct African development across the political economy terrain of the CFTA, and to ensure that the result is an outcome conducive to African development.

References

Bilal, S., B. Byiers and J. Vanheukelom. 2015. "Political-economy dynamics matter most to Africa's regional integration." *International Trade Forum* 8 (2): 20–21.

Byiers, B. 2016. *Political Economy of Regional Integration in Africa: What Drives and Constrains Regional Organisations?* Maastricht: European Centre for Development Policy Management (ECDPM).

Byiers, B., J. Vanheukelom and C. K. M. Kingombe. 2015. "A five lenses framework for analysing the political economy in regional integration." Discussion Paper 178. Maastricht: ECDPM.

COMESA (Common Market for Eastern and Southern Africa), EAC (East African Community) and SADC (Southern African Development Community). 2008. *Final Communique of the COMESA-EAC-SADC Tripartite Summit of the Heads of State and Government.* Kampala.

Davies, R. 2017. Debate of the State of the Nation Address, Cape Town, South Africa, 15 February.

ECA. 2011. *Economic Report on Africa: Governing Development in Africa – The Role of the State in Economic Transformation.* Addis Ababa: ECA.

———. 2012. *Economic Report on Africa: Unleashing Africa's Potential as a Pole of Global Growth.* Addis Ababa.

———. 2014. *Economic Report on Africa: Dynamic Industrial Policy in Africa.* Addis Ababa.

———. 2017. "African small island developing states." http://www.uneca.org/africansmallislanddevelopingstates/pages/african-small-island-developing-states. Accessed 5th April 2017.

Jones, E. 2013. *Negotiating Against the Odds: A Guide for Trade Negotiators from Developing Countries.* Basingstoke, UK: Palgrave Macmillan.

Mathieson, C. 2016. *The Political Economy of Regional Integration in Africa: The East African Community (EAC).* Maastricht: ECDPM.

OAU (Organisation for African Unity). 1963. *Founding Charter of the Organization of African Unity.* Addis Ababa.

Plaut, M. 2016. *Understanding Eritrea: Inside Africa's Most Repressive State.* London: C. Hurst & Co. Publishers.

Sommer, L., and D. Luke. 2017. *Smart Industrialization.* Addis Ababa: ECA.

UNDESA (United Nations Department of Economic and Social Affairs). 2017. *World Statistics Pocketbook.* New York: UN.

Endnotes

1   ECA calculations based on CEPII-BACI 2015 reconciled trade flows.

2   That is, all sectors and activities are subject to liberalization commitments unless explicitly excluded, which is generally more conducive to substantial liberalization.

3   Trade-Related Aspects of Intellectual Property Rights.

4   In Chapter 4 we elaborate on the CFTA as a tool for export diversification and African industrialization. This also underpins the attention that ECA has given to several aspects of structural transformation in its annual flagship report, the *Economic Report on Africa*, in recent years. In refuting economic and structural determinism, the underlying premise of these reports is that deliberate policy choices and action can change the status quo (ECA, 2011, 2012, 2014).

5   Arabic, English, French and Portuguese.

6   Article 3(3) Draft Tripartite Agreement.

7   Final Communique of the COMESA-EAC-SADC Tripartite Summit, October 2008 Heads of State and Government.

8   Acquis is a French term meaning "that which has been agreed." In the context of the TFTA it means that the negotiations should start from the point

the COMESA, EAC and SADC trade negotiations have reached. Tariff negotiations and the exchange of tariff concessions would be among Member/Partner States of the TFTA that have no preferential arrangements in place between them. This will both preserve the acquis and build on it.

Chapter 4
Revisiting the Case for the CFTA

This chapter revisits the case for the Continental free Trade Area (CFTA). It presents both the theoretical and empirical perspectives that inform the rationale, with a summary of the static and dynamic gains expected of the CFTA. The chapter then briefly looks at how the promotion of intra-African trade is valuable in contributing to Africa's industrialization. It concludes with a progress update on the CFTA negotiations as of July 2017.

Theoretical case

As articulated in *ARIA IV* (ECA, AU, and AfDB, 2010), liberalizing trade between two or more countries generally has positive welfare effects for those countries and leads to economic growth and poverty reduction. But these gains are not automatic. Flanking policies that are trade facilitating and measures to correct distributional distortions are also required (Chapters 5 and 6). Two sets of effects underpin the theory of trade liberalization: the static and the dynamic.

Static effects: Trade creation, trade diversion and modern trade theories

The traditional static effects of free trade areas were first hypothesized by Viner (1950) and concern two concepts related to the efficient allocation of factors of production: trade creation and trade diversion.

Trade creation refers to the increased level of trade that results from the removal of trade barriers within a free trade area. Trade is created when reduced trade barriers enable countries to better express their respective comparative advantage. By focusing their productive factors on where they have a comparative advantage, and trading with each other, countries generate more efficient economic outcomes through better allocation of resources and factors of production.

Trade diversion occurs when trade between countries within a free trade area replaces trade with third countries not party to that free trade area. While this result may benefit certain exporters within the free trade area, overall it is welfare decreasing. Trade is diverted from a more efficient third country in favour of a higher-cost producer from within the free trade area, leading to greater inefficiency and a loss of consumer surplus.

In theory, trade creation and trade diversion imply opposite effects on economic welfare. In practice, the net effect is generally positive (see "Empirical case" below).

Modern trade theories posit additional gains from free trade areas beyond those of the traditional Viner theory of static trade gains, which stem from the implications for producing firms, consumers, climate change and other factors. The following are hypothesized for the CFTA:

- Producers immediately gain from access to: cheaper inputs and intermediary goods from other African countries; a broader variety of inputs and intermediary goods; and larger markets for their products (Amiti and Konings, 2007; Estevadeordal and Taylor, 2013). This enables them to produce more efficiently and competitively and at greater economies of scale.

- Consumers immediately gain from: access to cheaper products from other African countries; and a broader variety of products (Broda and Weinstein, 2004). Both improve consumer welfare.

Continental trade integration also helps eliminate the challenges associated with multiple and overlapping trade agreements in Africa (Krueger and Bhagwati, 1995). More specifically, facilitating trade in food security products helps to mitigate productivity shocks induced by climate change (Ahmed et al., 2012). Where there is a food shortage, alternative food supplies may be more easily and affordably imported. Finally, enhanced access to agricultural inputs and intermediates, including improved seed varieties and machinery, can help producers of food products better adapt to climate change (Maur and Shepherd, 2015).

Dynamic effects

Dynamic gains from free trade areas are realized over the long run and can be more substantial than the static effects. As outlined in *ARIA V* (ECA, AU and AfDB, 2012), the CFTA is likely to realize dynamic gains in several areas, expanded here to seven:

- An enlarged regional market provides incentives for inward foreign direct investment (FDI) and cross-border investment. Most African markets are small, yet many industrial investments require large economies of scale to be profitable. An expanded African market creates the scale necessary for more investment.

- An integrated African market better facilitates competitive interaction between African firms, setting in motion dynamic gains from competition. In contrast, monopolies and oligopolies have little incentive to become more efficient, cut costs or innovate. Yet as monopolistic markets are pervasive across Africa, enabling African businesses to compete in each other's markets can unlock the competitive pressures necessary for long-run productivity growth (Melitz, 2003; Melitz and Ottaviano, 2008).

- Better access to imported inputs and intermediary goods lowers the cost of innovation. Firms may innovate with new combinations and varieties of inputs (Broda, Greenfield and Weinstein, 2006).

- The CFTA may cause trade diversion to African countries at the expense of third countries. While this implies negative static effects (discussed above), it can also increase the relative price of exportables in Africa, stimulating further investment, output and employment in these sectors.

- Greater intra-African trade is expected to extend economic growth and stability to Africa's less developed economies. Integration is likely to stimulate regional growth poles that are capable of generating externalities to less developed African countries. For instance, the formation of regional value chains (RVCs) around the South African automobile sector involves the sourcing of leather seats from Botswana and fabrics from Lesotho. Such spill-overs in regional trade can be particularly beneficial to weaker economies, with some analysis

finding that trade with a country's neighbours can reduce the risk of conflict (Calì, 2014).

- Trade diversification and a shift to trade in industrialized goods would improve Africa's long-run growth. Intra-African trade embodies a far larger share of industrial and value-added goods than Africa's trade with the rest of the world. Promoting such trade can generate industrial diversification in Africa and catalyse structural transformation.

- More broadly, regional agreements provide an excellent platform for cooperation and dialogue, including cooperation on infrastructure development, technology transfer, innovation, investment, conflict resolution and peace and security. Neighbouring countries are more likely to have a vested interest in supporting stability in countries with which they share established and valuable trade links.

Empirical case

Free trade areas are usually assessed through one of two approaches: ex-post evaluations that seek to estimate the observed impact of a free trade area using econometrics; or ex-ante evaluations that forecast the impact of a future free trade area using economic models. Here we assess the implications of the CFTA using both approaches, and then present an exposition of intra-African trade flows to reinforce the logic behind the CFTA.

The ex-post empirical literature on free trade areas is mixed. Abrams (1980) and Brada and Mendez (1985) found the European Community (EC) to have an insignificant effect on trade among members, whereas Bergstrand (1985) and Frankel et al. (1995) found significant effects. However, inherent in this analysis is a substantial challenge with endogeneity: The presence, or absence, of a free trade area is not exogenous, but rather the subject of many factors. The result has been to underestimate the positive effect of free trade areas on trade by as much as 75–85 per cent (Baier and Bergstrand, 2007).

Several ex-post studies estimate the long-run effects of a free trade area membership on bilateral trade to be quite large (Egger et al., 2011). Baier and Bergstrand (2007) find that, on average, a free trade area approximately doubles two members' bilateral trade after 10 years. A particular example is the North American Free Trade Agreement (NAFTA) for which Caliendo and Parro (2014) find intra-bloc trade to have increased by 188 per cent for Mexico, 11 per cent for Canada and 41 per cent for the United States.

The ultimate effect of a free trade area depends on the particular characteristics of member countries, including the compatibility of their trade profiles, pre-existing tariff structures and geographical proximity.

While such ex-post analysis of other trade agreements can help guide an indicative estimate for the impact of the CFTA on African trade, more tailored estimates can be gauged by ex-ante economic models.

Mevel and Karingi (2013) model the impact of the CFTA with the removal of all tariffs on trade between African countries. This analysis is then supplemented with the implied effects of improved trade facilitation between African countries using a database on trade costs. Trade creation effects are found to exceed and more than compensate for trade diversion effects. Under the CFTA reform, intra-African trade is estimated to increase by 52.3 per cent ($34.6 billion), compared with a baseline scenario without a CFTA, in 2022. Africa's industrial exports are forecast to enjoy the highest gains, expanding by 53.3 per cent ($27.9 billion). Real wages are estimated to increase for unskilled workers in the agricultural and non-agricultural sectors, as well as for skilled workers, and there is a small shift in employment expected from agricultural to non-agricultural sectors. Flanking the CFTA with trade facilitation measures is found to be important in maximizing the impact of the CFTA on Africa's industrialization and ensuring that all countries gain from the CFTA.

Chauvin et al. (2016) model the cumulative impact of the elimination of tariffs; a 50 per cent reduction in non-tariff measures; and a 30 per cent reduction in transaction costs. They find the short-run impacts in the first years after implementation are generally small but with larger and more positive long-run impacts. By 2027, the CFTA is estimated to increase Africa's welfare by 2.64 per cent. Notably, the reduction in non-tariff measures and transaction costs are found to contribute significantly to improving welfare gains. Chauvin et al. (2016) also link the modelled results to household survey data for a selection of African countries to assess the effect of the CFTA on subnational economic groups, including female or male-headed households, urban or rural groupings, and different income groups. They find the CFTA to have an asymmetric but positive effect on all the subnational groups, with the particular groups that gain most varying by country.

Three important messages derive from these studies. First, the importance of complementary policies that go beyond tariff reductions, which alone imply small and asymmetric impacts on African countries. Complementary policies are necessary to maximize the gains of the CFTA but also to ensure that its benefits are shared equally to produce a win-win outcome for all countries. Such measures include the reduction of non-tariff measures and transaction costs, such as those associated with improved regulatory transparency, harmonization of sanitary and phyto-sanitary regulations, the accreditation and mutual recognition procedures for technical barriers to trade and improved administrative conditions in customs. With the inclusion of such measures, welfare gains are enjoyed by all African countries (Chapter 6).

Second, the most important gains from the CFTA will be realized over the long run as the agreement contributes to the economic restructuring of African sectors towards more productive industrialized and export sectors, and to improved investments. (As detailed in Chapter 6, several measures can help ease this structural adjustment.)

Third, the recognition that such studies likely underemphasize the range of benefits derived from the CFTA, as modelling exercises struggle to capture and quantify the full gamut of CFTA benefits. They frequently overlook gains such as those facilitating trade in food security products, improving the stability of fragile countries, enhancing firms' access to inputs and intermediary goods, reducing the cost of innovation, improving intra-African competition, addressing the challenges linked to overlapping African trade agreements and RECs and providing a platform for cooperation and dialogue more broadly.

The CFTA, Africa's trade flows and industrialization

The prevailing story of Africa's exports since 2000 has been that of the strong impact of the commodities super-cycle. As Figure 4.1 shows, the bulk of Africa's impressive almost-three-fold increase in exports, from $194 billion in 2000 to $544 billion in 2014, is due mostly to the expansion of extractive exports and the commodity price boom.[1] This has contributed to Africa's headline growth figures but has not been conducive to the economic transformation Africa requires to industrialize and realize long-run sustainable growth.

In sharp contrast is the composition of Africa's intra-African trade. Extractive composition of intra-African trade shows that intra-African trade comprises a disproportionately large share of non-extractive exports. Looking at the most recent three-year average, this included $17 billion in processed industrial supplies, $10 billion in capital goods, $8 billion in processed food and beverages, $7 billion in transport equipment, another $7 billion in consumer goods, $4 billion in primary food and beverages and $2 billion in primary industrial supplies.

The growth of intra-African trade has helped to promote Africa's industrial export sectors since 2000. Despite amounting to just 18 per cent of Africa's total exports, intra-African exports have accounted for 57 per cent of the growth in Africa's exports of capital goods, 51 per cent of processed food and beverages, 46 per cent of consumer goods, 45 per cent of transport equipment, and 44 per cent of processed industrial supplies (Share of Africa's export growth in non-extractive export categories, intra-African vs the rest of the world). (Chapter 9 provides a more detailed assessment of Africa's trading relationship with the rest of the world (RoW), by presenting disaggregated data.)

The exceptional value of this intra-African trade for Africa's industrialized economic transformation provides the foundational logic behind the CFTA (Box 4.1). The fundamental rationale of the CFTA is to promote this trade through the removal of tariff and non-tariff barriers.

Figure 4.1

Africa's extractive industry exports and world commodity prices

a) Africa's extractive exports ($)

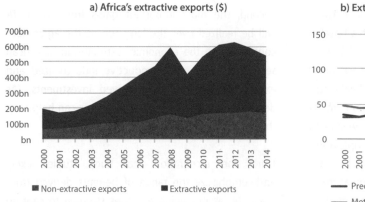

b) Extractive industry commodity prices

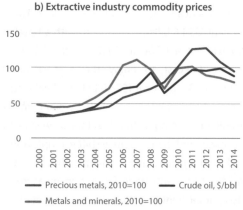

Source: ECA calculations using CEPII-BACI trade dataset and World Bank Commodities Market Data.

Figure 4.2

Extractive composition of intra-African trade

a) Intra-African extractive exports ($)

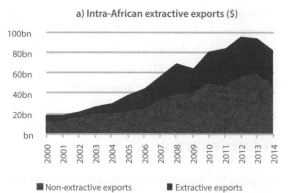

b) Extactive exports, RoW ($)

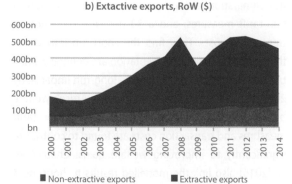

Source: ECA calculations using CEPII-BACI trade dataset and World Bank Commodities Market Data.

Table 4.1

Share of Africa's export growth in non-extractive export categories, intra-African vs the rest of the world

	Import category	Share of export growth attributable to each market (%)	
		Intra-Africa	Rest of the world
Food and beverages	Primary	18	82
	Processed	51	49
Industrial supplies	Primary	15	85
	Processed	44	56
	Capital goods	57	43
	Transport equipment	45	55
	Consumer goods	46	54

Source: CEPII's BACI dataset. Values compare the export growth between three-year averages of 1998–2000 and 2012–2014, and calculate the proportion of export growth attributable to each market such that **$Share\ Attributable_{i,j} = (Exp_{i,j,t} - Exp_{i,j,t-1})/(Total_{i,t} - Total_{i,t-1})$** *where i is the export category, j is the buying market, and t is the period. Exp is the value of exports of category i to market j while Total is the total value of exports from Africa of product j.*

Box 4.1

Using the CFTA as a vehicle for industrialization

The imperative of advancing Africa's industrialization should be kept in mind throughout the CFTA negotiation process. In particular, the final CFTA Agreement should aim to:

- Commit member states to an ambitious liberalization agenda for trade in goods, reflecting the importance of securing market access for African countries in other African countries, which is crucial for boosting intra-African trade in intermediates, developing manufacturing RVCs and reducing Africa's import bill for processed foods.
- Include provisions consistent with the imperative of industrial development under the CFTA industrial pillar. The continentally agreed programme for the Accelerated Industrial Development of Africa should serve as a building block for the industrial pillar, particularly its six objectives to integrate industrialization in national development policies; maximize the use of local productive capacities and inputs; add value to abundant natural resources; develop small-scale and rural industries; take maximum advantage of Africa's partnerships to enable the transfer of technology; and establish and strengthen financial and capital markets.
- Include a framework agreement on trade in services to help to boost intra-African trade in services, harness the capacities of African services suppliers and ensure competitively priced service inputs for African manufacturers. These can be achieved through progressive liberalization that consolidates and builds on existing achievements of the RECs.
- Contain a framework agreement on investment that provides common rules for state parties in introducing incentives for attracting investments to accelerate development and industrialization. This will help to avoid any race to the bottom and recognizes government procurement as a key policy tool for promoting the use of local suppliers.
- Include provisions for the free movement of economic operators (traders, business persons, investors, etc.) involved in trade in goods and services and in investment. This element is needed to transform the opportunities provided through liberalized trade in goods, services and investment and to maximize the use of regional productive capacities in industrial production.
- Harmonize product standards, conformity assessment and accreditation practices to achieve mutual product recognition and facilitate intra-African trade in manufactured goods, particularly agro-processed foods.
- Include flexible rules of origin with generous cumulation requirements to encourage local and regional processing and the development of African industrial supply chains.

Source: Sommer and Luke (2017).

Progress update: CFTA negotiations and scope

Negotiations for establishing the CFTA were launched in June 2015 by the Heads of State and Government of the AU at the 26th Ordinary Session of the AU Assembly in Johannesburg, South Africa. Th AU Assembly decision launching the CFTA urged the participation of all regional economic communities (RECs) and member states and called on the African Union Commission (AUC), UN Economic Commission for Africa (ECA), African Development Bank (AfDB), African Export-Import Bank and other development partners for support, with the aim to operationalize the CFTA by the end of 2017.

Following the launch, six meetings of the CFTA Negotiating Forum were held by July 2017, supported by eight meetings of the Continental Task Force, and two meetings each of the Technical Working Groups, the Committee of Senior Trade Officials, and the African Ministers of Trade (The remainder of 2017 will see these bodies convening frequently, with a further two meetings of the Negotiating Forum. Table 4.2 summarizes negotiation progress as of July 2017.).

The remainder of 2017 will see these bodies convening frequently, with a further two meetings of the Negotiating Forum. Table 4.2 summarizes negotiation progress as of July 2017.

As detailed in Chapter 9, free trade agreements can take many forms: Potential CFTA configurations were outlined in *ARIA VI* (ECA, AU, and AfDB, 2015). The CFTA negotiations are in progress and so it would be premature to provide a detailed outline of current expectations as to form and content.

On the basis of the draft of the negotiating text, and the negotiations and technical work undertaken, the envisaged scope of the CFTA covers agreements on trade in goods, services, investment, and rules and procedures on dispute settlement (Table 4.3). The constituent parts of these agreements and their appendices are expected to cover a range of provisions that aim to facilitate trade; reduce transaction costs; and provide exceptions, flexibilities and safeguards for vulnerable groups and countries in challenging circumstances. It is anticipated that agreements on intellectual property rights and competition policy will be tackled in phase 2 of the CFTA negotiations (Chapter 10). Crucially, countries are aligning their interests in a comprehensive agreement that achieves substantially more than tariff reductions and that offers safeguards and flexibilities, which are important for ensuring that the gains from the CFTA are maximized and shared equitably (discussed further in Chapter 5).

Though there remain substantive topics to discuss, the negotiations have achieved considerable momentum and build on a long history of African integration (Table

Figure 4.3

Institutional framework for the CFTA negotiations

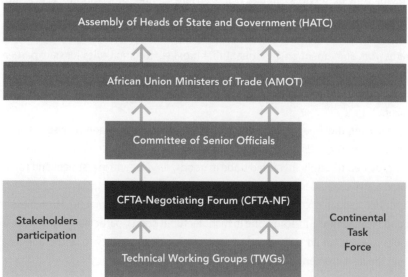

Table 4.2

Negotiation progress

Negotiating forum	Timeline	Progress
❶	February, 2016	Adoption of the Rules of Procedure.
❷	May, 2016	Adoption of 12 Negotiating Principles and Terms of Reference for the Services Technical Working Group.
❸	October, 2016	Adoption of remaining Terms of Reference for Technical Working Groups and opening discussions of Negotiating Modalities.
❹	December, 2016	Further discussions on Negotiating Modalities and commissioning of technical studies on services modalities and goods modalities.
❺	February, 2017	Review of modality options for goods and services and agreement on a range of modality elements. A draft text of the CFTA was presented and agreed to as a starting point for the text-based negotiations. This draft is to be refined with technical inputs at the Technical Working Groups.
❻	July, 2017	Refined modalities for both goods and services, including agreement on a 90% level of ambition for goods, the timeframe for liberalization, qualifications for sensitive products, a procedure for reviewing excluded products, and the scope for special and differential treatment to support less-developed state parties as well as a common approach for progressive services liberalization.

Table 4.3

Envisaged scope of the CFTA*

Protocol Establishing the CFTA	• Annex A: Agreement on Trade in Goods
	• Annex B: Agreement on Trade in Services
	• Annex C: Agreement on Investment
	• Annex D: Rules and Procedures on Dispute Settlement
Parts and appendices under negotiation	• Liberalization of trade (imports and export duties, NTBs and rules of origin)
	• Movement of persons and economic operators
	• Customs cooperation, trade facilitation and transit
	• NTBs
	• Technical barriers to trade
	• Sanitary and phyto-sanitary measures
	• Trade remedies and safeguards
	• Exceptions (general and security exceptions, balance of payments)
	• Agriculture, fisheries and food security
	• Technical assistance, capacity building and cooperation
	• Complementary policies (special export zones, capacity building and cooperation
Phase 2 negotiations	• Agreement on Intellectual Property Rights
	• Agreement on Competition Policy

*As of July, 2017.

Table 4.4

CFTA in the context of African integration

1963	Integration of African continent an aspiration at inauguration of the OAU
1979	Common African market first mentioned in the Monrovia Declaration
1980	Common market elaborated in the Lagos Plan of Action
1991	Continental Customs Union put forward in the Abuja Treaty
2000	AU established with integration as an objective
2012	AU Assembly adopts BIAT Action Plan and roadmap for establishing a CFTA
2015	African Tripartite Free Trade Area Signed
2015	CFTA negotiations launched by the AU Assembly
2016	AU Summit reaffirms its commitment to fast tracking the CFTA by 2017
2017	AU Heads of State and Government mandate President Mahamadou Issoufou of the Republic of Niger to champion the process of the CFTA to ensure that the 2017 deadline is reached

4.4). The CFTA has a notable commitment at the highest policy-making levels. The AU Summit in Kigali in 2017 reaffirmed the commitment of the AU Heads of State and Government to fast track the CFTA. Designing the CFTA at the technical working groups and negotiating forum meetings, and ensuring its effective implementation, are now the critical tasks at hand. As foreseen in the Abuja Treaty, the integration process is to culminate in the African Economic Community.

References

Abrams, R. K. 1980. "International trade flows under flexible exchange rates." *Economic Review* 65 (3): 3–10.

Ahmed, S. A., N. S. Diffenbaugh, T. W. Hertel and W. J. Martin. 2012. "Agriculture and trade opportunities for Tanzania: Past volatility and future climate change." *Review of Development Economics* 16 (3): 429–447.

Amiti, M., and J. Konings. 2007. "Trade liberalization, intermediate inputs, and productivity: Evidence from Indonesia." *The American Economic Review* 97 (5): 1611–1638.

Baier, S. L., and J. H. Bergstrand. 2007. "Do free trade agreements actually increase members' international trade?" *Journal of International Economics* 71 (1): 72–95.

Bergstrand, J. H. 1985. "The Gravity Equation in International Trade: Some Microeconomic Foundations and Empirical Evidence." *The Review of Economics and Statistics* 67 (3): 474–481.

Brada, J. C., and J. A. Méndez. 1985. "Economic integration among developed, developing and centrally planned economies: A comparative analysis." *The Review of Economics and Statistics* 67 (4): 549–556.

Broda, C., and D. E. Weinstein. 2004. "Variety growth and world welfare." *The American Economic Review* 94 (2): 139–144.

Broda, C., J. Greenfield and D. Weinstein. 2006. "From Groundnuts to Globalization: A Structural Estimate of Trade and Growth." Working Paper No. 12512. Cambridge, MA: National Bureau of Economic Research.

Calì, M. 2014. *Trading Away from Conflict: Using Trade to Increase Resilience in Fragile States*. Washington, DC: World Bank.

Caliendo, L., and F. Parro. 2014. "Estimates of the Trade and Welfare Effects of NAFTA." *The Review of Economic Studies* 82 (1): 1–44.

Chauvin, D., N. Ramos and G. Porto. 2016. "Trade, Growth, and Welfare Impacts of the CFTA in Africa." https://editorialexpress.com/cgi-bin/conference/download.cgi?db_name=CSAE2017&paper_id=749.

ECA (United Nations Economic Commission for Africa), AU (African Union) and AfDB (African Development Bank). 2010. *Assessing Regional Integration in Africa IV: Enhancing Intra-African Trade*. Addis Ababa.

———. 2012. *Assessing Regional Integration in Africa V: Towards an African Continental Free Trade Area*. Addis Ababa.

———. 2015. *Assessing Regional Integration in Africa VI: Harmonizing Policies to Transform the Trading Environment*. Addis Ababa.

Egger, P., M. Larch, K. E. Staub, and R. Winkelmann. 2011. "The Trade Effects of Endogenous Preferential Trade Agreements." *American Economic Journal: Economic Policy* 3 (3): 113–143.

Estevadeordal, A., and A. M. Taylor. 2013. "Is the Washington consensus dead? Growth, openness, and the great liberalization, 1970s–2000s." *Review of Economics and Statistics* 95 (5): 1669–1690.

Frankel, J., E. Stein and S. J. Wei. 1995. "Trading blocs and the Americas: The natural, the unnatural, and the super-natural." *Journal of Development Economics* 47 (1): 61–95.

ILO (International Labour Organization) and UNCTAD (United Nations Conference on Trade and Development). 2013. *Assessment Report: Towards a Continental Free Trade Area in Africa—Modeling Assessment with a Focus on Agriculture*.

Jensen, H., and R. Sandrey. 2015. *The Continental Free Trade Area – A GTAP assessment*. Stellenbosch, South Africa: Trade Law Centre. https://www.tralac.org/publications/article/7287-the-continental-free-trade-area-a-gtap-assessment.html.

Karingi, S., and S. Mevel. 2012. "Deepening Regional Integration in Africa: A Computable General Equilibrium Assessment of the Establishment of a Continental Free Trade Area followed by a Continental Customs Union." Paper for presentation at the 15th Global Trade Analysis Project Conference, Geneva, 27–29 June.

Krueger, A. O., and J. Bhagwati. 1995. *The dangerous drift to preferential trade agreements*. Washington, DC: American Enterprise Institute Press.

Maur, J. C., and B. Shepherd. 2015. *Connecting Food Staples and Input Markets in West Africa*. Washington, DC: World Bank.

Melitz, M. J. 2003. "The impact of trade on intra-industry reallocations and aggregate industry productivity." *Econometrica* 71 (6): 1695–1725.

Mureverwi, B. 2016. "Welfare Decomposition of the Continental Free Trade Area." Paper presented at the 19th Annual Conference on Global Economic Analysis, Washington, DC, 15–17 June. https://www.gtap.agecon. purdue.edu/resources/res_display.asp?RecordID=4978.

Saygili M., R. Peters and C. Knebel. 2017. "African Continental Free Trade Area: Challenges and Opportunities of Tariff Reductions." Policy Issues in International Trade and Commodities. New York and Geneva: United Nations.

Sommer, L., and D. Luke. 2017. *Smart Industrialization*. Addis Ababa: ECA.

TRALAC (Trade Law Centre). 2016. "Continental Wide Service Liberalization within Africa." Working Paper. Stellenbosch, South Africa. https://www.tralac.org/ publications/article/10876-continental-wide-service-liberalization-within-africa.html.

Viner, J. 1950. *The customs union issue*. New York: Carnegie Endowment for International Peace; London: Stevens & Sons.

Endnotes

1   Extractive exports here include petroleum oils (SITC 33), gas (SITC 34), non-ferrous metals (SITC 68), metalliferous ores and metal scrap (SITC 28), crude fertilizers and minerals (SITC 27), coal, coke and briquettes (SITC 32), as well as the remaining precious metals in HS 71, uranium (HS 2844), and the basic iron products of HS7201–HS7206.

Chapter 5
A Win-Win Approach to the CFTA: Sharing the Benefits

Sharing the benefits of the Continental Free Trade Area (CFTA) is important not only for reasons of equity, but also to ensure that the agreement actually works for countries at different levels of development. Trade agreements that are not win-win can remain unimplemented as partner countries have little interest in implementing them (Jones, 2013). If the gains are perceived as being captured by only a few countries, trade agreements may unravel (as seen with the earlier phase of the East African Community [EAC]).

This chapter acknowledges these challenges by assessing the distributional aspects of the CFTA and identifying the important support measures required at different levels. It is matched by Chapter 6, which outlines the policies critical to address these issues and to ensure win-win outcomes.

This is a "chapter of two halves." The first is an assessment of distributional issues *between* countries, looking at how countries with different economic configurations are likely to be affected in different ways by the CFTA, including via differing economic and tariff revenue channels. The second half assesses distributional issues *within* countries, including a review of structural adjustment costs and the particular challenges faced by some vulnerable groups.

Between countries

Opportunities and challenges
Many of the gains from the CFTA highlighted in Chapter 4 benefit all countries. For instance, the CFTA will help producers access a wider range of inputs and intermediary goods more affordably, and it will provide access to larger markets for their produce, enabling them to operate at greater scale. Africa's consumers have the potential to gain from access to a more affordable and broader variety of products, improving their welfare.

The CFTA is also expected to address Africa's multiple and overlapping trade agreements, facilitate trade in food-security products, enhance access to inputs necessary for adapting farming practices to climate change, stimulate inward and intra-African FDI, foster better competitive practices and lower the cost of innovation (among other factors).

Nevertheless, Africa's countries have a diversity of economic configurations and will likely be affected in different ways by the CFTA. (The foundational factors underpinning these differences were highlighted in Chapter 3.) A typology of African economies details the foundational factors likely to affect the distribution of CFTA gains. This is followed by a summary of the differentiated benefits and challenges expected of the CFTA and the accompanying measures required for those gains to be shared so that the CFTA is win-win for all African countries.

Table 5.1 shows the typology across four key dimensions for determining how each country will gain from the CFTA, describing the foundational economic and geographic factors within which each country's economic activities must operate.

Level of industrialization
African countries in the top half of the table are relatively more industrialized and will be better placed to take advantage of the opportunities for manufactured goods made possible by the CFTA (see Chapter 4). Their existing scale and capacities in manufacturing will enhance their ability to compete for new market opportunities, and it will make them attractive destinations for industrial investments to serve African consumers, particularly the growing middle class.

Still, the less-industrialized countries in the bottom half of the table can also benefit from the CFTA. By reducing transaction costs and facilitating trade and investment, the CFTA eases the creation of regional value chains (RVCs). Improved trade costs in the EAC have, for instance, enabled raw milk to be traded from Uganda for processing in Kenya, while milk packaging and spare parts from Kenya help support Ugandan milk

Table 5.1

Typology of African countries[1]

	Agriculture labour share >50%	Agriculture labour share <50%
Manufacturing value added >10% of GDP or >$1.85 billion	**Coastal** Ghana *(Resource rich)* Guinea-Bissau Kenya Madagascar Mozambique *(Resource rich)* Senegal *(Resource rich)* Tanzania *(Resource rich)* **Land-locked** Ethiopia Malawi Uganda	**Coastal** Algeria *(Resource rich)* Benin Cameroon *(Resource rich)* Congo, Dem. Rep. *(Resource rich)** Côte d'Ivoire *(Resource rich)* Egypt *(Resource rich)* Equatorial Guinea *(Resource rich)* Mauritius Morocco Nigeria *(Resource rich)* South Africa *(Resource rich)* Tunisia **Land-locked** Lesotho Swaziland Zimbabwe *(Resource rich)**
Manufacturing value added <10% of GDP and <$1.85 billion	**Coastal** Angola *(Resource rich)* Comoros Djibouti Eritrea *(Resource rich)* Gambia Guinea *(Resource rich)* Liberia Mauritania *(Resource rich)* São Tomé and Príncipe Sierra Leone *(Resource rich)* Somalia* **Land-locked** Burkina Faso *(Resource Rich)* Burundi Central African Republic *(Resource rich)** Chad *(Resource rich)** Mali *(Resource rich)* Niger *(Resource rich)* Rwanda South Sudan *(Resource rich)** Zambia *(Resource rich)*	**Coastal** Cabo Verde Congo, Rep. *(Resource rich)* Gabon *(Resource rich)* Libya *(Resource rich)* Namibia *(Resource rich)* Seychelles Sudan *(Resource rich)** Togo **Land-locked** Botswana *(Resource rich)*

* Denotes very weak economies within the top 10 states on the 2017 Fragile States Index (Fund for Peace, 2017).

Note: Countries are classified according to the agricultural labour share and manufacturing value added as a proxy for determining their level of industrialization. The countries are further subdivided according to whether they are coastal, land-locked and/or resource rich.

Source: Classification based on World Bank World Development Indicators and UNCTADStat. Most recent data available. Adapted from Sommer and Luke (2017).

processors. Integration has also fostered cross-border mergers of east African dairy companies.

The CFTA can create industrial sector opportunities to help less-industrialized countries increase their manufacturing footprint. However, such countries may require additional support in realizing these opportunities, including improving their productive capacities through increased FDI and intra-African investment, as well as implementing the programme for the Accelerated Industrial Development of Africa. It will also require domestic investments in education and training to ensure the necessary skills. Important initiatives include the Continental Strategy for Technical Vocation Education and Training and the Science, Technology and Innovation Strategy for Africa (2014–24).

To help firms—predominantly the small and medium-sized—engage in intra-African trade, investments must be made in trade information and the facilitation of access to trade finance. Factor market integration, including the improved movement of persons and cross-border investments, can be especially valuable in fostering RVCs. These support areas are among the seven clusters of the BIAT Action Plan, which is an important flanking policy for the CFTA.

It will also still be important to ensure that adequate safeguards remain for infant industries. Accessible trade defence instruments and infant industry provisions should be included in the CFTA to enable countries to defend their fragile industries as necessary (these aspects of the CFTA are discussed in detail in Chapter 6).

Agricultural sector size

Agriculture accounts for 32 per cent of Africa's GDP and employs 65 per cent of the labour force. It is therefore a sector where significant productivity improvements and great development gains can be made. Those countries in the top left quadrant of Table 5.1 will be particularly well placed to tap into new opportunities in the agro-industry and agro-processing sectors, helping to satisfy Africa's food security requirements and reduce its food import bill. This provides a natural progression from subsistence farming for these countries, given their existing productive capacities and knowledge in agriculture. (The African market has accounted for over 50 per cent of the growth in Africa's processed food and beverage exports since 2000.)

Accompanying measures to help boost the gains of the CFTA for these countries include trade facilitation and trade-related infrastructure, as envisaged in the Boosting Intra-African Trade (BIAT) Action Plan. The perishable nature of many agricultural food products means that they are particularly responsive to improvements in customs clearance times and logistics. Indeed, results from the Economic Community of West African States (ECOWAS) indicate that trade integration and trade facilitation significantly influence regional agricultural exports (Olayiwola and Ola-David, 2013). Africa is currently a net food-importing region. Also important are investments in productive capacities to help Africa feed Africa, including through mainstreaming the policy measures in the African Agribusiness and Agro-industries Development Initiative (3ADI) and the African Development Bank's (AfDB's) "Feed Africa: A Strategy for Agricultural Transformation in Africa 2016–2025." In particular, complementary investments in mechanization, rural infrastructure and increased agricultural access to credit will be crucial.

Resource endowments

The majority of African countries are classified as resource rich. Tariffs on raw materials are already low and so the CFTA can do little to further promote these exports. However, by lowering intra-African tariffs on intermediates and final goods, the CFTA will create additional opportunities for adding value to natural resources. Perhaps most important for these countries, the CFTA will offer opportunities for export diversification into other industrialized export sectors. The ambition of the CFTA is that it can reduce dependence on resource exports and to contribute to Africa's industrial development. The timing is now opportune: Commodity prices have fallen since 2012, providing an additional incentive.

Land-locked and coastal

The cost of being land-locked includes higher costs of freight and unpredictable transit times. This hampers integration into global value chains and de-links such economies from world markets. Land-locked countries, as a result, trade 30 per cent less, experience GDP growth that is weaker by about 1.5 per cent, and on average have had recourse to International Monetary Fund assistance longer than coastal countries (Arvis et al., 2007). Around 30 per cent of African countries are land-locked.

The industrialization of land-locked countries is particularly sensitive to the ease with which they can access port facilities in neighbouring coastal countries, because modern manufacturing relies on the import and export of components through regional and global value chains. The CFTA provides particular benefits: In addition to reducing tariffs, the CFTA is set to include provisions on trade facilitation, transit and customs cooperation. Indeed, these are recognized by the Almaty Programme of Action, adopted by the United Nations in 2003, as crucial components for supporting the development of land-locked countries. Initiatives found to be valuable include single-efficient clearance systems, customs reforms, computerized transit documentation and investments in road infrastructure (Arvis et al., 2007).

The Trade Facilitation Agreement (TFA) at the World Trade Organization (WTO) is another avenue of assistance open to African WTO member countries, which can support the implementation and operationalization of the CFTA and enhance intra-African trade. The dialogue around the TFA in the lead-up to its entry into force in February 2017 was focused on national commitments made. At the same time, the provisions of the TFA recognize the importance of implementing it well and offering capacity development support in a way that is conducive to regional and subregional integration. In the context of TFA implementation, the BIAT Action Plan could be a useful framework on coordinated action by African countries to support intra-African trade. The implementation of the TFA could also promote more inclusive benefits from trade through an easier environment for small and medium-sized enterprises, for women involved in trade and for other groups that generally face high barriers to trading.

Conflict and post-conflict states

Trade and trade policy can greatly affect the risk of conflict in some states, often via two main channels.

First, commodity-based export earnings such as oil and especially minerals, extricable through artisanal or small-scale mining, including alluvial gold and tantalum used in mobile phones, create incentives for conflict (Dube and Vargas 2013). These valuable resources can lead to battles over their control (Berman et al., 2014; Maystadt et al., 2014; Rustad et al, 2016). Once in control, their value can fund and sustain conflict. In contrast, the export revenues associated with other sectors, and especially labour-intensive sectors, such as basic agriculture or manufacturing, increase the opportunity cost of conflict by providing alternative incomes and livelihoods (Calì, 2014).

Second, increased trade with neighbouring countries is found to reduce the duration as well as the intensity of conflicts, especially when this trade occurs through regional trade agreements (Calì, 2014). Trade increases the incentive for contiguous countries to mitigate and abate conflict risks. Trade agreements provide a

further platform for cooperation and assistance with neighbouring countries.

Preferential trade agreements and trade facilitation, including that envisaged in the CFTA, can help foster stronger trade relationships between neighbours. It can help create new opportunities to diversify export earnings from commodities and extractive minerals and generate alternative incomes and livelihoods. However, already weak states tend to have especially limited productive and trade capacities. The CFTA will not be sufficient in itself to stimulate trade for these countries. Transit, logistics and trade-related infrastructure is also required, as are supportive measures to boost productive capacities.

Catering to different economic configurations through CFTA accompanying measures

The CFTA will provide a variety of opportunities that cater to the diversity of African countries, including the resource rich, agriculturally based or more industrialized. However, certain countries may require greater support. While the more-industrialized economies may be better placed to take advantage of new industrial export opportunities associated with trade creation and trade diverted from the rest of world, other countries may require measures to help them link to these value chains and develop their export sectors. Less-developed economies may experience challenges in satisfying complex rules of origin and meeting product standards. Their capacity to use trade remedies is also often weak.

The critical policies for supporting these countries are those proposed in the BIAT Action Plan, the "sister" initiative to the CFTA. Getting important provisions of the CFTA right, including those related to rules of origin and standards, will ensure that it is designed to take account of these countries' particular needs. While the CFTA is being designed to include such trade facilitation provisions, the BIAT Action Plan goes further by targeting additional constraints that are particularly inhibiting to the growth of intra-African trade. This includes clusters on trade policies, trade facilitation, productive capacity, trade-related infrastructure, trade finance, trade information and factor market integration (see Chapter 6).

Tariff revenue losses

It is expected that the CFTA will reduce tariff revenue generated by intra-African trade. The extent is now shown, first, in aggregate using a computable general equilibrium (CGE) model and, second, disaggregated across countries using a partial equilibrium (PE) model. The use of exclusion lists is discussed as a means of smoothing the tariff revenue impacts to ensure an equitable outcome for all countries.

Aggregate tariff revenue losses and welfare implications

Saygili et al. (2017) estimate the tariff revenue losses from the CFTA. They use a CGE model that estimates the long-run effect of the CFTA and then calculate two scenarios: the elimination of tariffs on intra-African trade, amounting to "full liberalization"; and Special Product Categorization, in which for each country the sector with the highest tariff revenue from African imports is excluded from liberalization. The second scenario aims to approximate the effect of partial tariff cuts and the use of exclusion lists.

In both scenarios, the welfare benefits exceed the tariff revenue costs for Africa as a whole, a finding that is consistent with other studies that integration can strongly contribute to economic development and is supported by the economic theory and quantitative evidence outlined in Chapter 4. Liberalization leads to welfare gains in the form of consumer surpluses, producer surpluses and efficiency gains that derive from improved access to imported products, as well as better specialization and economies of scale. In the second scenario, tariff revenue losses are reduced to $3 billion, from $4 billion in the first scenario, but the possible welfare gains are also reduced, from $16 billion to $11 billion.

Distribution of tariff revenue losses and impact of flexibilities across countries

Aggregate tariff revenue losses are modest relative to welfare gains, but this aggregation masks significant heterogeneity between countries. Here we evaluate the tariff revenue impacts at the country level using a straightforward partial equilibrium model and three scenarios: full liberalization, in which tariffs are

completely eliminated on all intra-African imports; a 1 per cent exclusion list; and a 5 per cent exclusion list.

The exclusion lists are modelled so that, for each country, the top 1 or 5 per cent of tariff lines (equivalent to 52 or 104 individual products at the HS6 level of detail, respectively) with the highest tariff revenue from African imports are excluded from liberalization. This allows a more efficient form of product exclusion than that modelled in the preceding subsection, in which the most protected sector was excluded. Doing so provides an approximation of the allocation of exclusion lists, though in practice their application will vary.

The model provides a short-run partial-equilibrium perspective. It comprises three parts: a "shock" elimination of tariffs on intra-African trade; an importer substitution effect, where consumers divert trade from original suppliers to new tariff-free African alternatives; and a demand effect, where consumers demand relatively more of a product as a result of it being cheaper.[2] The advantage of such a model is in generating results that demonstrate the immediate impact on tariff revenues in the short run. It also enables us to incorporate the effects of trade diversion and trade creation, which help to analyse highly specific changes to each country's liberalization schedule, allowing the detailed assessment of exclusion lists. Partial equilibrium and computable general equilibrium modelling of tariff revenue losses summarizes the merits and demerits of this modelling approach against those of the CGE model presented above.

The results show the tariff revenue losses as a share of total tariff revenue, for each country. They vary by country per their particular import and tariff profiles (Tariff revenue losses under different flexibility scenarios). Countries with high initial tariffs on intra-African trade, and with larger volumes of intra-African imports, experience the greatest revenue impact, especially the Democratic Republic of the Congo, São Tomé and Príncipe, and Zimbabwe, where tariff revenue losses from liberalizing African imports exceed 20 per cent of total tariff revenues.

The Democratic Republic of the Congo receives a large share of its imports from South Africa and Zambia, which have not yet liberalized under the Southern African Development Community (SADC) free trade agreement (FTA). This is similarly the case with Zimbabwe, where

Box 5.1

Partial equilibrium and computable general equilibrium modelling of tariff revenue losses

Two broad types of economic models are used for assessing the implications of trade agreements: partial equilibrium (PE) models and computable general equilibrium (CGE) models. Each approach provides a different perspective with its own advantages and limitations. A combination of both provides the fullest answer to assessing the impact of trade liberalization.

Level of detail for the model

PE: can provide very detailed results, at the individual product level and for each country with data. The data requirements for PE are less demanding than for CGE.

CGE: requires a degree of aggregation, both among products into broader groupings and among countries, especially when the analysis includes countries for which the required technical inputs, such as social accounting matrices, are unavailable. CGE modelling of African countries typically includes aggregations such as "Rest of West Africa" and "Rest of Central Africa," for instance.

Interaction between sectors

PE: excludes general equilibrium effects such as adjustment within and between firms, sectors and households. They thus represent a short-term perspective of the immediate impact of trade agreements.

CGE: better represents the medium to long run in which firms and households fully adjust their production and consumption patterns in response to changes in domestic and international prices. Capital and labour may also shift from one sector to another, and households may adjust their consumption patterns in response to changes in prices and incomes.

Macroeconomic adjustments

PE: represents the immediate short-run impact of trade liberalization and does not model macroeconomic adjustments, such as changes to the exchange rate, or account for their impact.

CGE: may incorporate long-term macro aggregates such as economic growth, investment and changes to the exchange rate.

Assumption or data driven

PE: relies on relatively few assumptions. The results from PE models are largely driven by the data they are based on.

CGE: a relatively large number of assumptions are required to produce CGE results (such as whether wages or unemployment adjust to clear labour markets, or savings or debt adjust to clear capital markets), and various elasticities determining the responsiveness of different values to different shocks.

CGE may be considered appropriate for estimating medium to long-run impacts and for implications that depend on the interaction of many sectors or macroeconomic adjustments. PE is valuable for short-run, highly detailed implications. Results of PE also depend on fewer assumptions and data are available for almost all African countries. The PE approach proves useful for comparing estimates of the immediate impact on tariff revenue losses at the country level across Africa.

99 per cent of tariff revenue is lost on imports from Southern African Customs Union (SACU) countries. Were the SADC FTA implemented in these countries, the impact of the CFTA would be far smaller. In São Tomé and Príncipe, 97 per cent of the tariff revenue losses accrue on mineral fuels from Angola.

The power of exclusion lists is also demonstrated. With even a 1 per cent exclusion list, equivalent to 52 products, tariff revenue losses for the Democratic Republic of the Congo fall from 36 per cent to 15 per cent. The average rate of tariff revenue losses for all countries falls from 8 per cent to only 1 per cent, if every country were to apply a 1 per cent exclusion list with full efficiency towards the goal of protecting tariff revenues. With a 5 per cent exclusion list, the tariff revenue losses fall to 0.3 per cent for the average country.

The exceptional efficacy of exclusion lists in this context is due to the particularly concentrated nature of intra-African trade: 1 per cent of tariff lines corresponds to 74 per cent of African imports for the average African country. For example, São Tomé and Príncipe imports a *total* of only 26 product lines from other African countries, from a possible total of 5,205 product lines. By excluding even a single product related to mineral fuels, that country can protect 97 per cent of its tariff revenues from African imports.

Further examples are illustrative. Fifty per cent of the tariff revenue losses accruing to Cameroon are due solely to liberalized imports of African petroleum oils, mostly from Nigeria. For the Central African Republic, the top 10 products account for 47 per cent of all African imports. For Gambia, the top two products—Portland cement and malt extract—account for 28 per cent of all its African imports.

The capacity for exclusion lists to limit tariff revenue losses is considerable. In practice, exclusion lists seek to achieve objectives other than just tariff revenue protection, such as retaining protection for infant industries and ensuring food security, and so the results provide a demonstrative upper limit of the effectiveness of such lists. Nevertheless, the results are powerful. With even a 1 per cent exclusion list, the average African country could reduce tariff revenue losses that would be implied by the CFTA from 8 per cent to 1 per cent of total tariff revenue. This stems from the strongly concentrated nature of current intra-African trade flows and the fact that for many countries, a lot of intra-African trade is already liberalized by regional economic communities (REC) FTAs.

Negotiators must exercise caution over the size of exclusion lists negotiated in the CFTA, so that overly liberal exclusion lists do not erode the value and benefits of trade liberalization with the CFTA. Doing so could, for instance, be achieved through the inclusion of an "anti-concentration" clause, in which the number of tariff lines that may be excluded in each Harmonized System (HS) chapter is limited, or "double-qualifying" exclusion lists would be used to account for, at most, a specified per centage of the *value* intra-African trade, rather than *number* of tariff lines.

Where exclusion lists may provide considerable value, though, is in helping to smooth the tariff revenue impact of the CFTA. This is important to ensure a win-win CFTA outcome in which no country is unduly threatened by tariff revenue losses. Countries in which the implied tariff revenue losses may be larger, such as the Democratic Republic of the Congo, can be accorded more flexibility for larger exclusion lists to help them bear the tariff revenue costs.

Figure 5.1

Tariff revenue losses under different flexibility scenarios

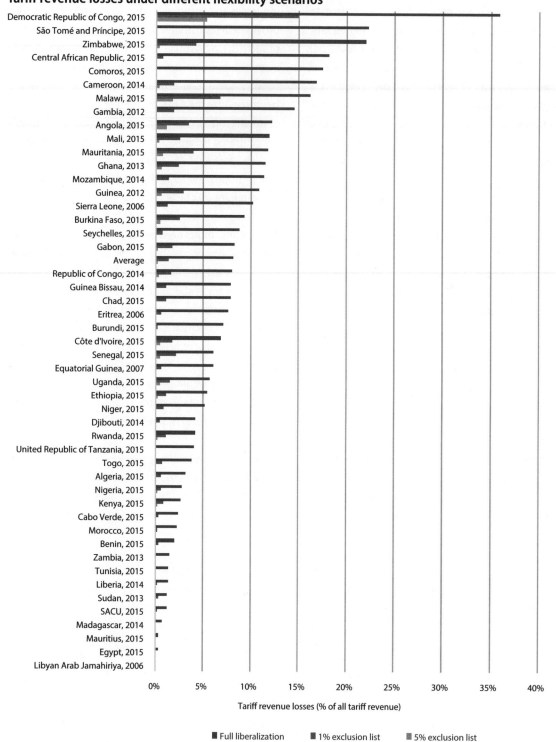

Tariff revenue losses (% of all tariff revenue)

■ Full liberalization ■ 1% exclusion list ■ 5% exclusion list

Note: Results derive from the described partial equilibrium model. The data require that SACU countries, which operate a fully effective customs union, are presented as a single entity.

Source: ECA calculations using CEPII-BACI dataset for 2015 trade flows and ITC tariff data for the specified date for each country.

Within countries

Structural adjustment costs

The CFTA is forecast to lead to higher levels of welfare in aggregate and in the long run. Related to this is the expectation that the agreement will expand Africa's industrial sector, diversify economic activity from its dependency on primary commodities, and contribute to Africa's industrialization and structural transformation. It is expected that factors of production within a country, including labour and capital, will shift across sectors towards those with expanding exports, and within sectors to more export-oriented firms.

It is important to consider the adjustment costs required for this transition in the long run. Structural adjustment costs can be defined as the "value of output that is foregone in the transition to new long-run production patterns because of the time taken to allocate factors from their pre- to their post-liberalization occupations" (Francois et al., 2011). In practice, this can mean obsolescence of skills, lower wages and unemployment for those in contracting sectors, while retraining and reskilling is required to enter expanding sectors. Likewise, capital may become underused or obsolete in a contracting sector and require reinvestment into an expanding sector.

The link between short-run adjustment costs and long-run benefits from trade liberalization can be shown using a simple stylized graph taken from Francois et al. (2011) (Adjustment paths after trade liberalization). Y_0 and Y_1 are the initial and long-run levels of output, respectively. After trade liberalization, output follows a j-shaped curve, first decreasing below the initial level (Y_0) but then gradually converging with a new higher long-run equilibrium (Y_1). The fall in the level of output below Y_0 during the first stages of adjustment is considered the structural adjustment cost.

Structural adjustment costs are concerned with the short run as economies undergo structural change and factors of production shift across sectors to align with new trading opportunities and threats. However, the transition process can be sluggish if capital and factor markets are not sufficiently flexible. For instance,

labour markets may be characterized by frictions and impediments to mobility, and exporting sectors subject to congestion externalities (Davidson and Matusz, 2004; Gaisford and Leger, 2000), which is what can lead to issues of underutilization of capital and to unemployment.

The severity of these adjustment costs can be mitigated by a measured and gradual approach to implementation: Rather than a shock elimination of tariffs, tariff reductions can be gradually introduced over a number of years (Cassing and Ochs, 1978; Gaisford and Leger, 2000; Davidson and Matusz 2000). The rationale is that as workers shift from import-competing sectors and seek new jobs in the expanding export sectors, "congestion externalities" will arise that increase the costs of adjustment. If the government removes trade barriers slowly, it can control the flow of workers, reduce congestion and smooth the adjustment process to minimize the social costs of adjustment (Davidson and Matusz, 2004).

The magnitude of structural adjustment costs is also associated with the extent of trade reform. Completely eliminating all tariffs on imports from all countries would imply a substantial shock to an economy, and correspondingly large adjustment costs. An FTA with a single other country would, conversely, amount to a far smaller shock and smaller adjustment costs.

There are three reasons why the CFTA is likely to amount to a relatively small trade shock:

- Intra-African trade accounts for only 14 per cent of total African imports and 18 per cent of total African exports.

- Most intra-African trade is between closely proximate countries or immediate neighbours, and much of it flows through existing REC FTAs.

- The CFTA will contain exclusion list provisions and safeguards, enabling members to omit the sectors that are most sensitive to liberalization.

The CFTA will nevertheless probably still entail modest structural adjustment costs. A gradual implementation may mitigate—but not fully eliminate—these costs, though such remaining costs may be addressed through two further mechanisms.

Figure 5.2

Adjustment paths after trade liberalization

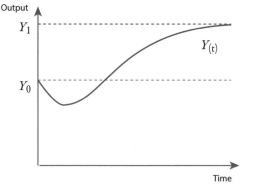

Source: Francois et al. (2011).

First, the particular trade flows causing the structural adjustments may be excluded from the exclusion list provision or through safeguard measures, both of which are to be built into the CFTA Agreement. Safeguard measures and product exclusions are not the ideal policy solutions. They create consumption distortions and present significant rent-seeking dangers (Gaisford and Leger, 2000). However, they may serve as an inferior but acceptable measure when better alternatives are not feasible. They may also allow negotiators to circumnavigate insurmountable political economy barriers that could otherwise slow or block the agreement.

Second, adjustment assistance may be applied to especially sensitive or vulnerable groups that face adverse effects from CFTA liberalization. Such adjustment assistance is considered among the flanking policies that governments can use to smooth the impact of the CFTA (Chapter 6). Here the idea is that a government may leverage the gains from liberalization realized by other groups, such as through tax revenue from an expanding export sector, to address the challenges faced by less fortunate groups. This amounts to compensating the losers from liberalization by using some of the gains accruing to the winners.

In either case, it is important to emphasize that adjustment assistance or safeguards should be considered strictly temporary to address the short-run nature of structural adjustment and should have a predetermined schedule by which they are phased out (Gaisford and Leger, 2000). The weight of CFTA adjustment costs must also be contextualized. In aggregate, they are likely to be modest and temporary, and need to be set against an indefinite stream of future higher incomes.

Vulnerable groups

Though structural adjustment costs may be small and may concern only the short run, it is particularly important to identify and address these costs when they fall on vulnerable or sensitive groups, four of which are being discussed. These groups may be less resilient to even small shocks or lack the resources necessary to reskill and seek new opportunities. Where possible, the CFTA and its accompanying measures should include provisions of particular benefit to such groups so

that they too can share the gains of the CFTA and are protected when necessary.

Smallholder farmers

Smallholder farmers represent some 53 per cent of Africa's agricultural producers. The CFTA promises large opportunities for agricultural exports across several sectors (Table 5.2). Wages of unskilled agricultural workers are also set to rise, though by a small amount (ILO and UNCTAD, 2013).

Nevertheless, smallholder farmers are usually connected to export markets through intermediaries. It will be important for the CFTA to include supporting measures that would promote the integration of smallholder farmers into larger value gains to ensure that they share these opportunities. Smallholder farmers can also be supported by simplified rules-of-origin requirements and with trade facilitation measures that help them to meet sanitary and phyto-sanitary export standards.

Smallholder farmers may also require capital and reskilling to focus their production on export opportunities and to shift from agricultural goods that may be more efficiently produced elsewhere. For instance, new seed varieties or fertilizers may be needed to take advantage of new exports. In the long term, this form of structural adjustment leads to more efficient production outcomes, but particular care is required in the short run to ensure that such farmers

Table 5.2

Africa's export volumes by agricultural and food sectors, and estimated growth with the CFTA (%)

	Growth
Paddy and processed rice	3.2
Wheat	26.0
Cereal	13.9
Oilseeds	3.9
Sugar cane and sugar beets	38.6
Cattle, sheep, goats and horses	4.2
Animal products and wool	0.5
Other agricultural products	1.7
Raw milk and dairy products	101.0
Meat products	26.2
Sugar	16.5
Other food products	17.0
Agriculture and food	9.4

Source: ILO and UNCTAD (2013).

are capable of these adjustments. CFTA monitoring mechanisms should be particularly sensitive to the effects on smallholder farmers, and that safeguards or product exclusions may be required if they require more time for adjustment.

Informal cross-border traders

Informal cross-border trade refers to the trade of goods or services that do not pass formally through customs controls and therefore escape the regulatory framework of taxation and other procedures set by governments.

Though cross-border trading contributes substantially to national economies and employment in Africa, traders are often pushed into the informal sector. This can be owing to problems faced in reading customs forms, accessing and comprehending opaque border procedures, understanding complex duty structures or affording tariffs. Such trading is particularly important as a source of employment for women from low-income households, with women accounting for some 70 per cent of informal cross-border traders (Ghils, 2013).

Once in the informal sector, cross-border traders face challenges. For example, border officials sometimes ask them to pay duties on commodities that should not attract any levies, and they can take advantage of informal traders' ignorance of the law and customs procedures (Mwanabiningo, 2015). Informal traders can be vulnerable to harassment, violence, confiscation of goods and even imprisonment. They also have poorer access to market information for determining prices, to information on policies and regulations and to credit.

The CFTA offers an opportunity to assist this vulnerable group and to make it easier for them to trade formally and under the greater protections and security afforded by such formality, partly because it will reduce tariffs, making it more affordable for such traders to operate through formal channels. However, accompanying measures should go further to benefit this group and to ensure that they are not disadvantaged relative to established formal traders.

For instance, trade facilitation and trade information measures generally make it easier for traders to operate through formal channels (Lesser and Moisé-Leeman, 2009). An example is the Simplified Trade Regime in the Common Market for Eastern and Southern Africa (COMESA), which simplifies clearing procedures and

the requirements necessary to qualify for the COMESA preferential duties for a common list of products. Other important support would be provisions for the free movement of economic operators, which should be designed not just to benefit large companies, but also small traders. Reinforcing these measures, a CFTA monitoring and evaluation mechanism should include an assessment of progress in alleviating the constraints faced by informal cross-border traders, particularly women.

Women

The African Union's (AU's) Agenda 2063 and the gender commitments under the UN's Sustainable Development Goals of Agenda 2030 are among the most recent continental and international affirmations of gender equality as a development priority. Yet unless the trend of gender disparities in wage earnings and absence from the labour force are reversed, Sub-Saharan Africa could lose up to $60 billion dollars annually (UNDP, 2016). Moreover, as a vulnerable group, African women achieve only 87 per cent of men's human development (UNDP, 2016).

Chauvin et al. (2016) estimate the differentiated impact of the CFTA on male- and female-headed households by linking a simulation of the CFTA to household survey data for six African countries with data. They find that both male- and female-headed households gain, but that the gains are unevenly distributed depending on the particular trade and tariff structures of each country, and the income and consumption characteristics of its households (Table 5.3).

In agriculture, women's participation is often concentrated in lower-value subsistence crops rather than cash crops for export, narrowing their opportunities to benefit from value addition and commercial export

Table 5.3

CFTA average welfare effects, by male- and female-headed households (%)

	Male-headed	Female-headed
Burkina Faso	8.70	13.47
Cameroon	7.13	6.39
Côte d'Ivoire	10.44	3.77
Ethiopia	6.26	8.52
Madagascar	2.10	2.61
Nigeria	6.47	5.44

Source: Chauvin et al. (2016).

opportunities due to the CFTA. The task is to make women's participation in agriculture more productive and to connect female agricultural workers to export food markets, enabling them to garner higher incomes (UNCTAD, 2014).

Women account for roughly 70 per cent of informal cross-border traders. The challenges for this vulnerable group are especially acute for women, particularly those related to harassment and discrimination by border officials and access to credit, training and information. Measures to assist informal cross-border traders should aim to benefit women. For example, trade facilitation measures should address issues to improve women's safety, such as storage facilities, accommodation, illuminated border areas, hygiene facilities and transport corridors.

The interests of women can be better reflected by their explicit involvement in the design and processes of the CFTA, including through national consultations and more female negotiators. Evaluating impacts on women also requires a monitoring and evaluation framework with gender-disaggregated data.

Youth

Sixty per cent of Africa's population are aged 24 or younger and are about to enter the workforce. If this increasing number of working age individuals can be employed in productive activities, Africa's youth bulge may become a demographic dividend. Otherwise, it may become a demographic disaster, as a large mass of frustrated youth become a potential source of social and political instability. Yet a shortage of opportunities for Africa's youth contributes to high youth unemployment and working poverty rates approaching 70 per cent (ILO, 2016). Aware of this, the AU Heads of State and Government have chosen as its theme for 2017: "Harnessing the Demographic Dividend though Investments in Youth."

The traditional approach to supporting youth has been to look at the labour supply side. The 2007 World Development Report, "Develop the Next Generation," set out a policy agenda focusing on education, skills upgrading, health and citizenship. Such support is also reflected within the AU Roadmap on Harnessing the Demographic Dividend through Investments in Youth, 2017, which includes pillars on education and skills development, health and well-being, and rights, governance and youth empowerment.

Structural transformation is required to produce new jobs for young people and to absorb these new entrants into the labour force. Countries that have been successful in this regard, such as China and the Republic of Korea, moved from a high share of employment in agriculture towards manufacturing first, then services. What will be important for Africa is restructuring economies away from capital-intensive commodities towards labour-intensive sectors, such as manufacturing, information and communications technology, and agriculture and agro-industries, to produce the jobs that can pull Africa's youth into the workforce. As recognized in the AU Roadmap on Harnessing the Demographic Dividend through Investments in Youth, 2017, this will require improved access to credit facilities to support entrepreneurs, initiatives such as tech incubators, and accelerators to support youth-led businesses, and trade liberalization.

Supporting Africa's youth requires a development strategy that goes beyond trade policy. Policies in education and skills development, such as the Continental Strategy for Technical Vocation Education and Training and the Science, Technology and Innovation Strategy for Africa (2014–24) are important, as are others in health and well-being and in youth empowerment. The CFTA can be an additional component. Most important, the CFTA can contribute to the kinds of export diversification and structural transformation that promote labour-intensive industry and help to "pull" Africa's youth into productive activities.

References

Arvis, J. F., G. Raballand and J. F. Marteau. 2007. "The cost of being landlocked: Logistics costs and supply chain reliability." Policy Research Working Paper No. 4258. Washington, DC: World Bank.

Berman, N., M. Couttenier, D. Rohner and M. Thoenig. 2014. "This Mine Is Mine! How Minerals Fuel Conflicts in Africa." Research Paper 141. Oxford, UK: Oxford Centre for the Analysis of Resource Rich Economies.

Calì, M. 2014. *Trading Away from Conflict: Using Trade to Increase Resilience in Fragile States*. Washington, DC: World Bank.

Cassing, J., and J. Ochs. 1978. "International Trade, Factor Market Distortions, and the Optimal Dynamic Subsidy: Comment." *American Economic Review* 68 69 (4) 950–955.

Chauvin, D., N. Ramos and G. Porto. 2016. "Trade, Growth, and Welfare Impacts of the CFTA in Africa." https://editorialexpress.com/cgi-bin/conference/download.cgi?db_name=CSAE2017&paper_id=749.

Davidson, C., and S. Matusz. 2000. "Globalization and labour-market adjustment: How fast and at what cost?" *Oxford Review of Economic Policy* 16 (3): 42–56.

———. 2004. "Should policy makers be concerned about adjustment costs?" In D. Mitra and A. Panagariya (editors), *The Political Economy of Trade, Aid and Foreign Investment Policies*. Amsterdam: Elsevier.

Dube, O., and J. Vargas. 2013. "Commodity Price Shocks and Civil Conflict: Evidence from Colombia." *Review of Economic Studies* 80 (4): 1384–1421.

Francois, J., M. Jansen and R. Peters. 2011. "Trade adjustment costs and assistance: The labor market dynamics." In M. Jansen, R. Peters and J. M. Salazar-Xirinachs (editors), *Trade and Employment: From Myths to Facts*. Geneva: International Labour Organization and European Commission.

Fund for Peace. 2017. Fragile States Index (database). http://fundforpeace.org/fsi/.

Gaisford, J. D., and L. A. Leger. 2000. "Terms-of-Trade Shocks, Labor-Market Adjustment, and Safeguard Measures." *Review of International Economics* 8 (1): 100–112.

Ghils, A. 2013. "How to help women cross-border traders in Africa?" *Bridges Africa*, 15 May.

ILO (International Labour Organization). 2016. *World Employment and Social Outlook 2016: Trends for Youth*. Geneva.

ILO and UNCTAD (United Nations Conference on Trade and Development). 2013. *Assessment Report: Towards a Continental Free Trade Area in Africa—Modelling Assessment with a Focus on Agriculture.*

Jones, E. 2013. *Negotiating Against the Odds: A Guide for Trade Negotiators from Developing Countries*. Basingstoke, UK: Palgrave Macmillan.

Karingi, S., and S. Mevel. 2012. "Deepening Regional Integration in Africa: A Computable General Equilibrium Assessment of the Establishment of a Continental Free Trade Area followed by a Continental Customs Union." Paper for presentation at the 15th Global Trade Analysis Project Conference, Geneva, 27–29 June.

Lesser, C., and E. Moisé-Leeman. 2009. "Informal cross-border trade and trade facilitation reform in sub-Saharan Africa." Trade Policy Paper No. 86. Paris: Organisation for Economic Co-operation and Development.

Maystadt, J.-F., G. De Luca, P. G. Sekeris, J. Ulimwengu and R. Folledo. 2014. "Mineral Resources and Conflicts in DRC: A Case of Ecological Fallacy?" *Oxford Economic Papers* 66 (3): 721–749. http://oep.oxfordjournals.org/content/66/3/721.

McKinsey & Company. 2013. *Reverse the curse: Maximizing the potential of resource-driven economies*. McKinsey Global Institute.

Mwanabiningo, N. 2015. *Deriving Maximum Benefit from Small-Scale Cross Border Trade between DRC and Rwanda*. London: International Alert.

Olayiwola, W. K., and O. A. Ola-David. 2013. "Economic integration, trade facilitation and agricultural exports performance in ECOWAS member states." Presentation at the 8th African Economic Conference on "Regional Integration in Africa," Johannesburg, South Africa, 28–30 October.

Rustad, S. A., G. Østby and R. Nordås. 2016. "Artisanal mining, conflict, and sexual violence in Eastern DRC." *The Extractive Industries and Society* 3 (2): 475–484.

Saygili M., R. Peters and C. Knebel. 2017. "African Continental Free Trade Area: Challenges and Opportunities of Tariff Reductions." Policy Issues in International Trade and Commodities. Study Series. New York and Geneva: United Nations.

Sommer, L., and D. Luke. 2017. "Smart Industrialization." Forthcoming. Addis Ababa: ECA

UNCTAD (United Nations Conference on Trade and Development). 2014. *Virtual Institute Teaching Material on Trade and Gender – Volume 1: Unfolding the Links*. New York and Geneva.

UNDP (United Nations Development Programme). 2016. *African Human Development Report*. New York.

Endnotes

1   The definition of "resource rich" adopted is that of the McKinsey Global Institute, which defines resource-driven countries as countries that meet at least one of three criteria: resource exports accounted for 20 per cent or more of total exports in 2011; resources on average accounted for more than 20 per cent of government revenue from 2006 to 2010; and resource rents were more than 10 per cent of GDP in 2010 or the most recent year for which data are available (McKinsey & Company, 2013).

2   This is very similar to the SMART and TRIST partial equilibrium models, and indeed uses the default TRIST demand and importer substitution elasticities (0.5 and 1.5, respectively). The analysis amounts to tariff reductions *within* the FTAs of existing RECs, where those FTAs do not already amount to full 100 per cent liberalization. Therefore, even countries that cover much of their imports within existing REC FTAs (Chapter 2) may still experience a significant import and revenue impact. The results of this approach are intuitive and transparent to a relatively non-technical audience, and rely on only a limited number of assumptions.

Chapter 6
A Win-win Approach to the CFTA: Critical Policies

This chapter builds on the content of Chapter 5 and elaborates on the critical policies and provisions that are needed to ensure that the gains of the Continental Free Trade Area (CFTA) are fully exploited and shared equitably.

It argues that negotiators must design the substantive content of the CFTA to support the aspirations for industrial development and structural economic change. To so so, they must "get right" six key components of the CFTA—non-tariff barriers (NTBs), rules of origin, investment and cross-border movement of persons, services liberalization and regulation, trade remedies, and monitoring and evaluation. This chapter identifies the critical challenges and policy recommendations for each of these components. It then outlines the Boosting Intra-African Trade (BIAT) Action Plan, which provides a framework for critical flanking policies that would support the CFTA. Lastly, it reviews the need for strategic logistics management to facilitate trade by buttressing investments in physical infrastructure.

Getting non-tariff barriers right

NTBs are impediments to trade and are particularly onerous in Africa; they include import bans, unjustified documentation and conditions, excessive border checks, and police stops. The average applied rate of tariff protection in Africa is 8.7 per cent, but other obstacles increase the cost of Africa's trade by an estimated 283 per cent (Sommer and Luke, 2017). Box 6.1 details the most common NTBs reported in Africa.

Getting NTBs right in the CFTA will mean including provisions to reduce these barriers. The CFTA is to include provisions on non-tariff measures, such as sanitary and phyto-sanitary standards and technical barriers to trade that can constitute some of the NTBs for cross-border trade in Africa. However, what will be especially important is targeting the particular NTBs that affect vulnerable groups to ensure that they gain from the CFTA.

Box 6.1

Typical non-tariff barriers in Africa

NTBs are particularly obstructive to small and medium-sized enterprises, informal cross-border traders, and women traders. Among the common NTBs reported in Africa are:

Customs and trade procedures, including non-standardized systems for imports declaration and payment of applicable duty rates; non-acceptance of certificates and trade documentation; incorrect tariff classification; limited and uncoordinated customs working hours; different interpretation of the rules of origin and non-acceptance of the certificate of origin; application of discriminatory taxes and other charges; and cumbersome procedures for verifying containerized imports.

Immigration procedures, for example, non-standardized visa fees and cumbersome or duplicative immigration procedures.

Quality inspection procedures, including delays in the inspection of commercial vehicles; cumbersome and costly quality inspection procedures; unnecessary quality inspections; non-standardized quality inspection and testing procedures; and varying procedures for issuing certification marks.

Transport-related requirements, such as non-harmonized transport policies, laws, regulations and standards; vehicle overland control systems; vehicle dimensions and standards; cross-border road permits; and prohibitive transit charges.

Road blocks, for example, numerous and uncoordinated road blocks by state agents.

Source: AU (2017).

Much can be learned by the success of NTB mechanisms employed by the regional economic communities (RECs) (Box 6.2). An effective NTB mechanism enables the reporting of NTBs by individual traders and includes an administrative structure that escalates issues to responsible governments and monitors their resolution.

Accordingly, it is recommended that the CFTA leverage the existing NTB mechanisms of the RECs rather than reinvent a wholly new mechanism. To do so the CFTA should extend the remit of the existing REC mechanisms to include trade between and within *all* RECs. The CFTA Secretariat may then assume the responsibility of coordinating these mechanisms across Africa.

Getting rules of origin right

Rules of origin are a foundational component of a free trade area. They aim to ensure that products traded within a free trade area really originate within a member country. Their objective is to avoid trade deflection and circumvention. For example, they would aim to stop third countries that are not party to the CFTA from re-exporting via one CFTA member state to another, illegitimately benefiting from the trade preferences that should be exclusive to the CFTA.

However, this primary objective must be balanced against excessively obstructionist rules of origin, which could be used as a protectionist measure against trade between CFTA member states (Estevadeordal et al., 2014). Moreover, overly burdensome rules of origin can prove particularly challenging for micro, small and medium-sized enterprises, including informal cross-border traders and smallholder farmers. Rules of origin are also tough to negotiate, especially for under-resourced negotiating delegations.

Getting the rules of origin right in the CFTA requires harmonizing rules of origin across RECs to facilitate regional value chains (RVCs), considering preferential rules of origin for less developed African countries and drawing lessons from how rules of origin have been negotiated in the Tripartite Free Trade Area (TFTA).

Regional value chains and harmonizing rules of origin in Africa

Numerous papers have highlighted the need to harmonize the rules of origin used across Africa in the CFTA (ECA, 2013a; UNCTAD, 2016; Draper et al., 2016). Harmonizing them would ease intra-African trade by reducing the complexity of complying with multiple sets

Box 6.2

Monitoring and reporting NTBs in the COMESA, EAC and SADC

The Tripartite Free Trade Area (TFTA) is yet to be finalized. However, the framework agreement (concluded in 2015) includes an NTB mechanism to coordinate the monitoring and reporting of NTBs in the three RECs.

Under the mechanism, NTBs are reported either online or by Short Message Service by individuals when they consider themselves to have faced a barrier in trading. Reporting is open to anyone, including drivers, travellers, business people or traders.

The report is forwarded by an administrator to nominated focal points in the reporting and offending countries, as well as to the REC or RECs concerned. Although responsibility for resolving the NTB lies with the sending country, RECs perform a facilitating function by providing capacity building or arranging meetings between countries where necessary. Progress is monitored on a publicly available website (http://www.tradebarriers.org), which updates the progress and whether any resolution action is under way.

The process includes concrete timelines for removing NTBs. Individuals can monitor and receive an update of progress made in resolving their complaint. The mechanism also retains a record of all complaints, and adds them to a database on NTBs. Since it was set up in 2009, the mechanism has registered 556 NTB complaints, 501 of which have been resolved.*

The Tripartite NTB mechanism is currently augmenting this service with an archive of NTBs in the Tripartite region. Estimated to be available for 12 Tripartite countries by the end of 2017, the mechanism will provide information on NTBs by tariff line and UNCTAD NTB category. Doing so will improve transparency and trade information on NTBs for businesses and traders in the Tripartite region.

Registered and resolved complaints as of 26 May, 2017 (for latest see http://www.tradebarriers.org).
Source: AU (2017).

of rules (Bhagwati, 1995). Doing so fosters inclusiveness by easing the use of rules of origin for smaller and less sophisticated traders (Corneja and Harris, 2007).

Preferential rules of origin in Africa

Africa's countries span various stages of economic development. The United Nations distinguishes between developing and least-developed countries (LDCs). To cater to this distinction, preferential rules of origin should be considered within the CFTA. They could help to ensure that Africa's less advanced countries are not excluded from CFTA opportunities by burdensome rules-of-origin requirements. Here rules of origin would be differentiated to provide less developed African countries with a set of rules that are easier to satisfy. Doing so can help spread the gains of the CFTA to smaller and less sophisticated businesses in Africa's less developed countries.

This initiative would not be without precedent. African countries have continually pressed for such special and differential treatment in the rules of origin discussions at the World Trade Organization (WTO), culminating in the Ministerial Decisions on preferential rules of origin in Bali, in 2013, and Nairobi, in 2015.

Drawing lessons from rules of origin negotiations in the TFTA

Agreement on the rules of origin was one of the stumbling blocks delaying conclusion of the TFTA. Central to this was the decision to negotiate product-specific rules of origin, entailing the highly onerous, time-consuming and technically demanding process of determining particular rules for over 5,000 products. Such an approach requires an intensely close relationship between negotiators and businesses and an in-depth understanding of the productive capacities of rival negotiating partners.

The TFTA's decision to use product-specific rules was motivated by some countries' request to ensure adequate protection of industries from trade deflection and circumvention. For instance, some countries worry that unsophisticated rules in textiles could allow third countries to access their markets through the affixation of highly limited value addition in their TFTA partner countries. Recent analysis suggests, however, that this fear is unwarranted, and that more general rules are not necessarily lax or lacking in rigor (Draper et al., 2016).

Though more sophisticated negotiating parties may possess the capability to negotiate product-specific rules of origin, they are difficult for less-developed countries with less well-resourced negotiating teams. Moreover, once negotiated, such rules can also prove difficult for less-developed countries to administer. At best, product-specific rules may allow tailoring to the exact specifications and requirements of trading businesses. At worst, they prove overly time-consuming to negotiate, potentially adding several years to the time taken to negotiate the CFTA. They also disproportionately advantage more sophisticated negotiating teams.

One solution draws on the novel approach of the Pan-Arab free trade area, which used general rules of origin over a transitionary five-year period, during which specific rules were negotiated. This technique enabled these countries to lock into their free trade area without delay, and to eventually graduate to product-specific rules within a specified period. Such a compromise could expedite the finalizing of the CFTA. Or, the CFTA could limit the use of product-specific rules to only the most controversial or sensitive products, and apply simple and liberal rules of origin as far as possible otherwise (AU, 2013; ECA, 2013a).

Getting investment and cross-border movement of persons right

Facilitating intra-African investment is crucial for allowing the flow of much-needed resources for the large-scale interventions required to transform Africa's agriculture and industry. Foreign direct investment (FDI), including intra-African investment, will be key. Indeed, one only needs to analyse the current construct of Africa's telecommunications sector to conclude that intra-African investment is important for getting entrepreneurs to innovate. The same is found in transport—road, rail and air, all of which are a showcase of strong intra-African investment. Financial services are no exception, with pan-African banks increasingly having continental, or at least regional, presence.

A CFTA that makes it difficult for Africans, including entrepreneurs, to move across the continent will be a missed opportunity. It should be designed to support African investors and improve weak business conditions.

The design of provisions for investment and cross-border movement of persons in trade agreements have typically been considered part of trade in services. The optimal decision would need to be informed by what the CFTA seeks to achieve and what would work in context. Any technical errors at this stage focus on limitations rather than facilitating access would create operational difficulties for the future and would be questionable in their value for African entrepreneurs. What is needed is a broader, forward-looking approach that boosts investment and movement for Africans to tap opportunities presented by the CFTA in agriculture, industry, services and investment.

Front-loading how these two important issues—of investment and movement of persons—can be incorporated in a pro-people manner in the CFTA would democratize the Agreement and allow African entrepreneurs to engage in (not just spectate at) the opportunities created by the CFTA.

Investment
The question for CFTA negotiators is whether they will wait for phase 2 to deal with investment, or instead use the opportunity presented by a discussion on supply of services through establishing commercial presence to determine an approach that will work for a comprehensive treatment of the key issues through the CFTA. The threshold question is whether it is appropriate and sufficient to limit the treatment of investment in the CFTA to a General Agreement on Trade in Services (GATS) mode 3 approach.

Mode 3 is the supply of services through an established commercial presence.[1] Service suppliers of a member state enter the territory of another, set up a branch or subsidiary presence on the basis of commitments made, and offer their services to consumers in the host country. This type of access is often found in the schedules of WTO members and is typically used by large companies. In the CFTA, it would entail, for example, large mobile telecommunications giants setting up branches to run their businesses in other African countries. Such companies would normally send their key personnel to lead these branches, which in turn would be offering their services through the presence of natural persons—mode 4—in what is known as intra-corporate transfers. These people would be beneficiaries of cross-border movement of persons.

A key development test for the CFTA will be its ability to deliver for all, and not just big business. This will require an approach that is sensitive to the bulk of African businesses that are micro, small and medium-sized enterprises, and it may require going beyond the General Agreement on Trade in Services (GATS) approach to consider a separate and dedicated CFTA chapter, annex or even agreement on investment.

Investment in Africa would also need to draw on the lessons of reforms to international investment agreements as a way to ensure a balance between investment protections, on the one hand, and investment promotion and facilitation (a core objective), on the other. Similarly, resolution of issues tied to the contribution of investment for attaining national development goals are key in designing the right approach, which would include careful consideration of provisions on "fair and equitable treatment," investor–state dispute-resolution mechanisms, illicit financial flows, corruption, good governance, endangered species and the environment.

It can be argued that these issues could always be placed as limitations to market access or national treatment in mode 3. However, at least two series of issues would arise: one related to scope—in light of the need to include investment in goods as part of the agreement, and one that conditions around market access, as provided in GATS Article XVI, seems to be of a defined scope and largely focused on quantitative-type measures. Such a scope would leave unanswered questions on how to treat issues concerning the need for investors to contribute to good governance as a precondition to accessing the market. Africa would be better served by a broader and more comprehensive treatment of investment issues in a dedicated chapter, annex or agreement on investment that includes services. This method can help provide an adequate scope for approaching investment provisions in the CFTA.

Cross-border movement of persons
The question for negotiators here is how to design an approach that does not take away from African entrepreneurs what they already have in their RECs, while creating new opportunities for inter-REC movement.

Traditional approaches to structuring movement of persons in a trade agreement tend to take the GATS mode 4 approach, where for a certain category of natural persons—typically intra-corporate transfers—members states would offer access for defined periods and on certain conditions. This is frequently inscribed as limitations on national treatment.

Conceptually, Africa needs an approach that focuses on supporting and facilitating people's movement. From a design perspective, it is important that negotiators focus on letting people in, especially those involved in MSMEs.

Several African countries have made GATS mode 4 commitments but also have gone further and deeper with their RECs beyond their mode 4 schedules. EAC, for example, has its Common Market Protocol[2] that has already taken large strides not only in movement of service suppliers, but also workers.[3] ECOWAS has its protocol on the free movement of persons,[4] as does COMESA.[5] All of them seek economic cooperation and integration, and it would be wrong to assume that there is a design difference in the intentions of these RECs and movement or persons in a trade agreement like the CFTA.

Where do solutions lie?

The key question is therefore: What sort of CFTA approach adds value to the RECs' achievements? An approach that focuses on scheduling limitations to access might not be the way to go. Rather, it would be important to think more about how to facilitate cross-border movement. Here again, the question of scope is critical: easing access for investors, traders and services suppliers, all in one instrument.

On investment, there is need for an approach with a good balance between protections and facilitation, all within the development prism. There is already a great body of work on which to build in the Pan African Investment Code, which itself has benefited from global and regional good practices in shaping new-generation, pro-sustainable development and international investment agreements. This is a good basis for a fully fledged investment chapter in the CFTA providing a framework for all categories of investors, including those in MSMEs. Because of the breadth of what is sought, it is proposed that this is not part of the services component of the negotiations, but rather

a stand-alone chapter. It would necessarily mean that all aspects related to the supply of services through establishment of commercial presence would be looked at—making the necessary changes—as part of the broader investment chapter.

On cross-border movement of persons, negotiators could consider an instrument—a separate annex for example—that focuses on facilitation and takes the best of what each of the RECs offers regarding the different steps a natural person takes to supply their services, trade their goods or invest in another African country. Such steps could include terms of accessing opportunities, applying for selection, and moving to other African territories for business, extensions and return.[6] A linked need would be regulatory cooperation in facilitating movement, including involving in the discussions all stakeholders, such as sector regulators, immigration officials, trade negotiators, civil society organizations and trade policy networks, to secure early buy-in on how this would work.

Investment and cross-border movement need to be thought through early, especially as both goods and services agreements are being negotiated now.

Getting services liberalization and regulation right

With a few exceptions, services have come to dominate the economic landscape. Globally they constitute about 70 per cent of GDP and 60 per cent of employment (World Bank, 2016), with cross-border services (excluding services investment) accounting for a quarter of world trade in 2014 in gross value terms (Loungani et al., 2017).

Services, both as inputs to production processes and as final products, are now seen as providing meaningful opportunities for developing countries to fast-track growth, reduce poverty and promote structural economic transformation.[7] This so-called "services revolution" has been attributed to "3Ts": *technology*, enabling services to be storable through digital means; *transportability*, undermining the necessity that services are often produced and consumed at the same time and place; and *tradability*, highlighting the challenges of restricting trade through government barriers for such services (Ghani and Kharas, 2010).

Services and services trade are also increasingly understood as fundamental components of goods trade (Swedish National Board of Trade, 2012). When decomposing the direct and indirect value added of imports that go into exports, estimates for 2007 put services trade at almost 50 per cent of the global total (Francois et al., 2013). Driven in large measure by the fragmentation of global production and the rise of global value chains, trade in goods and services is deeply interconnected. Getting services right in the CFTA requires a three-pronged approach, as outlined below.

Building on existing REC achievements

The starting point for services negotiations are the existing achievements (and challenges overcome) in the RECs; that is, building on what has worked and avoiding what has not worked. Learning from implementation challenges on the ground will be essential.

EAC—the REC most advanced in its liberalization of services—has faced many such challenges, including how member states interpret their schedule of commitments and the technical issues in the schedule. And the mode 4 (movement of persons) commitments were not clear, as they were linked to a separate schedule on movement of labour. However, achievements were secured with mutual recognition agreements for professional bodies, including accountants, architectures, engineers, veterinary surgeons and land surveyors. Such agreements are under negotiation for lawyers, pharmacists, medical professionals, land valuers and quantity surveyors.

Achieving the right levels of flexibility and ambition

Going beyond what the RECs have achieved in progressive services liberalization and regulatory cooperation requires a commitment that the CFTA fulfils its potential. As seen in the WTO's Trade Facilitation Agreement, being able to link targeted technical assistance, capacity building and support for regulatory reforms to the undertaking of (market access and regulatory) commitments is likely to create an amplifying effect. Ultimately, however, the approach must be realistic about member states' comfort level in committing to binding services reforms in trade agreements and to advancing with regulatory cooperation.

A highly flexible mechanism has the greatest chance of success. Flexibility is needed for the scope and depth of market access commitments and for the range of mechanisms needed for regulatory cooperation. Such flexibility should also enable differing levels of engagement among the variegated African Union (AU) member states.

For progressive liberalization, that flexibility would entail sticking with what member states know to some degree (for example, GATS-based, positive list) and being innovative to help in delivering more meaningful results. Starting from applied regimes, and making use of some form of standstill mechanism, constitutes prime examples, though member states may need to consider a non-uniform approach to these if horizontal application proves challenging. For regulatory cooperation, this involves deploying the most appropriate mechanism, formal or informal, based on different sector-specific variables, including the domestic regulatory environments across member states in the sector, approaches adopted within the RECs/AU (where relevant), global best/good practice and political economy dynamics.

The upshot may be harmonization in certain sectors (for example, where more than one REC already has made progress on regulatory cooperation, such as telecommunications or transport), mutual recognition agreements in others, treaties (for example, air transport, investment) or more informal approaches such as soft law or informal exchanges of information (including guidelines and voluntary standards). Even simple transparency exercises can help to reduce the informational costs faced by firms dealing with regulatory differences, and it could lay the groundwork for more in-depth cooperation in the future.

Overcoming challenges

There is a risk, however, that such efforts, if not adequately targeted and balanced in their ambition, could quickly evolve into "business as usual," with an eternal schedule of official meetings, missed deadlines and implementation (and compliance) deficiencies. For this reason, the process must be infused with a high level of credibility. For progressive liberalization, ensuring there is at least some use of the market access innovations touched on above will help to deliver real market opening and transparency, and prevent an approach that sees member states make commitments on paper that are already far-distanced from the actual conditions of African services firms. For the work on regulatory cooperation (an area less familiar to trade negotiators), ensuring that the process is supported by highly competent individuals, including those with strong local knowledge, and is adequately resourced, will be important to establish credibility among stakeholders from the outset. The use of specific targets over a certain period (for example, on the number of sectors, removal of restrictions, or negotiation of cooperation mechanisms) may also prove helpful. Establishing such credibility will help to situate such efforts as effective Aid-for-Trade vehicles and mobilization of resources for technical assistance and capacity building, including that for enforcement.

One option for the work on regulatory cooperation is to convene an African Regulatory Cooperation Forum as an inter-governmental body under the auspices of the African Union Commission (AUC). Such a forum would command authority and be well placed to pool national, regional and international expertise on the service sector's regulatory frameworks across the continent, and on good regulatory practices globally and elsewhere in the developing world. Additional technical partners, continental and international,[8] could provide important expertise, helping to boost the credibility of the Forum as an effective mechanism for regulatory cooperation, while supporting member states' regulatory reform efforts. The Forum could function in part as a knowledge platform for such cooperation. Engaging such key development partners, as well as the donor community, can similarly assist in mobilizing the requisite resources.

Establishing credibility among stakeholders is likely to have a positive knock-on effect for stakeholder inclusiveness (a common challenge in REC-level services integration experiences to date). An inclusive approach is needed to engage a broad range of actors, including trade officials, sectoral officials, regulators, qualification authorities and a range of non-state actors, including the private sector and consumer advocates. Such inclusiveness is needed not only to help ensure that the CFTA services agreement is crafted in such way as to deliver meaningful benefits to the people and workers of Africa, but also to ensure the necessary buy-in for putting plans into action.

Promoting the use of local expertise for regulatory cooperation work will also help to navigate the different consumer preferences, cultural and historical roots, and political economy considerations underpinning regulatory differences. And while it is important that any approach remains linked to negotiated market access outcomes, there are also advantages to removing them from the trade negotiating process, including mitigating narrower, mercantilist sentiments and enabling greater cross-pollination of trade and regulatory perspectives (both official and non-state).

The CFTA represents a unique opportunity for AU member states to "do services differently." For success, they must pursue an ambitious and realistic agenda, combining progressive liberalization and regulatory cooperation. To translate this into real new opportunities for African services firms, this work and its outcomes must be credible and inclusive.

Getting trade remedies right

Trade remedies (Box 6.3) are an important fail-safe for vulnerable groups in the CFTA and for countries wary that competition may damage their domestic industries. However, trade remedies can also be a covert means of protectionism.

Trade remedies are important in bringing the CFTA about. Countries are more willing to implement liberalization commitments if they have the flexibility to protect industries when necessary. Kucik and Reinhardt (2008) find countries with national trade remedy mechanisms to be more likely to join the WTO, agree to more tightly binding tariff commitments and lower tariffs.

Only Africa's most economically advanced countries have national trade remedy regimes in place, including Egypt, Morocco, South Africa (whose regime extends to cover the Southern African Customs Union [SACU] countries) and Tunisia. South Africa's first anti-dumping law goes back to 1914 (Joubert, 2005). Countries including Ghana, Kenya and Mauritius are at various stages of drafting trade remedy laws and setting up investigating authorities. A further 11 CFTA countries are not members of the WTO, and are not governed by WTO rules on trade remedies (Box 6.3).

What are trade remedies?

Trade remedies are trade policy tools that allow governments to depart from the usual WTO or FTA rules and take remedial action against imports that are causing material injury to a domestic industry. Their application is subject to certain substantive and procedural conditions outlined in the WTO General Agreement on Tariffs and Trade (GATT) from 1994. They are divided broadly into three categories.

Anti-dumping measures: These may be applied when an imported product is being "dumped" (that is, sold at or below its "normal" price) and when dumped imports are causing or threatening to cause material injury to domestic industry producing like products (or would materially retard the establishment of a domestic industry).

Countervailing measures: These are applicable when subsidized imports are causing or threatening to cause injury to the domestic industry producing the like products.

Safeguard measures: These can be applied when a product is being imported in such increased quantities and under such conditions as to cause or threaten to cause serious injury to the domestic industry producing like or competitive products. Unlike anti-dumping and countervailing measures, the application of safeguarding measures does not require an "unfair trade" action. Instead, the objective of safeguard measures is to provide a temporary remedy while facilitating structural adjustment of the industry affected by the imports.

The application of trade remedies between WTO member countries is governed by WTO law. However, some CFTA participants are not WTO members: Algeria, Comoros, Eritrea, Equatorial Guinea, Ethiopia, Libya, São Tomé and Príncipe, Somalia, South Sudan, Sudan and Western Sahara. As such, the CFTA requires trade remedy provisions to govern the use of trade remedies involving these countries.

Though all WTO members may apply trade remedies against each other in accordance with WTO law, the CFTA may include alternative trade remedy provisions to govern their use between CFTA member countries. For instance, African countries rarely resort to WTO-compliant trade remedies, because to do so is technically onerous and many such countries lack the requisite technical capacity or experience. The CFTA can therefore add value by either incorporating flexibilities into trade remedy provisions to ease their use by less developed countries or by supporting such countries in developing the necessary trade remedy regimes.

Getting trade remedies right in the CFTA will require providing for remedies that are both adequately rules-based and robust so as not to be exploited illegitimately as a means of protectionism, and sufficiently accessible for less-advanced countries. It will also mean helping African countries develop trade remedy regimes so that they are prepared not just for trade defence within the CFTA, but—perhaps more important—for defence against more advanced international competitors. Here the CFTA may take the TFTA approach as a starting point.

TFTA approach to trade remedies

The TFTA tried to compromise between demand for robust and rules-based trade-remedy provisions and flexibilities for less developed countries. It did this by adopting an annex with guidelines for Partner States to develop domestic trade remedy regimes (investigating authorities and supporting legislation) to be able to undertake investigations and impose measures.

The analysis behind this approach is that developing trade remedy regimes is desirable not just within the framework of intra-African trade, but also for a country's broader trade outside the continent where substantially more sophisticated competition exists. The annex on guidelines would help Partner States in setting up these regimes.

Need for a new CFTA approach to trade remedies

Trade remedy institutions require a high level of specialized legal and economic expertise that is prohibitively expensive to train and retain for all but the most advanced African countries. South Africa's trade remedy authority, which employs over 20 permanent staff, has an annual operational budget of around $25 million (Illy, 2013). The Egyptian equivalent, the Central Department of International Trade Policies, employs more than 200 people (Illy, 2013).

The limited financial resources of many African countries, often urgently required in sectors such as health care, education and infrastructure, cannot afford trade remedy regimes. Nor is capacity building a sufficient response. Trained officers are reportedly prone to leave for international organizations or to join the private sector (Illy, 2013). An approach that requires all African countries to have trade remedy regimes is unrealistic.

If the CFTA does not adequately cater to the trade defence requirements of less-resourced countries, these countries may resort to alternative instruments. The experience has been that African countries use import prohibitions, supplementary tariffs or voluntary export restraints, though compliance with WTO law is often questionable (Illy, 2013). Such measures can also cause inefficiencies, create scope for rent seeking and frustrate the interests of exporting countries. It is in the interests of all member states that an appropriate solution be found.

Moreover, Africa's evolving subregional structures make traditional national approaches to trade remedies increasingly ineffective. Africa's RECs are advancing their integration agenda to adopt common external tariffs and customs unions, in line with the expectations of the Abuja Treaty. Any border trade measure, such as anti-dumping or countervailing duties, has to be adopted and implemented by all members of common external tariffs or customs unions at the same time. Otherwise, the goods could easily escape the protective measure by transiting through other members, rendering impotent the remedying measures (Illy, 2013).

Getting trade remedies right in the CFTA will require regional investigating authorities. A regional approach can pool resources to ease the financial strain of supporting a remedy regime and benefit from gathering its required expertise more broadly. This would help extend trade remedies to small and less-developed African countries. Vulnerable groups and sensitive industries could then be better protected in more countries. This approach would also help ease such countries into ambitious liberalization schedules

to which they might otherwise be unable to commit, and would no doubt reduce the need for alternative and less-efficient forms of protection. It would also set up a system enabling these countries to protect themselves from more advanced international competitors.

Getting monitoring and evaluation right

Trade agreements are often criticized for failing to provide for systematic review of their impact on vulnerable communities. It is therefore recommended that provision be made in the monitoring and evaluation arrangements for periodic country reviews of economy-wide and sectoral impacts, including the effects on vulnerable groups.

A CFTA monitoring and evaluation mechanism must hence incorporate three functions. First, it must evaluate each country's compliance with the CFTA, including whether CFTA obligations are being met. Second, it must monitor progress being made with the Boosting Intra-African Trade (BIAT) Action Plan to identify successes and gaps. Third, it must monitor and evaluate how the CFTA is contributing to Africa's development goals and in particular its impact on vulnerable groups. Important in this will be the collection of gender-disaggregated data that can assess the gender impact of the CFTA, as well as the collection of data on vulnerable groups. This contrasts with the WTO Trade Policy Review Mechanism, a surveillance mechanism designed foremost for monitoring each country's compliance with WTO obligations.

A practical approach to monitoring and evaluation could usefully follow the approach of the Association of Southeast Asian Nations (ASEAN), which employed a self-assessment monitoring and evaluation "scorecard" that evaluated the progress of each country on an agreed list of priority measures. The scorecard was periodically reviewed and updated, and the findings published. The CFTA could adopt this system, agreeing on priority measures periodically to target implementation challenges and opportunities.

Beyond continental tariff liberalization: The BIAT Action Plan

Liberalization is not a panacea for intra-African trade. There are many binding constraints that limit Africa's trade potential. Studies show that while tariff reductions from the CFTA would increase intra-African trade by 52 per cent, additional trade facilitation measures would more than double it (Karingi and Mevel, 2012). The CFTA must therefore be accompanied by supportive measures to ensure both that the opportunities of the CFTA are fully exploited, and that these gains are shared equitably. Recognizing this, the AU Heads of State and Government adopted the Boosting Intra-African Trade (BIAT) Action Plan at the same 2012 AU Assembly meeting at which it was decided to establish the CFTA. The BIAT provides the framework for much-needed flanking policies that will support the CFTA.

The BIAT Action Plan brings together priority concerns around seven priority clusters (Box 6.4). Building on previous continental programmes and frameworks, it provides a basis for addressing the well-known trade barriers faced by African countries.

BIAT activities can address the challenges faced by countries and by vulnerable subnational groups to ensure that the CFTA is win-win, and its benefits are widely shared. For instance, trade facilitation measures help informal cross-border traders enter the formal sector, and are especially important for women traders. Improved trade information can help MSMEs and smallholder farmers recognize new trade opportunities.

Trade-related infrastructure is of particular value to Africa's land-locked countries, which struggle with trade transit issues. Factor market integration can facilitate the movement of businesspeople and cross-border establishment to spread RVCs into less-industrialized neighbouring economies.

Implementing the BIAT Action Plan

Three factors constrain implementation of the BIAT Action Plan.

Lack of an institutional structure. An implementing structure has been envisaged for the BIAT as part of a Draft Strategic Framework for the Implementation of the Action Plan for BIAT and for Establishing the CFTA (AU, n.d.). However, there was no concrete follow-up by any AU member state or REC. Folding the institutional structure of the BIAT into the CFTA's should ensure the combined implementation of the BIAT alongside the CFTA and avoid institutional duplication (a proposal made in Chapter 9).

Absence of monitoring and evaluation. The BIAT Draft Strategic Framework envisaged an institutional structure for this, but these institutions were not established. Successes already achieved at the national and REC levels cannot be clearly linked to the BIAT, nor can information on the various clusters of the BIAT be

Box 6.4

Summary of the seven priority clusters of the Boosting Intra-African Trade Action Plan

	Cluster	Activities
❶	Trade policy	Mainstream intra-African trade in national strategies; enhance participation by the private sector, women and the informal sector; boost intra-African trade in food products; undertake commitments to liberalize trade-related services; commit to harmonize rules of origin and trade regimes; promote "Buy in Africa" and "Made in Africa"
❷	Trade facilitation	Reduce road blocks; harmonize and simplify customs and transit procedures and documentation; establish one-stop border posts; adopt integrated border management processes
❸	Productive capacity	Implement the programme for the Accelerated Industrial Development of Africa, African Productive Capacity Initiative and Accelerated Agribusiness and Agro-industry Initiative (know commonly as 3ADI); establish integrated trade information systems; encourage investment; establish regional centres of excellence
❹	Trade-related infrastructure	Implement the Programme for Infrastructure Development in Africa (PIDA); mobilize resources for multi-country projects; pursue high-quality multi-country projects; ensure an enabling environment for private sector participation; develop innovative mechanisms (legal, financial, etc.) for multi-country projects
❺	Trade finance	Improve payment systems; set the enabling environment for financial services to provide export credit and guarantees; speed up the establishment and strengthening of regional and continental financial institutions (Afrexim Bank, Eastern and Southern African Trade and Development Bank and African Trade Insurance Agency)
❻	Trade information	Create interconnected centres of trade information exchange
❼	Factor market integration	Operationalize existing protocols and policies; facilitate movement of businesspeople; harmonize rules on cross-border establishment; conclude agreements on mutual recognition of qualifications

monitored. However, with the AUC, ECA through its African Trade Policy Centre has recently launched an initiative to monitor progress across the BIAT clusters at the REC level. The African Regional Integration Index, which was launched by the ECA with the AUC and AfDB, also monitors progress on several dimensions of regional integration (see Chapter 2). Nevertheless, a continental framework for tracking progress would grant a better understanding of the status of implementation and help to identify gaps. BIAT and CFTA monitoring and evaluation could be combined for economies of scope.

Poor resourcing of BIAT initiatives. Funding for policy proposals is a persistent challenge in developing countries. Domestic resource mobilization presents the greatest untapped financial source of funds for development, but requires strengthened tax administration, lowered tax avoidance and reduced illicit financial flows. Tapping the private sector for certain types of trade-facilitating investments and public–private partnerships are other important modalities for generating funding for BIAT initiatives. To complement these efforts, Aid-for-Trade can be better targeted to support CFTA and BIAT implementation (Chapter 8). Aid-for-Trade in Africa has in fact been growing as a resource, more than doubling from 2006 to 2014, to over $15 billion.

Strategic logistics management: Buttressing investments in physical infrastructure

A major objective of Africa's regional transport infrastructure is to enhance the competitiveness of its countries, particularly those that are land-locked. Improved infrastructure, both hard (physical) and soft (policy/service), would boost intra-African trade. Most regional infrastructure programmes on the continent have trade and transport facilitation aspects that deal with non-physical barriers to transport and trade.

A combination of strong cross-border infrastructure and efficient transport services is required. Africa's trade facilitation initiatives are vital to cope with the predicted increases in trade. These initiatives are in line with the provisions of the WTO agreement on trade facilitation, which deals with issues on the release and clearance of goods, border agency cooperation, and

formalities connected with import, export and transit among other things.

African regional organizations and countries increasingly recognize that investments to improve transport corridor infrastructure or construct alternative routes to the sea are necessary but not sufficient to ensure a smooth flow of goods. They also recognize that investment gains for physical infrastructure in access and mobility—particularly savings in travel time and transport costs—along regional transport corridors are undermined by non-physical barriers.

Recent studies in Burundi, Rwanda and Tanzania confirmed findings from previous research on the performance of transit corridors in Africa: that transport costs are high and delays excessive due in part to high port dwell times, numerous stops (including at weighbridges and police checkpoints) and cumbersome border-crossing procedures. The dwell time at the Port of Dar es Salaam was more than twice the time that goods spend on the road, while that of imports to Burundi was 75 per cent of the total time between the cargo discharge at Dar es Salaam and arrival at final destination in Bujumbura (Lisinge, 2017).

The studies also showed that there were more than 10 weighbridges in Tanzania that contributed to transit transport delays. These weighbridges generally had limited working hours, with some of them closing at 6 pm. There were also numerous police checkpoints, some of them too close to each other—an issue that is sensitive and associated with national security concerns (Lisinge and Gatera, 2014; Lisinge, 2017).

The desire to overcome these non-physical barriers has contributed in mainstreaming strategic logistics management and the supply chain approach not only in the continent's regional infrastructure initiatives, but also in managing existing corridors. This explains why trade and transport facilitation is a key focus of the Programme for Infrastructure Development in Africa as well as the Trans-African Highway network, and it is a major preoccupation of RECs.

Trade facilitation is a priority for Africa's trade stakeholders because they recognize that reaping the full benefits of the CFTA hinges on regular implementation of such measures. To that end, trade documents, standards and customs procedures need to be simplified and harmonized, and should conform to international and regional regulations. The logistics of moving goods through ports, and the movement of documentation associated with cross-border trade, also have to be made more efficient. In addition, the environment in which trade transactions take place, including the transparency and professionalism of customs and regulatory environments, needs improvement.

RECs have made great strides in addressing these issues, usually in concordance with the provisions of the WTO Trade Facilitation Agreement. For instance, EAC has relevant trade-related documents such as its Treaty, Customs Management Act and tariffs on its website. Similarly, COMESA introduced the Regional Payment and Settlement System in 2012, resulting in a faster and more cost-effective transfer of funds. Several one-stop border posts are operational in Africa, including those at Chirundu between Zambia and Zimbabwe, and Cinkase between Burkina Faso and Ghana. Several such posts also exist under the framework of EAC at multiple locations between Kenya, Rwanda, Tanzania and Uganda.

In terms of the movement of goods intended for import under control, as well as formalities connected with import, export and transit, up to 11 countries on the continent reduced the number of documents required for import and export between 2007 and 2013, and many of them are moving to electronic submission of documents (ECA, 2013b). Several countries have introduced single-window systems, including Cameroon, Ghana, Mauritius, Senegal and Tunisia. Electronic cargo management has also gained ground, including the use of cargo-tracking systems and electronic management of customs warehouses.

On the transit of goods, customs cooperation and exchange of information, and institutional arrangements, most RECs have regulatory frameworks. They have harmonized or introduced vehicle load and dimension controls, road transit charges, carrier licence and transit plates, third-party motor insurance schemes, road transport customs transit declaration documents and regional customs bond guarantee schemes. Most of these measures exceed the scope of the WTO Trade Facilitation Agreement, which does not explicitly deal with transport infrastructure. On institutional arrangements, the RECs Transport Coordination Committee and the African Corridor Management Alliance have important coordinating roles at the regional level. Several countries also have national committees on trade facilitation (ECA, 2013b; Valensisi, Lisinge and Karingi, 2016).

References

AU (African Union). 2013. "Orientation Paper for the Development of Rules of Origin for the Continental Free Trade Area (CFTA)." Yaoundé. Unpublished.

———. 2017. *Survey of the non-tariff barriers reporting and monitoring mechanisms used by regional economic communities in Africa.* Addis Ababa. Unpublished.

———. n.d. *Draft Strategic Framework for the Implementation of the Action Plan for Boosting Intra-African Trade and for Establishing the Continental Free Trade Area.* Addis Ababa.

Balchin, N., B. Hoekman, H. Martin and M. Mendez-Parra. 2016. *Trade in services and economic transformation.* Supporting Economic Transformation. London: Overseas Development Institute.

Bhagwati, J. 1995. "US Trade Policy: The Infatuation with FTAs." Discussion Paper Series 726. New York: Columbia University.

Cornejo, R., and J. Harris. 2007. *Convergence in the Rules of Origin Spaghetti Bowl: A Methodological Proposal.* New York: Inter-American Development Bank.

Draper, P., C. Chikura and H. Krogman. 2016. "Can Rules of Origin in Sub-Saharan Africa be Harmonized? A Political Economy Exploration." Discussion Paper 1/2016. Bonn: Deutsches Institut für Entwicklungspolitik.

ECA (Economic Commission for Africa). 2013a. *Harmonizing Policies to Transform the Trading Environment: Assessing Regional Integration in Africa VI.* Addis Ababa.

———. 2013b. *Trade Facilitation from an African Perspective.* Addis Ababa.

Estevadeordal, A., J. Blyde, J., Harris and C. Volpe. 2014. *Global Value Chains and Rules of Origin.* Geneva: E15Initiative.

Francois, J., M. Manchin and P. Tomberger. 2013. "Services Linkages and the Value Added Content of Trade." Policy Research Working Paper 6432. Washington, DC: World Bank.

Ghani, E. and D. O'Connell. 2014. "Can service be a growth escalator in low-income countries?" Research Working Paper 6971. Washington, DC: World Bank.

Ghani, E., and H. Kharas. 2010. "The Service Revolution in South Asia: An Overview." In Ejaz Ghani (editor), *The Service Revolution In South Asia.* New York: Oxford University Press.

Giovanni V., R. Lisinge and S. Karingi. 2016. "The Trade Facilitation Agreement and Africa's Regional Integration." *Canadian Journal of Development Studies* 37 (2): 1–21.

Illy, O. 2013. "Trade Remedies in Africa: Experience, Challenges, and Prospects." Working Paper. Princeton, NJ: Princeton University.

Joubert, N. 2005. *Managing the Challenges of WTO Participation: Case Study 38—The Reform of South Africa's Anti-Dumping Regime.* Geneva: World Trade Organization.

Karingi, S., and S. Mevel. 2012. "Deepening Regional Integration in Africa: A Computable General Equilibrium Assessment of the Establishment of a Continental Free Trade Area followed by a Continental Customs Union." Paper for presentation at the 15th Global Trade Analysis Project Conference, Geneva, 27–29 June.

Kucik, J., and E. Reinhardt. 2008. "Does Flexibility Promote Cooperation? An Application to the Global Trade Regime." *International Organization* 62 (3): 477–505.

Lisinge, R. T. 2017. "Managing Africa's Regional Transport Infrastructure Programmes: Partnerships and Performance." Doctoral dissertation. Maastricht: Maastricht School of Management.

Loungani, P., S. Mishra and C. Papageorgiou. 2017. *World Trade in Services: Evidence from a New Dataset.* Washington, DC: International Monetary Fund.

Sommer, L., and D. Luke. 2017. "Smart Industrialization." Forthcoming.

Swedish National Board of Trade. 2012. *Everybody is in Services – The Impact of Servicification in Manufacturing on Trade and Trade Policy.* Stockholm.

UNCTAD (United Nations Conference on Trade and Development). 2016. *African Continental Free Trade Area: Policy and Negotiation Options for Trade in Goods*. Geneva.

World Bank. 2016. World Development Indicators (database). http://data.worldbank.org/data-catalog/world-development-indicators.

Endnote

1   See Article 1 (2) (c) GATS.

2   http://www.eac.int/integration-pillars/common-market. Accessed on 1 June 2017.

3   Ibid.

4   http://documentation.ecowas.int/download/en/legal_documents/protocols/PROTOCOL%20RELATING%20TO%20%20FREE%20MOVEMENT%20OF%20PERSONS.pdf. Accessed on 1 June 2017.

5   See http://www3.nd.edu/~ggoertz/rei/rei120/rei120.05tt1.pdf. Accessed on 1 June 2017.

6   See Kategekwa, Opening Markets for Foreign Skills: How can the WTO Help? http://www.springer.com/gp/book/9783319035475. Accessed on 1 June 2017.

7   See for example Ghani and O'Connell (2014) and Balchin et al. (2016).

8   Such as UNCTAD, OECD, International Finance Corporation, International Trade Centre, WTO, International Organization for Standardization and ARSO.

Chapter 7
Financing for Bringing the CFTA About

Bringing the Continental Free Trade Area CFTA about will require financing for its implementation. Getting the most out of it will also require financing for its flanking policies, including the Boosting Intra-African Trade (BIAT) Action Plan. Ensuring that the CFTA is win-win for all countries necessitates an approach that considers the different resource capacities of CFTA member states.

This chapter outlines the areas where support will be required and assesses the different means to secure financing. It looks at domestic resource mobilization, a proposed 0.2 per cent African Union (AU) levy and Aid-for-Trade (including what works and what doesn't under that initiative), after presenting an assessment framework for financing.

Framework for assessing the financing of the CFTA

In the short run, governments face implementation costs associated with the introduction of new reforms obliged by the agreement and with changes to tariff revenue. Throughout the medium term, the private sector will face costs linked to the structural readjustment of the economy as it reacts to new opportunities and competitive pressures. Governments will want to invest in flanking policies to help their economies adjust and take advantage of the agreement, as well as to support any groups that could be vulnerable to changes in trade. Long-run costs include the maintenance of the trade reform infrastructure, such as new institutions.

The CFTA implementation costs can be framed as those affecting the private sector and the public sector (Table 7.1). The private sector incurs structural adjustment costs while the public sector faces tariff revenue losses, implementation costs and flanking policy costs.

Structural adjustment of the private sector
The private sector bears the principal costs of structural adjustment—those entailed by reallocating factors of production, such as labour and capital, from their pre- to post-liberalization occupations.

The structural adjustment costs expected of the CFTA are likely to be relatively small because of the limited size of intra-African trade, the pre-existing coverage of regional economic community (REC) free trade areas, and the use of exclusion list provisions and safeguards. A gradual approach to liberalization and flanking policies should be used to ease these costs for especially sensitive or vulnerable groups. Still, these costs will be felt by certain private businesses and personnel.

In practical terms, businesses may need to repurpose capital and organization to reflect changes in business

Table 7.1

Framework for assessing CFTA adjustment costs

CFTA adjustment costs (aggregate)	Private sector	Labour	Obsolescence of skills
			Training costs
			Personnel costs
		Capital	Underutilized capital
			Obsolete machines or buildings
			Cost of shifting capital to other activities
			Investments to become an exporter
	Public sector	Lower tariff revenues	Reduced revenues on intra-African imports
		Implementation costs	CFTA institutional costs
			Implementing costs of trade reform
		Flanking policy costs	Social safety net spending
			Compensatory mechanisms
			CFTA flanking policies (BIAT)

Source: Adapted from Francois et al. (2011).

opportunities and competition. Workers may require reskilling and training to respond to these changes.

Public sector: Lower tariff revenues

At the foundation of any free trade area is a reduction in tariffs, and by implication, lower tariff revenues. This is a cost borne by governments, but one that affects the households and firms that are recipients of government spending. But tariff revenue losses are likely to be modest, amounting to 8 per cent of total tariff revenue on average in a scenario in which the CFTA amounted to full liberalization of all products (see Chapter 5). Again, this stems from the low value of intra-African trade and the fact that much of this is already covered by pre-existing REC FTAs. Exclusion list provisions will further limit revenue losses. A 1 per cent exclusion list could reduce average revenue losses from 8 per cent to 1 per cent of total tariff revenue, while a 5 per cent list could reduce losses to 0.3 per cent. Revenue losses will affect countries unevenly, and a flexible approach to exclusion lists should be used to smooth their impact more equitably. Nevertheless, as a free trade area, the CFTA will lower tariff revenues.

Public sector: Implementation costs

Trade agreements include obligations that can require countries to change domestic practices, initiate reforms or establish new entities, including revamping customs operations, establishing domestic institutions and setting up mechanisms for trade facilitation.

One example is with the obligations often contained within competition chapters of free trade agreements. Competition provisions aim at guaranteeing that liberalization will not be undermined by anti-competitive business practices within countries. To accomplish this, agreements may call for the establishment of legal institutions that can proscribe measures against anti-competitive practices, and for the development of competition policy and regulations within a country (Dawar and Mathis, 2007). Countries that do not already have such institutions may be called on to establish an authority to undertake this role and enforce these provisions.

Another example is seen with non-tariff barrier (NTB) provisions, which may oblige countries to abolish the technical, or sanitary and phytosanitary, trade barriers between member countries when they lack justifiable domestic policy purposes. In doing so, they typically oblige countries to establish mechanisms to facilitate coordination between member countries for identifying, monitoring and resolving NTBs (see Chapter 6).

The CFTA will require its own institutional structure, including a CFTA Secretariat and additional implementing structures. Costs may be minimized, however, by reliance where possible on pre-existing national, regional and continental structures (Chapter 8).

The CFTA is conceptualized as building on the established RECs of the AU. The provisions envisaged in the CFTA do not amount to wholly new trade ideas, but to expanding the achievements of the RECs to the continental level. In this way, the CFTA architecture can rest on and reinforce the institutions already required by the RECs. For instance, NTB institutions that currently address trade issues within RECs may simply expand their mandate to include inter-REC trade. There are probably costs associated with implementing CFTA provisions and reforms, but by using pre-existing structures, the CFTA may harness economies of scope.

Public sector: Flanking policies

Implementing the BIAT measures will incur costs, though the exact amount is not available. However, it is possible to gauge the funding gap for different components related to the BIAT clusters. The Programme for Infrastructure Development in Africa (PIDA) comprises projects focused on a more interconnected and integrated Africa that will require substantial improvements in power generation, transport logistics, information and communications technology infrastructure and water resources. The total estimated cost of implementing all the projects identified in PIDA to address projected infrastructure needs by 2040 is $360 billion. The PIDA Priority Action Plan includes 51 priority infrastructure "back-bone" projects and programmes requiring $68 billion in investments by 2020.

The capacity gap of course extends beyond infrastructure. Reviewing Africa's skills shortage, the African Capacity Building Foundation estimates Africa to have a gap of as many as 4.3 million engineers and 1.6 million agricultural scientists and researchers with the number needed to implement the AU's first 10-year plan of Agenda 2063. Alongside these are gaps in effective institutions for development.

These costs are not obliged by the CFTA, but relate to programmes and activities important for leveraging its opportunities.

Financing the CFTA and BIAT Action Plan

Financing in Africa has to be increasingly based on domestic public and private resources (ECA and AU, 2012, 2013). At the United Nations conference on Financing for Development, Addis Ababa, Ethiopia, in July 2015, it was agreed that that domestic resources represent the largest untapped source of funds for financing development goals.

Improved self-financing also mitigates the political economy issues discussed in Chapter 3. An overreliance on development assistance risks perpetuating donor-driven, rather than Africa-led, initiatives, and fostering donor "signalling," where actions are taken superficially to satisfy donor obligations rather than to drive development. Such moves reduce ownership and responsibility for projects, which in turn stifle implementation, which can be particularly sensitive in international trade where donor countries may have alternative trade policy priorities.

Unpredictability of aid is a further challenge for budgetary planning and staffing, especially as much of Africa's integration agenda is dependent on donor financing (Table 7.2). Such financing can be fragmented when provided as project aid, not budget support, and when amounts and timing are unpredictable. Different accountability relations can also raise transaction costs.

African governments must commit to enhancing domestic revenue collection; making tax systems fairer,

more transparent and effective; and strengthening development aid for building the capacities of its tax administrations. Doing so will require tackling corruption, weak institutional capacities, a narrow tax base and pervasive tax avoidance and evasion by wealthy individuals and multinational corporations. Even minor improvements in domestic resource mobilization can contribute to the costs of implementing the CFTA and its measures.

The African Union's 0.2 per cent levy

An important proposal for Africa's self-financing is the "0.2 per cent levy on all eligible imported goods into the continent to finance the AU Operational, Program and Peace Support Operations Budgets" (AU, 2016a). This proposal was adopted by the AU Assembly at its July 2016 Summit in Kigali and aims to ensure that the AU "is financed in a predictable, sustainable, equitable and accountable manner with the full ownership by its member states" (AU, 2016a). The intention is for this funding mechanism to be introduced before the end of 2017 (AU, 2016b).

The AU total budget in 2016 amounted to $417 million, of which only 44 per cent was provided by member states, with the remainder from international donors, including China, the European Union (EU), the United Kingdom, the United States and the World Bank (AU, 2015). The 0.2 per cent levy proposal is intended to raise $1.2 billion to fully fund the AU operational budget, finance 75 per cent of the AU programme budget, 25 per cent of its peace and security operations budget, and the peace fund as determined annually (AU, 2016b). Included within the programme budget will be the CFTA and other flagship projects.

Table 7.2

Degree of donor dependency by REC and the AU (%)

Entity	Percentage of budget (for available budgets)
IGAD	90
SADC	79
COMESA	78
EAC	65
ECOWAS	N/A—though largely self-funded by 0.5% ECOWAS levy on imports into ECOWAS
AU	44

Source: ECDPM (2016).

However, questions have been raised as to the whether the levy would be compliant with Africa's existing international obligations. Principally this concerns compatibility with World Trade Organization (WTO) law and with regional trade agreements (RTAs).

Compatibility with WTO law: Challenges and solutions

At the 7 December 2016 meeting of the General Council of the WTO, the issue of the AU 0.2 per cent levy was raised by the United States, which expressed expectations that implementation of the levy would be consistent with WTO agreements, including the most-favoured nation (MFN) principle (WTO, 2017). The EU and Japan both welcomed the initiative but also expressly reaffirmed the statement of the United States and the need for WTO compliance. Compatibility issues with the AU levy and WTO law are threefold.

First, the proposal intends to apply the levy on goods imported "into the continent," which implies discrimination among WTO members: African WTO members would not face the levy, while those outside Africa would. The proposal would therefore be incompatible with Article I of the General Agreement on Tariffs and Trade (GATT) on MFN treatment, which requires that all WTO members be treated equally. MFN treatment is the most important foundational principle of the GATT.

Second, tariff-binding schedules under Article II of the GATT could be affected. Such schedules are commitments not to increase rates of duty beyond specified and agreed levels. Some African countries could either have certain tariffs bound at zero per cent or have their applied rates already equal to their bound rates, and would therefore be unable to raise these without breaking their bound-tariff commitments at the WTO.

Products covered by the schedules under Article II are also bound from the imposition of new "other duties or charges." The date that "other duties or charges" were bound, for the purposes of Article II, is 15 April 1994. Thus the levy cannot be applied as a new duty or charge beyond what would constitute a normal customs tariff.

Third, Article II of the GATT permits the imposition of "fees or other charges commensurate with the cost of services rendered." Article VIII on Fees and Formalities connected with Importation and Exportation further clarifies that any fee or charge connected to the import of goods must "be limited in amount to the approximate cost of services rendered and shall not represent an indirect protection to domestic products or a taxation of imports or exports for fiscal purposes." The AU levy is not applied for any related import service, which for example, would include fees for import inspection and the operation of digital customs systems. And so the AU levy would not be permitted as an acceptable fee or other charge.

In response, the first issue is one that can conceivably be addressed by the CFTA. Article XXIV of the GATT permits a group of countries to derogate from their commitment to MFN treatment and discriminate against other WTO members if they enter into regional FTAs or customs unions. By forming such a free trade area, the CFTA can circumvent the MFN treatment required by Article I.

However, note must be taken of Article XXIV 5.b requiring that the formation of a free-trade area not result in duties to other countries being higher or more restrictive than those existing prior to the formation of the free-trade area. The AU levy may be permissible in that it constitutes a separate parallel initiative, rather than a levy resulting from the formation of the CFTA. The AU levy is a different and separate issue, and it should not be mixed with the CFTA.

There may also be an issue of sequencing. It is intended that the AU levy be implemented before the end of 2017. While it is also the intention that the CFTA negotiations be concluded by this point, it may take member states longer to begin implementing the Agreement. Even if the CFTA permits a derogation from MFN treatment through Article XXIV, there may be an interim period during which the CFTA has yet to be constituted to afford this derogation.

Finally, some African countries may be members of the WTO and the AU, but not party to the CFTA. In this case the CFTA cannot provide them with the legal cover to discriminate between WTO member countries.

The second issue may be harder to address. In theory, tariff binding commitments can be exceeded with the agreement of other WTO members. However, WTO members that are "suppliers with a substantial interest" of a product affected by an increase in a tariff above its bound rate may apply for compensation. Compensation is calculated on the basis of the difference in the tariff rates and trade flows.

The third issue implies that the AU levy cannot bypass the former issues by considering itself a "fee or other charge," in the sense of Article II.2c).

Four solutions are possible.

Option 1 – Apply for a WTO waiver: African countries may apply for a WTO waiver in accordance with Article IX of the Marrakesh Agreement. Waivers grant permission for WTO members to not comply with normal commitments. Indeed, the above statement on the AU levy by the United States at the 7 December 2016 meeting alludes to the possible need for a WTO waiver.

The terms and conditions governing the application of a waiver, and the date on which a waiver would terminate, are determined by the WTO Ministerial Conference. Any waiver granted for more than one year is reviewed annually. At each review it could be extended, modified or terminated. A waiver cannot therefore permit an indefinite derogation from WTO law, but it may enable African countries to apply such a levy as a reasonable means of self-financing until replacement through domestic resource mobilization is possible.

Furthermore the waiving of a WTO obligation is expressly afforded only in "exceptional circumstances." This can require due legal justification and possibly the exchange of other concessions. African countries would need to spend political capital on this issue and balance it against other important issues on the WTO Ministerial Conference agenda.

Still, Africa's status as the world's least-developed region and the part-allocation of the levy towards financing peace and security are reasonable grounds on which to assume that, with sufficient political diplomacy, such a waiver could be secured.

If it is decided that Africa's WTO members should seek a WTO waiver, sequencing should be considered. The request for a waiver would have to be submitted to the WTO Ministerial Conference for consideration. Ministerial Conferences are usually held every two years, with the next meeting scheduled for December 2017.

Option 2 – Ring-fence existing tariff revenue: The AU levy could be designed to avoid violating WTO law. The above compatibility issues concern the application of an AU levy as an additional charge on imports into the continent. Were the levy to be expressed not as an additional charge but as a share of existing tariff revenue collected on these imports, it would not contravene WTO law. In such a formulation, the levy would not collect new revenue but ring-fence existing tariff revenue for the purposes of the AU. This is reportedly the approach to be taken by Kenya, which is to carve out the 0.2 per cent levy from a pre-existing import charge.

Option 3 – Ad hoc measures to address the binding schedules of Article II of the GATT: Were the CFTA or a waiver to provide legal cover against contravention of MFN treatment, the application of ad hoc measures could address the violation of the binding schedules of Article II of the GATT. In such an approach, the AU levy would be designed so that African countries would be permitted to forgo the requirement to apply the levy on tariff lines already at the bound rate. In such circumstances, the AU levy might require African countries to provide instead the equivalent amount from an alternative source.

Option 4 – Consider WTO law: Across Africa, levies have been in place for many years, including the Economic Community of West African States (ECOWAS) 0.5 per cent levy and the East African Community (EAC) 1.4 per cent joint infrastructure levy—as well as national levies, such as Ghana's 0.5 per cent Export Development and Agriculture Investment Fund levy. The legal certainty of these is not always clear.

Most developed countries have, throughout the history of the WTO, been hesitant to resort to litigating against less-developed African countries. Nevertheless, as seen in the US statement on the levy and in the comments from the EU and Japan, these economies appear to be of the opinion that any AU levy should be WTO compliant. Other developing country members of the WTO may also be less hesitant to litigate than previously.

Aversion to such a contravention of WTO law need not concern the actual amount of trade involved, nor the burden of the levy. What may be of foremost concern is the perception of precedence set by violation of these rules. Moreover, these are rules that African countries benefit from in the great share of trade conducted outside the continent. In the interest of Africa itself, it might be imprudent to contribute to the violation of important WTO laws.

Compatibility with regional trade agreements: Challenges and solutions

The second important concern is compatibility between the AU levy and Africa's regional trade agreements (RTAs). Several African countries are negotiating, or are planning to negotiate, trade agreements with third countries. It must be assured that within these agreements there is also legal cover for the imposition of the AU levy. Without expressly exempting the AU levy from these agreements, its elimination would be required on imports originating from the countries party to those agreements.

There is a precedent for this approach. Article 11 of Annex 1 of the ECOWAS-EU Economic Partnership Agreement (EPA) provides a carve-out for the ECOWAS 0.5 per cent levy by permitting the maintenance of the "autonomous financing arrangement of the West African Organizations responsible for regional integration […] until a new financing method has been set up." However, no existing RTA to which an African country is party includes provision for the AU levy. Three solutions are possible here.

Option 1 – Include carve-outs for the AU Levy in future RTAs: Provisions permitting the AU levy to be maintained on imports can be included in all future RTAs. Negotiating for such permissions may, however, require the offering of compensating concessions to the partners of such RTAs.

Option 2 – Renegotiate pre-existing RTAs to introduce carve-outs for the AU Levy: In addition to Option 1, African countries may renegotiate pre-existing RTAs and, through such negotiations, introduce provisions that permit the AU levy to be maintained on imports originating in the other countries party to these agreements. This may involve difficult renegotiations and require compensating concessions to the partners in these RTAs.

Option 3 – Refrain from applying the AU Levy on countries party to existing RTAs with Africa: The AU levy may be designed so that African countries party to existing RTAs are permitted to forgo the requirement to apply the levy on trade with these partners. In such circumstances, the AU levy might require African countries to provide, instead, the equivalent amount from an alternative source. If desired, the AU levy could also permit African countries to forgo the levy in *future* RTAs if the equivalent funds are supplied from an alternative source.

New approaches to resourcing

Innovative means of financing are needed (ECA and AU, 2013). Strategies include leveraging pension funds, insurance funds, private equity, the diaspora market and public–private partnerships and stemming illicit financial flows.

Pension funds have considerable potential. Africa's pension market is underdeveloped in all but a few countries and is dominated by state-owned schemes (ECA, 2014). Learning from successes in countries such as Botswana, Kenya, Mauritius and South Africa could open up new sources of capital (ECA and NPCA, 2013).

Insurance funds are an underdeveloped source for long-term financing. Most of Africa's insurance companies are small and provide short-term non-life products, rather than long-term life and savings products. The infancy of Africa's insurance markets means that they are not risk free and reforms will be required to improve regulations. But the market is growing rapidly and could exceed $15 billion by 2022 (Kurt, 2012).

Private equity has grown rapidly in several African countries, but remains concentrated in a few countries and sectors. Private equity is dominated by the extractive industries, which account for some 46 per cent of all cross-border mergers and acquisitions by private firms in Africa (UNCTAD, 2013).

The **African diaspora** is another source of funds: 120 million Africans save up to $53 billion in destination countries every year (AfDB, 2010). African governments can capture some of these savings through sovereign bonds, such as Eurobonds. Ethiopia was the first African country to issue a diaspora bond in 2011, which it used to help finance its Renaissance Dam project. Sound sovereign-bond issues require forward-looking and comprehensive debt management structures (ECA and AU, 2014).

Public–private partnerships have proved an important source, particularly for financing infrastructure development. Beyond infrastructure, public–private partnerships have been extended to other sectors, such as agriculture in Tanzania. Issues remain, however, with high up-front costs, redistributive factors in output pricing, long pay-back periods and foreign exchange risks.

Illicit financial outflows are a considerable drain on Africa's ability to self-finance but—illicit by definition—are difficult to estimate. The Economic Commission for Africa (ECA) estimates that Africa loses as much as $50 billion annually from them, roughly twice what it receives in official development assistance (ODA) (ECA and AU, 2015). Counter-measures include improving the international exchange of tax information, fighting corruption and abuse of entrusted power, requiring multinational companies to publicly disclose their operations country by country, and addressing abusive transfer pricing, trade mis-invoicing, tax evasion and aggressive tax avoidance (ECA and AU, 2015).

Aid-for-Trade

For Africa's lower-income countries, ODA remains important. The distribution and objectives of ODA differ from other international financial flows. Given its primary mandate to directly target development, improve welfare and reduce poverty, ODA remains

essential in supporting many developing countries, especially the poorest with little access to private finance and low levels of domestic resources. In fact, ODA remains the largest international resource for countries with a gross national income (GNI) of less than around $2,000 per capita (Development finance flows by OECD/DAC members and international financial institutions: Share in per capita GNI). Thirty-seven African countries have per capita GNI below this amount.

The importance of ODA relative to private investments, remittances and other official flows is decreasing in lower-middle-income countries (LMICs) and upper-middle-income countries (UMICs). Yet it can still contribute to their development through mobilizing private flows, leveraging private investment and facilitating trade. If developing countries want to attract resources for building trade capacities, they need think innovatively and consider how ODA grants can leverage other resources, such as private loans or other finance.

ODA will remain an important source of funding to help ensure that Africa's less-developed countries can implement the CFTA and its flanking policies. It may also remain important for Africa's lower-middle-income countries over the short run as they mobilize further their domestic resources. Aid-for-Trade, an initiative launched in 2006, is the particular vehicle of choice for leveraging ODA for the CFTA. Regional Aid-for-Trade is especially relevant.

Figure 7.1

Development finance flows by OECD/DAC members and international financial institutions: Share in per capita GNI

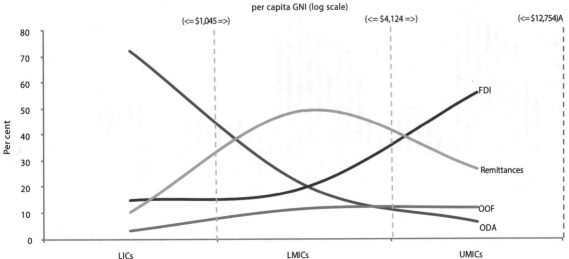

Note: OECD/DAC is the Development Assistance Committee of the Organisation for Economic Co-operation and Development.

Source: OECD Development finance statistics.

Levels of regional Aid-for-Trade

Aid-for-Trade is well suited to the CFTA flanking policies, especially to the BIAT Action Plan, which has projects with targets for ODA. Aid-for-Trade has been adopted as an African policy priority by the AU Heads of State and Government. Since 2011, Africa has been the main recipient of Aid-for-Trade.

In 2015, the continent received 35 per cent of total disbursements, totalling over $14 billion, more than three times the average amount during the 2002–05 baseline period. Although only a small portion of this targets regional programmes directly, all national programmes are aimed at building trade capacities. At the sectoral level, there are substantial differences in regional and subregional disbursements compared with overall flows.

Since 2002, economic infrastructure has on average accounted for more than 50 per cent of total Aid-for-Trade disbursements, while building productive capacity has consistently been the most important component of disbursements for regional and subregional programmes. The share of total disbursements to building productive capacities dropped 11 basis points since the 2006–08 average of 53 per cent to 42 per cent in 2015, whereas building productive capacity represented 70 per cent of the regional Aid-for-Trade figure (figure 7.2 and 7.3).

Regional and subregional Aid-for-Trade, as defined in the Organisation for Economic Co-operation and Development (OECD) Creditor Reporting System (CRS), constitutes a small share of total Aid-for-Trade flows, but has been rising steadily since the start of the Aid-for-Trade Initiative in 2006. In 2002–05, total regional and subregional Aid-for-Trade disbursements averaged around $1.2 billion. It reached $6.2 billion in 2015. Multi-regional programmes constitute the largest category, with 58 per cent of regional Aid-for-Trade disbursements in 2015 (average). Total multi-regional disbursements since 2002 reached $21 billion. Almost 40 per cent is associated with German funding for the Climate Investment Fund, an $8.3 billion programme providing 72 developing and middle-income countries with much needed resources to manage the challenges of climate change and reduce their greenhouse gas emissions. At the regional and subregional level, the share of Aid-for-Trade disbursed to Africa is, on average, four times higher than that those disbursed to Asia. No doubt this reflects the high priority African leaders place on regional integration.

Between the 2002–05 baseline average and 2015, regional aid for trade to Africa increased from $357 million to $1.6 billion, with 60 per cent of the increase due to a $700 million allocation to the African Development Fund for those defined by the AfDB as fragile states. Building productive capacity is the dominant sector with $1.1 billlion, followed by

Figure 7.2

Aid-for-Trade disbursements by region and sector ($ billion, 2015 constant prices)

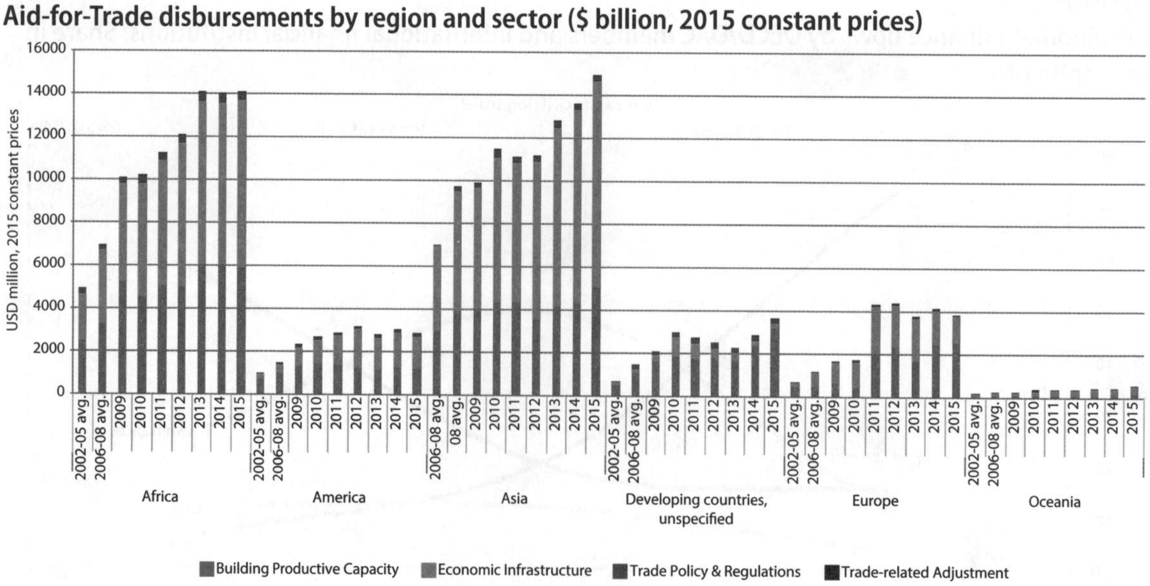

Legend: Building Productive Capacity | Economic Infrastructure | Trade Policy & Regulations | Trade-related Adjustment

Note: Data extracted 17 August 2017.

Source: OECD/DAC CRS.

Figure 7.3

Regional and subregional Aid-for-Trade disbursements by region and sector

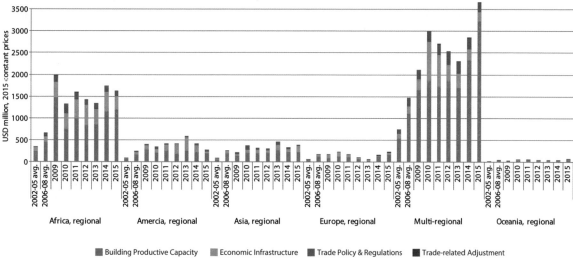

Note: Data extracted 17 August 2016.

Source: OECD/DAC CRS.

Figure 7.4

Regional Aid-for-Trade to Africa, disbursements by sector

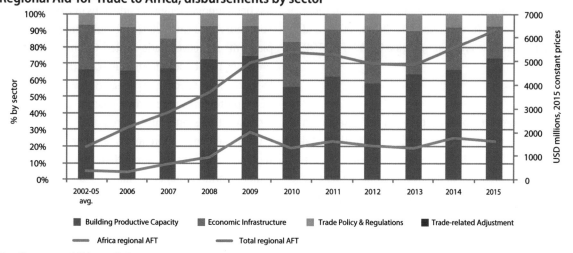

Note: Data extracted 17 August 2017.

Source: OECD/DAC CRS.

trade-related infrastructure with $300 million (Figure 7.4). Although the shares have fluctuated, building productive capacity and economic infrastructure have consistently dominated regional Aid-for-Trade flows. The literature on binding constraints to trade suggests that this focus is well merited, and case studies reviewed below display a number of successful projects.

Regional Aid-for-Trade successes: What works and what doesn't

Regional Aid-for-Trade initiatives have generated considerable successes in certain areas. Highlights include addressing NTBs, investing in regional soft and hard infrastructure, fostering regional cooperation, reducing investment-related costs, harmonizing regional trade arrangements, furthering institutional and human development, and supporting operations of the RECs. Challenges include engaging stakeholders and prioritizing the needs of poor and vulnerable groups.

World Bank Group

The World Bank's strategy for regional integration in Sub-Saharan Africa is implemented with the RECs and the AU. It is based on four pillars: building regional hard and soft infrastructure, promoting international cooperation for economic integration, providing regional public goods, and improving alignment between regional and national planning (World Bank, 2011). An evaluation found good performance related to regional infrastructure development, institutional cooperation for economic integration, and management of regional public goods (IEG, 2011).

United Kingdom

A 2016 Inquiry into the UK–African Free Trade Initiative found that the different programmes funded by UKAID made progress in cutting tariffs, harmonizing regional trade arrangements, improving hard and soft trade infrastructure and cutting red tape through modernizing customs systems, procedures and facilities. The initiative also helped to facilitate coordination and reduce investment-related costs between governments and stakeholders across borders and leveraged private sector investment funding from Development Finance Institutions. Nevertheless, the inquiry found that more work is needed to further reduce tariffs and NTBs, and negotiate a credible and wide-ranging CFTA (APPG-TOP, 2016).

Germany

Germany fosters regional cooperation and integration through the provision of technical and institutional support to different RECs. The results in each REC are found to be supportive of the overall strategy to create a multi-regional FTA. The German approach focuses on the EAC Secretariat and combines institutional and human development. For instance, the EAC Secretariat received assistance to develop a template for mutual recognition of professional qualifications to facilitate the free movement of labour and services in EAC.

One area in which EAC has been successful is assisting trade in services (Chapter 6). Germany also supported a project in East Africa to create a WTO-compatible legal framework for regional quality assessments. However, stakeholder engagement was found insufficient to create a sense of ownership among private sector operators (OECD and WTO, 2015a).

Sweden

The Swedish Government has engaged with TRALAC—a capacity-building organization for trade-related capacity in Africa—to improve regional trade integration. TRALAC supports the concurrent

negotiation of trade in goods and services by producing and disseminating studies and research to inform the development of several key messages for trade policy makers, negotiators and other trade policy stakeholders on the continent. In particular, TRALAC became involved in the CFTA negotiation process by engaging with key stakeholders and delivering messages in a timely and non-technical manner. It also contributed to well-formulated CFTA provisions on services for investment generation, industrial development and regional integration.

Given the preliminary phase of the CFTA, it is too early to assess how TRALAC messages have influenced the negotiating agenda. However, it is safe to say that TRALAC has generated debate and stimulated further engagement.

United States

The US Agency for International Development (USAID) has been funding regional trade hubs in West, East, and Southern Africa since 2002. The hubs provide regional platforms to deliver trade-related technical assistance on issues that benefit from multi-country approaches. In particular, support is directed to implementing RECs' protocols and improve custom procedures to facilitate trade and further regional integration. A multi-stakeholder approach is used in creating the regional platforms to strengthen the legitimacy of regional arrangements at national and local levels. Many activities are directed to engage the private sector. The Borderless Alliance is a good example of this approach. The Alliance is a platform of private sector operators (traders, transporters, producers) working with public institutions to advocate for greater regional trade integration in West Africa. It identifies barriers inhibiting regional trade and uses data to drive decision making. The West Africa Trade Hub provides financial resources and technical expertise to boost the impact of the Alliance's advocacy.

USAID found that private sector involvement helps in building stronger political will for tackling vested interests, but it could also create asymmetric incentives. Thus ex-ante analysis and understanding of the incentive structure is fundamental for planning trade-related activities and may help avoid complications in implementation.

China

China is supporting regional integration through the China-Africa Cooperation Forum, in operation since 2000. Among South–South providers, China is arguably the highest profile supporter of regional integration in Africa. The engagement of other South–South providers consists of creating links between their trade, investment and development aid interventions. Apart from China,[1] there is no institutionalized emerging-economy approach to regional integration in Africa (Dube, 2016).

Multi-donor

One multi-donor programme is TradeMark East Africa (TMEA), supported by Belgium, Canada, Denmark, Finland, the Netherlands, Sweden, the United Kingdom and the United States. Since 2010, TMEA investors have contributed $560 million towards the delivery of around 150 projects in Burundi, Rwanda, South Sudan, Uganda and Tanzania. TMEA estimates that for every $1 spent, there will be a return of $30 over 10 years. An example is the Customs Business Systems Enhancement Project to increase the efficiency of the Uganda Revenue Authority. In March 2014, this programme combined with the reforms introduced under the Single Customs Territory to yield results. The time to clear and transport goods from port arrival to goods clearance fell from an average of 18 days to four days, for an estimated annual savings of $373 million.

The Infrastructure Consortium for Africa addresses regional infrastructure integration. It serves as a platform to broker donor financing of infrastructure projects. Similarly, PIDA promotes regional economic integration by bridging Africa's infrastructure gap. PIDA aims to accelerate the delivery of regional and continental infrastructure projects in transport, energy, information and communications technology, and trans-boundary water.

The Enhanced Integrated Framework is a multi-donor fund supporting least-developed countries (LDCs), based at the WTO. It provides financial and technical support to build trade capacity in 48 LDCs and three "graduated" countries. It is designed for the trade challenges faced by LDCs and helps them to address trade constraints and become integrated with global markets. In its first phase, from 1997 to 2006, the Framework provided support for 134 projects with a total allocation of $200 million.

Other notable Aid-for-Trade initiatives in Africa

The AfDB supports regional economic integration through its regional infrastructure and trade development programmes. The AfDB is also providing support for trade facilitation measures, including before-and-after border issues, one-stop border posts, coordinated border management and customs reform and modernization. In conjunction with these programmes, it is tackling non-tariff measures along transport corridors and advocating reforms within RECs and regional member countries (AfDB, 2015).

The Africa Trade Fund—financed with seed money from Canada and hosted at the AfDB—facilitates consultations to remove bottlenecks at borders, reduce waiting times and improve safety and security. The Fund works with border agencies to streamline border processes, modernize customs, upgrade logistics and reduce trader costs.

Canadian Aid-for-Trade funding also contributes to the African Trade Policy Centre (ATPC), in ECA. The main objective of ATPC is to contribute to increased, inclusive intra-African trade flows. In doing so it prioritizes enhanced formulation, implementation and monitoring of inclusive trade related reforms, action plans and frameworks by the RECs and national governments for reducing barriers to trade within Africa. It targets the increased integration of gender, including women enterpreneurs, and youth into trade policy design at AU and REC levels. And it aims to increase the participation of private sector operators and civil society organizations in regional and continental dialogues on the AU's trade agenda. ATPC has been closely involved in supporting the CFTA negotiations.

Japan's support for regional integration in Africa consists of capacity building for RECs and regional development banks to better plan, finance and execute infrastructure programmes. Japan's International Cooperation Agency has also dispatched technical experts to support regional bodies in harmonizing policies and regulation, such as those related to vehicle overload controls and procedures (OECD and WTO, 2015b).

Support from the EU to CFTA is channelled through the third AU Support Programme, which covers all the priorities of the Joint Africa–EU Strategy, such as sustainable and inclusive development and growth and continental integration, as well as private investment, infrastructure and continental integration. Cooperation with the AU under these priority areas serves a double purpose of enhancing EU–Africa dialogue on key policy areas of mutual interest, and of supporting the AU's role in steering the implementation of continental strategies. EU support includes the provision of technical expertise to the AU as well as expert studies on CFTA negotiations and the establishment of a private sector consultation mechanism. Support is also under consideration to implement the BIAT Action Plan (with a focus on trade facilitation and productive capacities) and to strengthen the AU's role in implementing the WTO Trade Facilitation Agreement.

France, like most other bilateral donors, has not formulated a specific strategy to promote regional economic cooperation in Africa. On the basis of sector strategies, regional integration is considered a tool to achieve the overall objectives of French development assistance. This is particularly the case for building infrastructure and creating a vibrant private sector. The focus is on West and Central Africa (AfDB, 2012).

Why are regional projects difficult?

Despite the undeniable positive impact of a regional approach to tackling trade-related constraints, the share of regional projects in Aid-for-Trade to Africa appears sub-optimally low. Initiatives such as the Enhanced Integrated Framework that is aimed at supporting LDCs' trade capacity development have virtually no footprint in regional initiatives. Several challenges can make regional Aid-for-Trade difficult.

- **Stakeholder engagement**: Regional Aid-for-Trade is still insufficiently understood and appreciated in national line ministries and among stakeholders. This is a problem for mainstreaming regional Aid-for-Trade into national development plans.

- **National ownership and commitment**: Insufficient attention is devoted to building strong national ownership and commitment before establishing regional institutions.

- **Uneven distribution of costs and benefits across countries**: Regional programmes may affect countries differently. This complicates the

prioritization of regional approaches to multi-country trade-related barriers.

- **Overlapping processes of regional integration**: Countries are involved in different processes of integration, making it more difficult to align national policy with different regional frameworks.

- **Donor support for regional institutions rather than projects**: Donors tend to focus on supporting regional institutions rather than tackling regional trade-related constraints directly. These institutions display varying human, legal and institutional capacities, which can constrain their capacity to implement projects.

- **Coordination challenges**: There is often a lack of coordination between national and regional development programmes even when these are funded by the same donor. Coordination is also often weak when several donors are involved in the same regional integration programme. Coordination becomes even more complicated when the private sector and civil society become involved as development actors in regional programmes.

- **Technical challenges**: For multi-country and regional Aid-for-Trade to be effective, regulatory equivalence, in which the standards of regulation are "equivalent" in each country, is often required. This is problematic for regional Aid-for-Trade and for its potential to boost regional integration.

More widely, it is hard to assess the impact of regional Aid-for-Trade. Many of the key results are dependent on the enabling policies and regional economic integration agenda pursued in an imperfect policy, economic and social environment.

How can Regional Aid-for-Trade programmes be improved to support the CFTA?

Despite the challenges, regional economic integration programmes have been one of the success stories of the Aid-for-Trade initiative. Funding for such programmes has increased fourfold since 2002 with developing countries and their development partners devoting both political and financial capital to regional public goods issues. Nevertheless, regional Aid-for-Trade programmes may be improved to support the CFTA in four ways:

- There must be better mainstreaming of regional initiatives within national planning. This remains a challenge, given the national focus to most aid programming and the various obstacles to aligning national priorities with regional programmes.

- Regional Aid-for-Trade projects must be better aligned with Africa policy frameworks, such as the BIAT Action Plan. In this way, projects can foster improved ownership on the part of stakeholders, which in turn is necessary to ensure the success of regional projects.

- The private sector needs to be more closely involved in regional Aid-for-Trade projects than it has been previously.

- Institutional mechanisms need to be developed to ensure smooth in-country coordination for regional and subregional programmes.

References

AfDB (African Development Bank). 2010. *Infrastructure Deficit and Opportunities in Africa*. Economic Brief 1 (September). Tunis. http://www.afdb.org/fileadmin/uploads/afdb/Documents/Publications/ECON%20Brief_Infrastructure%20Deficit%20and%20Opportunities%20in%20Africa_Vol%201%20Issue%202.pdf.

———. 2015. *Regional Integration Policy and Strategy (RIPoS) 2014–2013: Integrating Africa—Creating the Next Global Market*. Abidjan.

APPG-TOP (All-Party Parliamentary Group on Trade Out of Poverty). 2016. *Inquiry into the UK's Africa Free Trade Initiative*. London.

AU (African Union). 2015. *Budget of the African Union for the 2016 Financial Year*. Addis Ababa.

———. 2016a. *Assembly of the Union: Decisions and Declarations*. Twenty-Seventh Ordinary Session, 17 – 18 July. Addis Ababa.

———. 2016b. *Guidelines on the Implementation of the Decision on Financing the Union*. Addis Ababa.

Dawar, K., and J. H. Mathis. 2007. "Consumer protection, competition and RTAs: Some lessons for developing countries." In P. Brusick, A. Alvarez and L. Cernat (editors), *Competition Provisions In Regional Trading Arrangements: How to Assure Development Gains*. Geneva: United Nations Conference on Trade and Development.

Dube, M. 2016. "Could emerging economies accelerate regional integration in Africa?" *Bridges Africa*, 15 September.

ECA (Economic Commission for Africa) and AU. 2012. *Economic Report on Africa: Unleashing Africa's Potential as a Pole of Global Growth*. Addis Ababa: ECA.

———. 2013. *Economic Report on Africa: Making the Most of Africa's Commodities—Industrializing for Growth, Jobs and Economic Transformation*. Addis Ababa: ECA.

———. 2014. *Economic Report on Africa: Dynamic Industrial Policy in Africa*. Addis Ababa: ECA.

———. 2015. *Illicit Financial Flows: Report of the High Level Panel on Illicit Financial Flows from Africa*. Addis Ababa: ECA

ECA and NPCA (New Partnership for Africa's Development, Planning and Coordinating Agency). 2013. *Mobilizing Domestic Resources for Implementing NEPAD National and Regional Programmes and Projects—Africa Looks Within*. Draft report. Addis Ababa: ECA.

ECDPM (European Centre for Development Policy Management). 2016. *Political Economy of Integration in Africa: Synthesis Report*. Maastricht.

Francois, J., M. Jansen and R. Peters. 2011. "Trade adjustment costs and assistance: The labor market dynamics." In M. Jansen, R. Peters, and J. M. Salazar-Xirinachs (editors), *Trade and Employment: From Myths to Facts*. Geneva: International Labour Organization and European Commission.

ICAI (Impact Commission for Aid Impact). 2013. *DFID's trade development work in Southern Africa*. London. http://icai.independent.gov.uk/wp-content/uploads/DFIDs-Trade-Development-Work-in-Southern-Africa-Report.pdf.

IEG (Independent Evaluation Group). 2011. *The Development Potential of Regional Programs: An Evaluation of World Bank Support of Multicountry Operations*. Washington, DC: World Bank.

Kurt, K. 2012. "Insurance in Sub-Saharan Africa: Gearing Up for Strong Growth." A Swiss Re presentation made at the African Insurance Organisation meeting, Mauritius, 2 October.

OECD and WTO (World Trade Organization). 2011a. *Monitoring Exercise Case Story No. 85*.

———. 2011b. *Monitoring Exercise Case Story No. 145*.

———. 2011c. *Monitoring Exercise Case Story No. 142*.

———. 2015a. *Monitoring Exercise Case Story No. 67*.

———. 2015b. *Monitoring Exercise Case Story No. 7.*

UNCTAD (United Nations Conference on Trade and Development). 2013. *World Investment Report 2013: Global Value Chains—Investment and Trade for Development.* Geneva.

World Bank. 2011. *Partnering for Africa's Regional Integration: Progress Report on the Regional Integration Assistance Strategy for Sub-Saharan Africa.* Washington, DC. http://documents. worldbank.org/curated/en/151701468006936079/ Africa-Partnering-for-Africas-regional-integration-progress-report-on-the-regional-integration-assistance-strategy-for-Sub-Saharan-Africa.

WTO. 2017. *Minutes of the Meeting Held in the Centre William Rappard on 7 December 2016.* Geneva.

Endnotes

1   And as distinct from the vehicles created and employed by traditional partners to foster African regional integration.

Chapter 8
CFTA Governance

In governance, what is needed is function rather than form—a point made in Chapter 3, which emphasized the importance of institutional structures for regional integration that are practical rather than idealistic.

This chapter frames the Continental Free Trade Area (CFTA) governance in the context of the African Union (AU) reform and the fluidity of the negotiations on the CFTA institutional form. It proposes five "guiding principles" for forming the CFTA institutions, with a CFTA institutional structure that aspires to meet these guiding principles, but also emphasizes practicality by relying on existing institutions where possible.

The changing role of the regional economic communities (RECs) in the CFTA is discussed, drawing on the CFTA's own "negotiating guiding principles" and the Abuja Treaty. Recommendations for institutional structures, including those related to dispute settlement and the role of national courts, are based on what works in Africa's RECs.

CFTA architecture with the restructuring of the African Union

In discussing the institutional framework for the CFTA, one needs to keep in mind that the AU, as an inter-governmental institution, is going through reform itself. The purpose of this reform is to improve efficiency of the organization; elaborate on a sustainable funding approach that reduces dependence on foreign donor funds; and determine a framework for a coordinated response to Africa's most pressing challenges.

On the one hand, this AU reform provides an opportunity for member states to discuss and determine how the AU can be reformed such that flagship projects like the CFTA can be better institutionalized and implemented. On the other, designing an institutional framework for the CFTA will be extremely complicated if the main aspects of AU reform have not been finalized. Member states might then try to define an institutional framework for the CFTA without a clear idea of the future institutional arrangements of the AU itself. Some member states might even wish to set up a totally independent institution for the CFTA, such as a specialized agency of the AU, which would have an entirely separate legal personality but could be governed through the AU's policy organs. A more extreme form could be an "African WTO," which under international law would be a new international and inter-governmental organization for implementing the CFTA Agreement.

It is possible to design the CFTA insitutions with consideration of the principles driving the reform of the AU. Primarily, these reforms are to streamline the most important initiatives through the AU while transforming it into an efficient and effective organization. It would be reasonable to envisage CFTA structures operating within a reformed AU. Possibilities include hosting the CFTA institutions in the African Union Commission (AUC), either as a standalone department of the AUC or in the existing AUC Department for Trade and Industry.

Figure 8.1

Situational options for the CFTA institutions

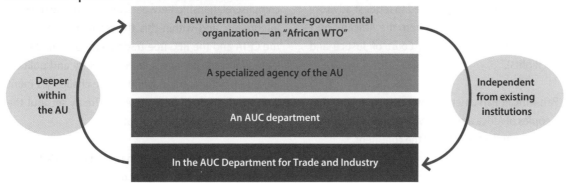

Alternatively, CFTA institutions could be located outside the AUC, but remain within the remit of the AU as a specialized agency.

This decision will depend on several elements: the extent to which member states want the CFTA institutions to operate independently from existing AU structures or to link closely to existing AU structures; costs; AU inter-linkages and economies of scope; and authority (Figure 8.1).

Institutional architecture envisaged in the Abuja Treaty

To reflect on what the governance architecture of the CFTA should be, it is important to outline the institutional architecture that the Abuja Treaty contemplated for the African Economic Community (AEC). Doing so reveals the "institutional pegs" onto which the CFTA structures will be hooked. The Abuja Treaty envisaged the primary organs of the AEC to be the Assembly of Heads of State and Government, Council of Ministers, Pan-African Parliament, Economic and Social Commission, Court of Justice, General Secretariat, and Specialized Technical Committees.[1]

The Assembly—renamed the Summit after the founding of the AU—was to be the supreme AEC organ.[2] It comprises the Heads of State and Government of the signatory States. The Assembly would be assisted by the Council of Ministers in its functions and the Assembly would, on recommendation of the Council, make decisions and give directives on regional economic activities, approve the AEC's programme of activity including its budget, and determine the contributions of each member state.[3]

The Council of Ministers of the AEC is effectively the Council of Ministers of the AU[4] and is responsible for guiding all the activities of all subordinate AEC organs.[5] Like the Assembly, it is empowered to request advisory opinions on any legal question from the African Court of Justice (currently, the African Court of Justice and Human Rights).[6]

The Pan-African Parliament is intended to ensure that "the peoples of Africa are fully involved in the economic development and integration of the continent."[7]

The Economic and Social Commission, which comprises ministers responsible for economic development planning and integration, is empowered to participate in the meetings of the Council of Ministers. The Commission's primary responsibilities include those to prepare policies, programmes and strategies for cooperation in economic and social development in Africa, as well as between Africa and the international community, and to make recommendations to the Council.[8]

The Court of Justice and Human Rights is to ensure "the adherence to law in the interpretation and application" of the Treaty and to determine disputes submitted to it under the Treaty, although the Assembly could decide to expand its jurisdiction.[9] Decisions of the Court are "binding on member states and organs of the Community,"[10] and the treaty provides that the functions of the Court should be carried out "independently of the member states and the other organs of the Community."[11]

The Specialized Technical Committees span the whole spectrum of economic, trade, industrial, educational, health, labour and human resources cooperation. Each committee would have a representative of each member state.[12]

Under the AU Constitutive Act, all these organs established under the Abuja Treaty are now considered those of the AU.

New thinking for the Abuja Treaty

The treaty underpinning the CFTA must be well designed. For the CFTA, the framework is currently provided by the Abuja Treaty. But it is an old document, adopted in 1991 and ratified in 1994. It addresses an Africa very different from today's, and it predates lessons in integration from around the continent and elsewhere. For instance, new guidance is needed to rationalize the complex relationship between continental and regional integration, and within this the relationship between the CFTA and the REC free trade areas. Lessons can be learned from experiences with monetary and political unions elsewhere in the world. These challenges merit a reconsideration of how the Abuja Treaty sets out the pathway to continental integration.

African continental integration should not hide behind the Abuja Treaty but reopen debate on how best to integrate the continent. It may be that the pathway to continental integration envisaged in the Abuja Treaty can be amended to take stock of Africa's achievements in the last 26 years and the challenges overcome along this path.

Five guiding principles for a CFTA institutional structure

Owing to the AU reform, the AU institutional structure is an unsettled foundation on which to build the CFTA institutional structure. Under negotiation, the CFTA institutional structure is also flexible. This merits an approach that emphasizes the principles which should guide the eventual form of the CFTA institutions. Five guiding principles are considered important in constructing the CFTA institutions:

- **Use the Abuja Treaty as the backbone for the CFTA institutional form**. The Abuja Treaty provides endorsement of Africa's integration agenda at the highest level and the vision and guidance for continental integration. The Treaty informs the goals and expectations of the CFTA, which in turn frames what is needed by its institutional structure. As outlined above, the Abuja Treaty may need to be revisited to improve how well it achieves this function.

- **Use and empower existing structures of African integration where available**. These structures exist across Africa and at the national, regional and continental levels. Examples include the REC institutions and the national bodies that report to the RECs. They already possess considerable experience in the integration process that may be leveraged in implementing the CFTA, which would help to avoid institutional duplication, generate economies of scope and reduce costs.

- **Ensure that the institutions of the CFTA are accessible to the African people**. The institutional architecture of the CFTA should not exist at a level beyond reach of the people of Africa. This is important both to ensure that the CFTA is win-win—leaving nobody behind—but also because the long-term sustainability of the project requires ground-level buy-in and support.

- **Support the joint implementation of the BIAT Action Plan alongside the CFTA**. The Boosting Intra-African Trade (BIAT) Action Plan is necessary for ensuring that the benefits of the CFTA are fully realized and shared both across and within African countries. Joint implementation and synergies between the BIAT Action Plan and the CFTA can be realized if there are strong linkages between the institutions charged with their implementation. Better linkages between the BIAT Action Plan and the CFTA can also keep down institutional duplication and costs.

- **Develop practical, rather than idealistic, institutional forms**. Although ideal institutional structures offer aspirations, it is important to consider how to get there. This can mean prioritizing low-cost and easily implementable first steps.

Proposed CFTA institutional structure

Fully recognizing the challenges of fluidity with the envisaged CFTA institutional structure under negotiation and the AU undergoing reform, we now outline a proposed institutional structure for the CFTA to help frame the five guiding principles.

- The structure adopted by the Abuja Treaty should be the platform on which to build a governance framework for implementing the CFTA, so that the proposed institutional structure is consistent with the Treaty.

- The proposed CFTA structures can lean on and incorporate those already established under the RECs and at the national level to meet the second guiding principle.

- In meeting the third guiding principle, the proposed structures must extend down to the country level and give individuals the right to enforce compliance of CFTA obligations in national courts. However, appeals could be addressed at regional courts and subsequently the African Court of Justice and Human Rights so that citizens see the bigger picture on regional and continental jurisprudence developed through the additional layers of integration. In addition to national institutions, this will also require dispute settlement arrangements that are accessible to individuals (see the next subsection).

- The implementing structure for the BIAT Action Plan should be considered. In particular, folding the implementing structure for the BIAT Action Plan into that for the CFTA can help realize the fourth guiding principle.

- The proposed institutional structure recommends putting pragmatism over idealism by leveraging and reinforcing existing regional and national institutions to implement the CFTA, rather than creating new, idealistic alternatives.

Figure 8.2 illustrates the proposed institutional structure, which builds on that of the AU, the Abuja Treaty and the Draft Strategic Framework for the Implementation of the BIAT Action Plan and for establishing the CFTA (AU, n.d.). The components are discussed subsequently.

The AU Assembly is the highest decision-making organ of the CFTA and provides overall oversight of the administrative and organizational arrangements.

The Council of Ministers responsible for Trade provide leadership for implementing the CFTA and includes ministers responsible for trade in each member state. It provides strategic oversight for the CFTA and may take all measures it deems necessary for implementing the CFTA, including promoting policies, strategies and measures. It may establish and delegate responsibilities to ad hoc or standing committees, working groups or expert groups, and consider and take action on the reports and activities of the CFTA Secretariat.

The Committee of Representatives supports the implementation of the CFTA and comprises representatives designated by the governments of the member states. It may establish and delegate responsibilities to ad hoc or standing sub-committees and technical working groups, and submit periodic reports, proposals, resolutions, recommendations or

Figure 8.2

Proposed CFTA institutional structures

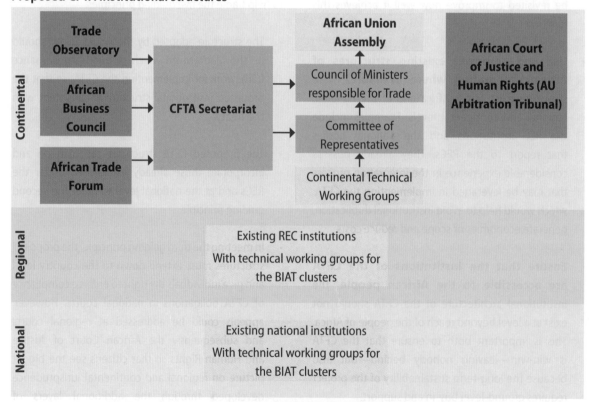

Note: The blue boxes represent the institutional structures outlined in the CFTA draft text. The green box is the link to existing AU architecture. The yellow boxes incorporate the proposal to combine the BIAT structures envisaged within the BIAT Strategic Framework with those of the CFTA. The orange boxes consider additional components anticipated as operating with the CFTA architecture.

opinions to the Council of Ministers responsible for Trade. Among the Technical Working Groups that report to the Committee of Representatives will be Continental Technical Working Groups, covering each of the seven BIAT clusters.

The CFTA Secretariat provides administrative support for implementing and enforcing CFTA provisions, facilitates the establishment of a monitoring and evaluation mechanism, serves as a depository of notifications from member states as required under the CFTA, convenes and services meetings of the member states as necessary for implementing the CFTA, provides and facilitates technical cooperation and capacity development programmes, serves as a secretariat to CFTA arbitration tribunals, and carries out any other responsibilities that may be assigned to it by the Assembly, Council of Ministers responsible for Trade, or Committee of Representatives.

The Trade Observatory will be responsible for monitoring and evaluation of the implementation of the BIAT Action Plan and the CFTA. Its responsibility will be to gather trade information, with a crucial role as the trade information bank for monitoring and evaluation and will serve as an essential part of the monitoring and evaluation mechanism.

The African Business Council is a necessary continental platform for aggregating and articulating the views of the private sector in the continental policy formulation processes. It can play an advisory role in continental policy formulation and will communicate its views and positions through the CFTA Secretariat. It should be composed of the chairs/representatives of umbrella (regional) associations/business councils that represent private sector interests, such as chambers of commerce and industry, small and medium-sized enterprises, women entrepreneurs and women in trade, sectoral associations such as banking and finance, and farmers, etc. It may be invited to meetings of the Ministers responsible for Trade in an observer capacity.

The African Trade Forum can serve as a Pan-African platform for reflection and discussion on the progress and challenges of continental market integration. It will be organized every year by the AUC and the UN Economic Commission for Africa (UNECA) jointly. Participants can include all stakeholders in the development of intra-African trade: member states; RECs; representatives of

continental and regional private sector, of civil society, and of women's organizations; research institutes; heads of major African cross-border enterprises; and development partners.

Continental Technical Working Groups: It is proposed that among the Technical Working Groups responsible to the Committee of Representatives would be seven dedicated to each of the BIAT clusters. These will support oversight of CFTA and BIAT technical and policy issues. Experts from the REC Secretariats and Regional Technical Working Groups can be included in these Continental Technical Working Groups.

Regional institutions: Engagement at the regional level can be through the existing REC institutional arrangements to avoid institutional duplication and to leverage existing resources. The RECs can develop region-specific programmes to enhance implementation of the BIAT and the CFTA, including Technical Working Groups for each of the BIAT clusters. Although the BIAT Strategic Framework envisages Regional Technical Working Groups, Regional Steering Committees and Regional Ministerial Oversight Committees, it is not realistic to expect these "best practice" institutions to be set up in the immediate term. Nor is a one-size-fits-all approach appropriate to cover the wide range of REC capabilities or to reflect existing REC achievements. Instead, the regional CFTA institutions should leverage and reinforce what exists in the RECs.

National institutions: The most important first step in approaching the institutional structure will be the requirement of each CFTA partner state to designate or create a ministerial agency that will be responsible for implementing and communicating on CFTA issues. This follows the successful approach used in the East African Community (EAC), in which lead agencies for each country were charged with coordinating implementation and application of EAC commitments at the national level (Box 8.1). The national institutions can be responsible for implementing the CFTA and BIAT at the country level, and should be resourced to engage with regional and continental arrangements, including National Technical Working Groups for each of the BIAT clusters. Again, while the BIAT Strategic Framework foresees national Technical Working Groups, National Steering Committees, and National Ministerial Oversight Committees, these are more feasible as an ideal to which to aspire in the medium to long run. In the short term, member states should give CFTA responsibilities to existing ministries or agencies charged with regional integration and coordination with the RECs.

Role of the RECs in the CFTA

This subsection outlines the evolving role of the RECs in the CFTA across the following four dimensions.

RECs as experienced institutions in guiding the CFTA

In the Declaration on the launch of the negotiations for the establishment of the CFTA, the AU Assembly "URGE[D] all Regional Economic Communities [...] to participate effectively in the CFTA negotiations." The RECs are unrivalled in their experience and expertise in African trade integration. The lessons learned by the RECs are vital inputs into the conceptualization, negotiation and implementation of the CFTA. In recognition of this, they comprise a substantial portion of the experts in the CFTA Continental Task Force, which in 2012 was constituted by the Assembly of Heads of State and Government of the AU to spearhead the CFTA negotiations and ensure completion by the end of 2017. The RECs perform a vital role in the development of the CFTA.

RECs as building blocks of the CFTA instructional structure

The RECs are explicitly recognized as building blocks of the CFTA within the CFTA negotiating guiding principles. It is envisaged that the RECs coordinate and administer Regional Technical Working Groups, Regional Steering Committees and Regional Ministerial Oversight Committees for the implementation of the CFTA and associated BIAT Action Plan. The RECs will also administer the regional Monitoring and Evaluation Committee for the CFTA. The REC institutional structures for the CFTA will then feed into those at the continental level.

RECs as operators of substantive components of the CFTA

Consistent with their role in the CFTA institutional architecture, the RECs will remain vital for implementing many of the substantive components of the CFTA. Both within and between them, the RECs will be required to operate mechanisms such as those intending to address non-tariff barriers (NTBs) or to mediate trade remedies and disputes (see previous sections).

RECs on graduation of trade policy to the continental level

To the extent that a key objective of the CFTA is the rationalization of multiple trade regimes on the continent and the creation of a continent-wide economic space, the free trade areas of the RECs cannot coexist with the CFTA. It should also be recalled that the CFTA will be more than a traditional trade agreement and will embody elements of a single market (for example, by reducing non-tariff restrictions and promoting trade in services) and an economic union (for example, by moving towards the harmonization of regulatory policies). This means that the RECs that are not already customs unions or are not on a trajectory towards a customs union will cease to have a role in trade policy.

The preeminent authority for trade policy will graduate to the continental level as the CFTA contributes to a consolidation of Africa's overlapping "spaghetti bowl" of free trade areas. It is expected that the RECs will contribute to continental-level trade policy through their roles in the CFTA institutional architecture or as customs unions where this applies. This will enable Africa to operate as a stronger, consolidated trading body in its negotiations with its trading partners, such as the European Union (EU), the United States, and the emerging market economies (Chapter 9). Moreover, consolidating this role to the continental level will enable Africa to economize on the resources currently required to undertake these activities in each of the RECs. REC FTAs as building blocks of the CFTA and preservation of the acquis draws on the CFTA negotiating guiding principles to outline practically how African trade policy will transition to the continental level.

Box 8.2

REC FTAs as building blocks of the CFTA and preservation of the acquis

The envisaged role of the RECs draws on the CFTA Negotiating Guiding Principles, adopted by the African Union Ministers of Trade in May 2016. The Negotiating Guiding Principles help outline the desired vision of the CFTA. Most relevant to the RECs are the following two principles.

1. REC free trade areas as building blocks of the CFTA

"The CFTA shall build on and improve upon the process that has been made in the trade liberalization and integration programmes of Regional Economic Communities: AMU, CEN-SAD, ECCAS, ECOWAS, IGAD, COMESA, SADC and EAC."

The importance of the RECs as building blocks for the CFTA is also reaffirmed by the fact that the Assembly considered that the REC initiatives in the area of trade should be consolidated in order to achieve the CFTA by the indicative date of 2017. This is illustrated by the Decision on Boosting Intra-African Trade and Fast Tracking the CFTA (Assembly/AU/Dec.394(XVIII)) whereby the Assembly decided that "the CFTA should be operationalized by the indicative date of 2017, based on the framework, Roadmap and Architecture, with the following appropriate milestones:

i)   Finalization of the East African Community (EAC)–the Common Market for Eastern and Southern Africa (COMESA)–Southern African Development Community (SADC) Tripartite FTA initiative by 2014;

ii) Completion of FTA(s) by Non-Tripartite RECs, through parallel arrangement(s) similar to the EAC-COMESA-SADC Tripartite Initiative or reflecting the preferences of their Member States, between 2012 and 2014;

iii) Consolidation of the Tripartite and other regional FTAs into a Continental Free Trade Area (CFTA) initiative between 2015 and 2016;

iv) Establishment of the Continental Free Trade Area (CFTA) by 2017 with the option to review the target date according to progress made.

This decision appears to provide the way the CFTA should be built: through the establishment of free trade areas at the regional economic community level, the AU member states would prepare for the establishment of a CFTA.

2. Preservation of the acquis

"The CFTA shall build on and improve upon the acquis of the existing REC FTAs and shall not reverse or be inconsistent with the Acquis of the Union including but not limited to the Constitutive Act, the Abuja Treaty and other relevant legal instruments of the Union."

REC FTAs as building blocks of the CFTA and preservation of the acquis (continued)

By stating that the CFTA must build on and improve upon the level of trade liberalization and integration achieved in the RECs, it is implied that the CFTA must not merely add another layer and another free trade area to the existing "spaghetti bowl" of overlapping regional free trade areas, but instead go beyond the level of liberalization and integration achieved by the RECs. If this ambitious principle is satisfied, it is implied that the regional free trade areas will be superseded by an improved level of liberalization within the CFTA. However, consistent with the preservation of the acquis, the CFTA additionally must not unravel the REC FTAs.

In practice, the particular modalities for tariff reductions or liberalization in the CFTA will likely require REC FTAs to persist as "islands" until the tide of liberalization envisaged by the CFTA rises above them in the medium to long term. Otherwise, the CFTA will fail in its objective of rationalizing and consolidating the overlapping RECs into a single pan-Africa area and merely add another layer of liberalization. On the other hand, immediately replacing the REC FTAs would not satisfy preservation of the acquis, as the CFTA will not immediately begin at the 100 per cent liberalization achieved by the most successful REC FTAs. What is required is a transition. The Abuja Treaty, in relation to Africa's trade, envisages the adoption of "common policies" by 2020, indicating a timeline for such a transition.

The other remaining role for RECs in trade will be the formation of REC customs unions. These can remain as "islands" of further integration within the CFTA framework.

Dispute settlement arrangements

To give the obligations in the CFTA legal certainty and predictability, it will be important to establish a dispute settlement mechanism that would be compulsory and binding as well as fast and efficient. Where diplomatic and alternative mechanisms have failed, this dispute settlement system would allow CFTA member states to bring cases against each other on the application or interpretation of the rights and obligations created by the CFTA Treaty.

For this system to be effective, it has to build on the experiences of the RECs, in particular by initially encouraging those member states considering litigation to first engage in direct negotiations (COMESA approach to non-litigious dispute settlement). Failure of negotiations would be followed by mediation, conciliation and other negotiated means of settling disputes through the CFTA institutional framework before resorting to litigation.

In the CFTA, where negotiations, mediation or conciliation fail to produce an outcome within six months, there ought to be a CFTA Dispute Settlement Committee as a next step that would be charged with the responsibility of resolving such a dispute between states, represented by government authorities. The decision of the CFTA Dispute Settlement Committee

would be legally binding on the parties to the dispute. However, it is important that this process be expedited so that it can provide for timely resolution of disputes (Proposed dispute settlement arrangements).

Pending the establishment of the African Court of Justice and Human Rights, which will replace the African Court of Human and Peoples' Rights, and on the entry into force of the Treaty for the Establishment of the CFTA, the AU Assembly could either convene a commercial chamber in the existing African Court of Human and Peoples' Rights or establish a specialist ad hoc committee to hear appeals from the decisions of the CFTA Dispute Settlement Committee. To be an effective dispute settler, this Chamber ought to

Table 8.1

Proposed dispute settlement arrangements

Non-litigious methods	
Step 1	Direct diplomatic negotiations
Step 2	Mediation and conciliation through CFTA institutions
CFTA dispute settlement	
Step 3	CFTA Dispute Settlement Committee
Step 4	Convene a commercial chamber in the African Court of Human and Peoples' Rights;* or Establish a specialist ad hoc committee

Companies and individuals, as well as member states not signatories to the Protocol on the Statute of the African Court of Human and Peoples' Rights, can have petitions referred by the AUC.

COMESA approach to non-litigious dispute settlement

Non-litigious methods of resolving trade problems are an important feature of Africa's RECs (Gathii, 2016). For example, in its February 2014 COMESA Council of Ministers meeting, the COMESA Secretariat was empowered to investigate the removal of the contentious NTBs, which the state that had imposed them argued were justified; the Secretariat was tasked with confirming that the NTBs were supported by legitimate policy goals.

In three instances, the COMESA Secretariat facilitated the hiring of consulting firm KPMG to undertake a cost assessment of the three contentious NTBs relating to COMESA's rules of origin. The involvement of a third-party facilitator is incorporated in COMESA's NTB Regulations. These NTBs concerned soap from Mauritius to Madagascar; palm oil from Kenya to Zambia; and regriderators and freezers from Swaziland to Zimbabwe (COMESA Secretariat, 2016).

COMESA has another innovation that could be replicated in the CFTA. COMESA member states that have a complaint against another member states are required to write to that member states requesting clarification. This communication has to be copied to the COMESA Secretariat. If the member states from which additional information is sought do not respond, the Secretariat then writes to the member states seeking a response. Where there is no resolution, the matter is taken up by the COMESA Committee on Trade and Customs. This committee has authority to receive complaints on COMESA treaty violations. The committee may then submit a report to the Council of Ministers or to the COMESA Secretary General requesting that investigations be undertaken. The COMESA Treaty empowers the Council of Ministers to make binding decisions on member states in order "to promote the attainment of the aims of the common market."**

This committee is established under Article 13(k) of the COMESA Treaty.

*** Article 9(2)(g) of the COMESA Treaty. See also Article 9(2)(d) empowering the Council to "…issue directives, take decisions, make recommendations and give opinions in accordance with the provisions of this treaty." Another institutional feature in COMESA is the Inter-Governmental Committee that comprises Permanent/Principal Secretaries from COMESA Coordinating Ministries in all member states.*

comprise eminent jurists in international trade law, commerce and allied areas.

In addition, for CFTA parties that are not signatories to the Protocol on Amendments to the Protocol on the Statute of the African Court of Justice and Human Rights, the AUC could be empowered to refer disputes relating to the CFTA to the African Court of Justice and Human Rights for a binding determination of a dispute

---

Figure 8.3

Proposed CFTA dispute settlement structure

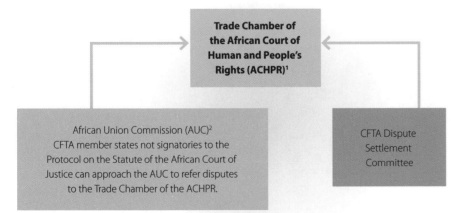

1 To be replaced by the African Court of Justice and Human Rights.
2 The AUC can receive petitions brought by companies and individuals from CFTA member states that have not signed a declaration under Article 34 (6) of the African Charter on Human and People's Rights and refer such disputes to the Trade Chamber of the ACHPR.

that involves them. Figure 8.3 shows the proposed dispute settlement structure.

For AU member states that have not signed a declaration, under Article 34(6) of the Protocol to the African Charter on Human and Peoples' Rights, in allowing individual access to the Court (including suits by private actors), consideration could be made to allow the AUC to receive such individual petitions from companies and individuals in those AU member states and for the Commission to consider whether or not to file a reference on behalf of such individual claimants in the African Court of Human and Peoples' Rights in cases involving alleged infringement of CFTA rights and obligations.

The Role of National Courts

The CFTA dispute settlement arrangements will be inter-governmental. To ensure that the individuals' rights under the CFTA are fully implemented, national courts of the CFTA member states will be important, as these courts can give individuals the right to enforce compliance of CFTA obligations nationally. National courts can be used to decentralize compliance. National courts work best where the provisions of the CFTA Treaty are made part of domestic law.

There are good precedents for using national courts to enforce regional economic community commitments. For example, Kenyan courts have a series of decisions, stretching more than a decade, that enforced Kenya's COMESA obligations on sugar imports.[13]

References

AU (African Union). n.d. *Draft Strategic Framework for the Implementation of the Action Plan for Boosting Intra-African Trade and for Establishing the Continental Free Trade Area*. Addis Ababa.

COMESA (Common Market for Eastern and Southern Africa) Secretariat. 2016. "All but Four Non-Tariff Barriers resolved." http://www.comesa.int/all-but-four-non-tariff-barriers-resolved/.

Gathii, J. 2016. "The Variation in the Use of Sub-Regional Integration Courts between Business and Human Rights Actors: The Case of the East African Court of Justice." *Law and Contemporary Problems* 78 (4): 37–62.

Endnotes

1   Article 7 of the Treaty for the Establishment of the African Economic Community (1994) (also referred to as the Abuja Treaty).

2   Article 8.1 id.

3   Article 8.3 (h) and (i) as well as Article 8(4) id.

4   The treaty refers to the OAU but since the OAU is now defunct and its activities taken over by the African Union, I have used the reference African Union. See Article 11.1 id.

5   Article 11.3(b). Article 11.2 confers on the council the responsibility for the functioning and development of the community.

6   Article 11.3 (f). Similar power to Assembly Article 83 (k) id.

7   Article 14.1 id.

8   Article 16(a)

9   Article 18.2 and Article 18.4 respectively.

10   Article 19.

11   Article 18.5.

12   Article 25.1 and 25.2.

13   See for example, in Transouth Conveyors Limited and Others Versus Kenya Revenue Authority and Others, Misc. Court of Appeal No. 120 of 2007 consolidated with Misc. Civil Appeal No. 136 of 2007 (Judgment of 30 May 2008, http://kenyalaw.org/caselaw/cases/view/44874/), which found in part that companies that had brought sugar into Kenya were entitled to do so duty free because they complied with the preconditions for importation contained in an agreement between Kenya and COMESA.

Chapter 9
The CFTA in a Changing Trade Landscape

The Continental Free Trade Area (CFTA) is being negotiated in an evolving trade landscape. The multilateral trading system is in crisis after the failure of the Doha Round and populist anti-globalization sentiments in several large trading nations. The rapid rise of emerging market economies has caused a fundamental shift in the trade patterns of many African countries. The controversies surrounding the Economic Partnership Agreements (EPAs) and Brexit require new thinking on restructuring trade relations with Europe. Africa's trading relationship with the United States, having developed under the African Growth and Opportunity Act (AGOA), is likely to transform into reciprocal arrangements by 2025 in a post-AGOA agenda. The so-called "mega-regional" trade agreements that once threatened Africa's preferential trade with established partners, now have evolved into a different threat of protectionism. Finally, new modes of trade such as e-commerce are putting pressure on demands for new trade rules.

Chapter 4 introduced the concept of "external factors" as critical junctures in the political economy of the CFTA. These may offer windows of opportunity to speed up processes, alter political priorities or reshape the incentive environment for different CFTA stakeholders. Alternatively, such changes may require a downscaling of ambition or even stall efforts towards the CFTA as reform windows narrow or close. This chapter expands on these concepts, assessing the implications of the biggest tremors in Africa's trading landscape.

Rise of the mega-regionals or of protectionism?

The rise of regional trade agreements was triggered by another external factor: a profound slowdown in multilateral trade negotiations at the World Trade Organization (WTO) and the "death of the Doha round" (*Financial Times*, 2015). This critical juncture spawned the proliferation of negotiations on regional trade agreements, including mega-regional trade agreements (MRTAs), as a means of circumventing the

multilateral impasse and developing new trade rules among groups of willing countries.

Trade, however, occurs not between countries in a vacuum but in the context of a global trading environment; the MRTAs threatened to have spill-over effects for excluded countries, including many in Africa. Trade between mega-regional members would have increased at the expense of third countries outside the agreements.

The MRTAs of note here are the Transatlantic Trade and Investment Partnership between the European Union (EU) and the United States; the Trans-Pacific Partnership (TPP), originally comprising the United States and 11 other Pacific Rim countries; and the Regional Comprehensive Economic Partnership (RCEP), covering the Association of Southeast Asian Nations (ASEAN) group of countries and others, notably China and India, and conceived largely as a rival to the TPP.

The implications for Africa would be higher competition and erosion of preferences in MRTA markets resulting in trade diversion. Estimates by Mevel and Mathieu (2016), using a model in which all three of these agreements are implemented, see Africa's net exports falling by $3 billion (equivalent to 0.3 per cent) in 2022 compared with the baseline. They also found a further concentration of Africa's exports in energy and mining, largely on the back of reduced agricultural and industrial exports to China and India. The impacts would be felt most severely by certain sectors of particular countries, such as African textile producers, which would face competition from Vietnam and other highly efficient Southeast Asian producers, undercutting the textile preferences granted to African countries, for instance through AGOA.

The potential impacts extend beyond the conventional focus on tariffs and trade diversion, however. The MRTAs have been conceived to include new disciplines, such as e-commerce, competition policy and labour standards, and deeper commitments to existing disciplines,

Figure 9.1

Membership of mega-regional trade agreements

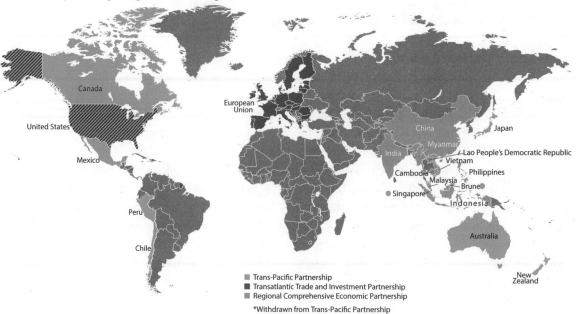

■ Trans-Pacific Partnership
■ Transatlantic Trade and Investment Partnership
■ Regional Comprehensive Economic Partnership
*Withdrawn from Trans-Pacific Partnership

such as government procurement, services and trade facilitation, which extend their remit beyond traditional "shallow" trade agreements and instead amount to "deep" agreements (Lawrence, 1996; Baldwin, 2014a; Ueno, 2013). This could create new discriminatory arrangements against outsiders but also establish norms for the *multilateralization* of new and deeper issues (Melendez-Ortiz, 2014; Draper et al., 2014). By eroding WTO's status as the forum for creating new trade rules, MRTAs undermine the voice that outsiders, including Africa, have in shaping these rules. The WTO may be increasingly sidelined as the international rule-making body. Yet to export to these markets, outsider countries would still have to play by their rules (Baldwin, 2014b).

On the other hand, elements of deep regional trade agreements can also benefit Africa; the MRTAs would also include provisions with no enforceable preferences (Baldwin, 2014a). For instance, disciplines on certain services and many other issues often lack a legally and administratively feasible discriminating mechanism that can be used for identifying and restricting the nationality of firms that use those disciplines. In such circumstances, the agreements are merely a vehicle for locking in domestic reforms that are applied multilaterally. Furthermore, regulatory convergence and harmonization of diverse norms, standards and regulations are argued to also reduce trade costs to the benefit of outsider exporters (Baldwin, 2014a). The

analogy here is to the EU, whereby an outsider country can export to a single bloc of countries with harmonized regulations, compared with the complexity of accessing 28 different markets.

Any discussion on MRTAs needs to touch on the recent emergence of political populism in developed countries and its apparent attachment to protectionism. On 14 January 2017, the subheading to one of the articles in *The Economist* referred to "a protectionist entering the White House." Nine days later President Donald Trump signed a presidential memorandum withdrawing the United Stated from the TPP. The incipient perception was of protectionism with immediate implications for the viability of concluding MRTAs.

A second disruption stems from Brexit and the disengagement of the Untied Kingdom from the EU, in an apparent rejection of European regional integration, marking a break from the world's most ambitious regional integration project.

Yet it is unclear whether these events really signify impending protectionism that will undermine MRTAs. Certainly the United States has left the TPP, but this may merely create a more enticing gap to be filled by the Regional Comprehensive Economic Partnership or for China to be included in the "rump" TPP (*Financial Times*, 2017). Alternatively, the TPP could go ahead without the United States (Reuters, 2017). Recent

Smartly sequencing trade agreements

It will be important for Africa to "smartly sequence" its trade policy reforms to ensure that deeper regional integration takes place before the inevitable gradual opening up of African markets to the rest of the world, and before the main MRTAs are fully established. This will allow African countries to harness the economies of scale and learning by doing that is needed to develop competitive regional value chains (RVCs) and industries, which are then well positioned to compete internationally and integrate into global value chains.

Such sequencing calls for:

- Fast implementation of the CFTA to avoid any trade losses from the anticipated increase in reciprocity in Africa's trade agreements with the rest of the world and from the rise in MRTAs.[1]

- Well-managed and appropriately phased tariff reductions on imports into Africa would enable African industries to adapt. African countries must make smart choices when negotiating reciprocal versions of EPAs and AGOA and when negotiating new trade agreements with trading partners outside the continent. Tariffs on intermediate and capital goods not produced locally should be removed first,[2] which would cut the costs of industrialization and foster domestic value addition. Tariffs on intermediates and capital goods for which some domestic and regional production exists should be removed next, followed by tariffs on finished products. This sequencing would support Africa's industrialization, development of RVCs and technological catch-up, while providing temporary protection for local producers to guard against premature de-industrialization (Sommer et al. 2017).

political analysis on the rise of this populism finds less evidence of its origins in economic insecurity, which would incite protectionism, than in a cultural backlash against liberalism (Inglehart and Norris, 2016). Or as held by Paul Krugman in a *New York Times* op-ed, "Trump is wimping out on trade" and softening his protectionist rhetoric (Krugman, 2017). If this is so, the MRTAs may likely yet resurge.

Still, the apparent rise of protectionism is not restricted to the United Kingdom and the United States. Nor is it restricted to tariffs. A WTO report on G20 Trade Measures (2016), found that new trade-restrictive measures are being applied by the G20 group of countries at the fastest rate since monitoring began in 2009. A large share of them are trade-remedy actions against imports of industrial products. Within the G20, the majority of new measures are applied by Russia, China, India and Indonesia (European Parliament, 2015). After the global financial crisis, developing countries increasingly used anti-dumping remedies, and increasingly applied them to imports from other developing countries (Bown and Kee, 2011). While a "China reaction" accounts for a moderate share of the increased use of trade remedies, there is a growing use of trade-restrictive measures in developing countries to defend against imports from other developing countries.

Implications

The CFTA was seen to be critical for Africa's trade in the context of the MRTAs. Implemented in parallel with the MRTAs, the CFTA was found, in modelling work by Mevel and Mathieu (2016), to substantially improve the outcomes for Africa, increasing intra-African exports by $27.5 billion (equivalent to 3 per cent). Moreover, the gain was estimated to benefit all African countries and to be especially beneficial to expanding Africa's industrial products.

With the TPP on hold, there is conceivably a reduced immediacy for the CFTA. Yet, the MRTAs may resurface, and rather than disincentivizing the CFTA, this apparent hiatus gives Africa some breathing room.

In recent years there has appeared to be a rise in protectionist sentiment and tendencies. This is not restricted to developed countries, but increasingly concerns trade-remedy actions applied by developing countries against imports from other developing countries. Africa is not yet a primary target for such means of trade defence, but the trend highlights external risks for Africa's trade with the rest of the world.

New trade issues for the WTO and CFTA

The part of the trade landscape that has not altered is the WTO Doha Round. With little progress being made, developed countries have increasingly pressed to close the Round and move on to negotiate new issues. This will likely remain their focus at the upcoming WTO Ministerial Conference in Buenos Aires in December 2017. Developing countries have resisted this approach and demanded the conclusion of the Doha Round, which includes critical issues for developing countries, such as agricultural subsidies.

Energy has coalesced around the emergence of "new" trade issues at the WTO. While negotiations cannot begin on these issues without agreement by all WTO members, discussions have progressed to inform what will eventually become negotiations on these issues. Attempts are being made to convert these discussions into a mandate to negotiate new rules. The new issues include proposed rules on e-commerce, micro, small and medium-sized enterprises (MSMEs), domestic regulation of services and investment facilitation, as now discussed.

e-commerce

E-commerce concerns the online sale or purchase of goods or services (OECD, 2011). It is frequently cited for its potential as a revolutionary new trade route of the 21st century that could reduce market costs for MSMEs, connecting them to international markets. In Africa, however, e-commerce is substantially constrained by inadequate infrastructure, digital education, digital regulations and Internet penetration (Budree, 2017). This creates a digital divide and knowledge gap, such that Africa's economies lag behind the digital development of the advanced countries and are less competitive in this area.

Proposals for new e-commerce rules aim to limit policy space to ensure open access for businesses operating through these channels. Suggested rules include prohibiting customs duties and non-discrimination, forbidding data localization, safeguarding network competition, ensuring unrestricted cross-border data flows, promoting a free and open Internet, protecting critical source code and limiting policies on technology transfers[3] (Proposed e-commerce rules).

The concern is that these rules are being driven by established e-commerce companies that want to cement their market dominance in the digital world. Azmeh and Foster (2016) argue that such rules reduce the policy space for latecomer economies to promote their online businesses, foster technology transfer and

implement digital industrial policy. Data localization laws, for example, can be imposed to require that businesses set up data centres within the countries in which they are operating, similar to how local content requirements work. However, Bauer et al. (2014) find the

---

Box 9.2

Proposed e-commerce rules

Prohibiting digital customs duties — on electronically transmitted products, such as books, music, videos and software.

Non-discrimination principles — require that national treatment be provided to e-commerce goods and services.

Data localization rules — prohibit rules requiring that the storage, routing, processing or other use of data be within the territory of a country.

Safeguarding network competition — enables digital suppliers to build networks in the markets they serve or to access such facilities and services from incumbents.

Enabling cross-border data flows — enables companies and consumers to move data without restriction.

Free and open Internet rules — targets governments that block certain websites for commercial or political reasons, as well as similar initiatives by private companies.

Protecting critical source code — requires that businesses do not have to hand over their source code or proprietary algorithms to their competitors or to pass them along to a state-owned enterprise. Trade secrets (including source code) are not covered by the Agreement on Trade-Related Aspects of Intellectual Property Rights (TRIPS), however.

Ensuring technology choice—prohibits governments from forcing foreign businesses to use specific local technologies when they invest in an economy.

No technology transfers — prohibits governments from requiring companies to transfer technology, production processes or other proprietary information.

imposition of such laws to have a significant negative impact on economic growth, reducing domestic investments and contributing to welfare losses. They estimate that the welfare impact of such laws in India amounted to the equivalent of an 11 per cent loss to the average monthly salary and argue that any gains from data localization are too small to outweigh losses in the general economy.

Rules that strengthen intellectual property rights, such as those protecting critical source code, arguably make it more difficult for new entrants to a market to imitate the successes of those already established. Such rules can, however, help to ensure that online transactions and related businesses are unhindered and so promote the development of related industries.

Other e-commerce proposals, promoted by developing countries and better reflecting their interests, concern trade facilitation for e-commerce, infrastructure gaps to enable e-commerce, access to payment solutions and online security.

Rules on micro, small and medium-sized enterprises

Proposals for addressing MSMEs at the WTO largely concern intellectual property rights. (MSMEs include entrepreneurs, start-ups, businesses, researchers and investors.) New rules would tighten and spread intellectual property rights to better cover the operations of MSMEs. Though it is argued that doing so could foster transparent and predictable intellectual property rules for such entities, it could also lock out developing country businesses from these areas.

Almost all African businesses are MSMEs. Support to them is thus vital in ensuring a successful CFTA. The flanking policies in Chapter 6 will be crucial for this purpose. As this is already part of the CFTA agenda, it is questionable whether Africa needs disciplines at the level of the WTO given the associated risks to policy space.

Rules on domestic regulation of services

Several developed economies (including Australia, the EU, Japan and New Zealand) have proposed a package of rules for the WTO Ministerial Conference that is scheduled to be held in Buenos Aires in December 2017 on Domestic Regulation in Services.

These rules "apply to measures by members relating to licensing requirements and procedures, qualification requirements and procedures, and technical standards affecting trade in services where specific commitments are undertaken."[4] These disciplines must apply to all levels of government—central, regional and local.

The proposals include the following key elements:

- The measures relating to licensing and qualification requirements, procedures and technical standards must be "objective and transparent."

- The regulator must "administer in an independent manner."

- The technical standards must be developed according to "open and transparent processes."

- Detailed transparency requirements (all aspects of licensing and qualification requirements and procedures and technical standards) must be published including timeframes for processing, as well as fees and procedures for monitoring compliance.

- Fees must be reasonable and transparent and cannot restrict the supply of the service.

- They must allow for prior comment, i.e. foreign industry players are allowed to comment on regulations that are being developed domestically, etc.

Developing countries may be challenged on the basis of these disciplines when implementing measures intended to support development of domestic industries.

Investment facilitation

Some members are also seeking a mandate at the December 2017 Buenos Aires Ministerial Conference to negotiate investment facilitation rules. Proposals were submitted in March–April 2017 by, Brazil, China and Russia, suggesting detailed transparency requirements that would require listing the criteria used in licensing requirements and the appraisal of potential investors.

A concern here is that these rules could mean that markets are open to investors without conditions, unless adequate criteria and conditions have already been put in place. This could be used to force countries to open up sectors for investment beyond what is desired by these countries.

Implications

The CFTA can be a means of solidifying a common African position at the WTO to give Africa a single, strong voice, including on the new WTO issues. However, there is no requirement for any of the new issues to be included in the CFTA (although, as discussed in Chapter 10, negotiators way wish to consider issues of e-commerce as a topic of the second phase of CFTA negotiations).

In all cases, the new issues divert attention in the WTO from the remaining Doha Round issues, which are of particular value to developing countries. The new issues can thus be perceived as a way to circumnavigate the Doha Round interests of developing countries, enabling more advanced countries to pursue their alternative interests. African countries must be wary of how such new rules could restrict their policy space or strengthen intellectual property rights. Consideration should be given for the CFTA to establish a platform for solidifying a common African approach to these new issues.

Traditional trading partners: Brexit and the EU

In what is commonly dubbed Brexit, the United Kingdom intends to exit the EU as a result of a 23 June 2016, referendum in which 51.9 per cent of those who cast a valid vote, voted to leave. This has the following three main implications or lessons for regional integration in Africa and the CFTA.

A direct effect on Africa's trade with the United Kingdom

Brexit has a direct effect on Africa's trade with the United Kingdom. Work by Mold (2017), finds a small increase in African exports to the United Kingdom due to trade diversion, under a scenario in which the United Kingdom falls back on WTO provisions for its trading with the EU. Certain African exporters have sensed this possibility, such as those in the Citrus Growers' Association of Southern Africa, who suggested that revised UK plant health regulations on citrus imports could help them improve access to the United Kingdom market (Luke and MacLeod, 2016). On the other hand,

the effects of the British pound's devaluation have had immediate negative effects not just for African goods exports, but the dollar value of UK aid, investment, remittances and tourism in African countries (Mendez-Parra et al., 2016).

Brexit enables the United Kingdom to undertake a renewed trade policy towards Africa which, at most, could better support the CFTA by targeting continental Africa (Luke and MacLeod, 2017). However, Brexit also creates risks to Africa's trade. The preferential regimes of the UK for Africa through the current trade policies of the EU, including the Everything But Arms (EBA) initiative, Generalised System of Preferences (GSP), and the EPAs may be disrupted or excluded from the new UK trade policy. Were the United Kingdom to turn more protectionist or offer fewer preferences than the EU does, the UK trade arrangements could have potentially large negative effects for African and other developing countries (te Velde, 2016).

A "catalyst" for African countries to exit the Economic Partnership Agreements

Brexit reduces the cost for African countries to leave the EPAs by removing from the EPAs one of the EU's largest markets for key African products. The United Kingdom accounts for about 11 per cent of Africa's exports to the EU, but among agricultural exports, it takes in 67 per cent of beef, 41 per cent of tea and spices, 31 per cent of wine, and 22 per cent of Africa's fruit exports to the EU (The United Kingdom's share of EU's agriculture imports from Africa, 2014).

The effect is to undermine the case for the EPAs in particular countries for which these products are of especial value. Stevens and Kennan (2016), identify the United Kingdom as accounting for 29.3 per cent of Ghana's "sensitive exports" to the EU, 27.3 per cent of Kenya's, 15.5 per cent of Namibia's and 9.6 per cent of Swaziland's. Ghana, which had long deliberated over the EPA, recently signed an interim Ghana EPA because of its strategic significance for priority fish, processed cocoa, fruit and vegetable exports, yet within the EU the United Kingdom accounts for over 50 per cent of some of these imports from Ghana.

Consequently, Brexit has sparked fresh EPA concerns while reigniting those already largely doused. It was, for example, the ostensible reason for Tanzania's decision

Table 9.1

The United Kingdom's share of EU's agriculture imports from Africa, 2014

No.	Product	Value ($ million)	Share of EU imports (%)
1	Fruit	813	22
2	Vegetables	394	17
3	Fish	329	8
4	Cocoa	289	5
5	Wine	167	31
6	Tea and spices	166	41
7	Fresh cut flowers	128	11
8	Sugar	126	10
9	Beef	66	67
10	Banana	61	10
11	Tobacco	59	6
12	Coffee	46	5
13	Seeds and nuts	41	7
14	Edible oils	15	3
	Other agriculture	99	11
	Total agriculture	2,802	11

Source: Reconciled bilateral trade flows from the CEPII-BACI dataset.

to postpone signing its East African Community (EAC) EPA.

Lessons for African regionalism

Brexit is a cautionary tale for African integration, and a lesson in the risks of integration generally. Central to the case for Brexit was the perception that European integration had diminished UK sovereignty and that the decisions affecting UK citizens were instead being made by unaccountable European bureaucrats in a foreign capital. Africa is a continent all too familiar with its own, albeit much darker, struggle for sovereignty: Indeed, sovereignty is the first principle of the 1963 charter for the Organisation for African Unity. The lesson for Africa is that perceptions of sovereignty matter, and moves towards pan-African unity must be cautious.

Other implications

At best, a new UK trade policy can contribute to the CFTA by orientating towards and supporting African continental integration. This can be buttressed by the United Kingdom's substantial development assistance, roughly $16 billion, which is reportedly to be increasingly focused on trade-related projects (*Financial Times*, 2016; DfID, 2017).

Brexit has fundamentally shifted the negotiating cards held by the EU in its EPA negotiations with Africa. This has already proved catalytic for certain countries

in turning their back on the EPAs, but may be more constructively leveraged to reopen discussions with the EU for better achieving the trade interests of Africa, including continental integration and the CFTA.

Brexit is, in an admittedly very different context, a rejection of regional integration. African leaders must heed this caution and ensure that integration projects in Africa, including the CFTA, are cognizant of the potential pitfalls of integration and responsive to their root causes, including perceptions of loss of sovereignty.

United States: Beyond AGOA

The African Growth and Opportunity Act (AGOA) has been the cornerstone of the United States–Africa trading relationship since 2000, and forms an important component of US development policy towards Africa. The legislation provides significantly enhanced market access to the United States for qualifying Sub-Saharan African countries and has been especially valuable in promoting African textile and apparel exports. Several AGOA beneficiaries, including Kenya, Lesotho, Madagascar, Swaziland, Ghana, Ethiopia, and Mauritius, have achieved some export diversification through textiles and apparel.

Beyond such notable success stories, AGOA is generally considered to have fallen short of achieving its transformation potential. Included within AGOA preferences are oil, gas and petroleum exports, which still account for the majority of AGOA exports (Figure 9.2). Over 2001–15, the value of AGOA exports was largely determined by the impact of the commodities super cycle on oil, gas and petroleum exports. In 2015, 55 per cent of US imports from Africa were oil or energy-related products, and since AGOA's inception, petroleum products have averaged around 80 per cent of exports. While AGOA has facilitated the production and export of certain processed and manufactured products to the United States, this has yet to lead to any fundamental change in the structure of African exports to that market.

In 2015, AGOA was renewed for another 10 years with new provisions, such as an emphasis on National Utilization Strategies, which are designed to ensure that African countries are better prepared to take advantage of AGOA opportunities.

The *Beyond AGOA* report, released by the US Trade Representative in September 2016, lays out US intentions for the future of AGOA beyond this 10-year renewal. It argues that provision of unilateral preferences for Africa is untenable while Africa negotiates reciprocal agreements with other regions and countries, and while other providers of non-reciprocal preferences to Africa, such as the EU, move towards reciprocal arrangements.

Beyond AGOA frequently alludes to the increasing commercial and domestic pressure in the United States for reciprocal arrangements with Africa. It also presents Africa's rising economic significance, in terms of development improvements and increasing economic size, suggesting that with these opportunities American businesses could be "left out" in the competition with other trading partners with which Africa is developing reciprocal agreements. Chief among this competitive scramble is the EU with its EPAs, and China, which is frequently mentioned in the Report. China does not yet have serious reciprocal agreements under negotiation in Africa, but it overtook the United States in 2004 as the second-biggest supplier of Africa's imports (after the EU) and in 2012 as the second-biggest destination for African exports (again after the EU).

The Report hints heavily at a multilayered approach to engaging different African countries based on their divergent characteristics and appetites, such as levels of development, wealth and readiness for expanded trade engagements. This suggests an approach of pre-selecting "can-do" countries as regional leaders for individual free trade areas, after which other countries can be folded into these agreements when ready.

Figure 9.2

Exports to the United States by category for AGOA-qualifying countries

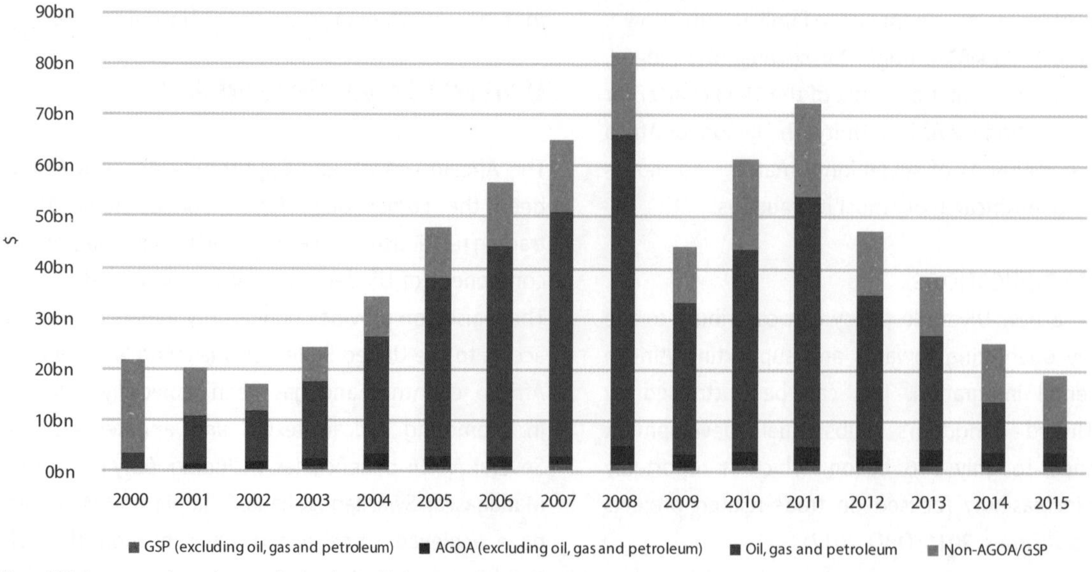

■ GSP (excluding oil, gas and petroleum)   ■ AGOA (excluding oil, gas and petroleum)   ■ Oil, gas and petroleum   ■ Non-AGOA/GSP

Note: GSP denotes products that would already qualify for access into the United States through the United States GSP preference scheme without AGOA. AGOA denotes products that benefit from additional AGOA-related preferences. Non-AGOA/GSP denotes exports to the United States that do not enjoy any preferential market access scheme.

Source: AGOA.info.

This presents a serious challenge to African regional integration, with the risk of fragmenting, rather than consolidating, African integration—despite "African regional integration" being stated as one of the three underlying principles of any new United States–Africa trade framework and the Report also identifying "small fragmented markets" as among Africa's key challenges to its competitiveness.

The Report ostensibly draws lessons from the EPAs, suggesting that the failure of EPA negotiations is due to regional approaches that draw in too many countries of divergent characteristics and interests. Ironically, then, the one concluded EPA (with SADC) is actually with the continent's most divergent countries, because it includes South Africa, Africa's most advanced economy.

The United States is likely drawing lessons instead from its experiences in Latin America and the failure of the FTAA (see Chapter 3), in which a one-size fits all trade agreement with no flexibilities for its less developed members was ultimately rejected by the 34 countries of the Americas. However, there is caution for Africa from the FTAA experience also. It resulted in the fragmentation of regional integration in Latin America (see Box 3.1 and associated text).

When considering its options beyond AGOA, Africa should remain cautious of such fragmentation and should instead press for a comprehensive continental agreement with the United States that is supportive of the CFTA.

Implications

African trade policy makers should be aware that such a US approach to individual "can-do" FTA countries may again be the desire of the United States and would present a major critical juncture against African continental integration. This is all the more reason to ensure the conclusion and implementation of the CFTA before 2025, so that African countries are prepared to address the United States as a single, cohesive and stronger entity, and individual FTAs do not pick apart the African regional integration agenda. The window of opportunity to secure the CFTA is now open—but will not remain so indefinitely.

Rise of emerging market economies: Brazil, China, India and Turkey

The rise of emerging market trade with Africa—we focus here on Brazil, China, India and Turkey—is momentous. Rank of Africa's export partners by value and Figure 9.3 show the rising importance of these countries in Africa's trade over the 15 years 2000–14. While the EU, Africa's most important trading partner in terms of value, has remained Africa's number one export destination, the United States, traditionally Africa's second-most

Figure 9.3

Rank of Africa's export partners by value

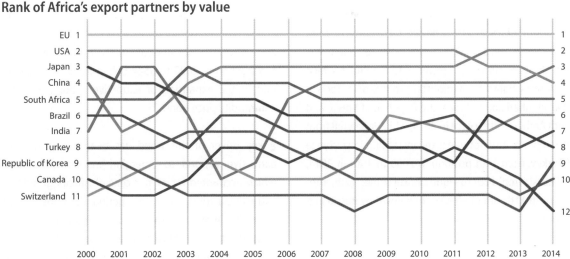

Source: ECA calculations using CEPII-BACI trade dataset.

Figure 9.4

Rank of Africa's import partners by value

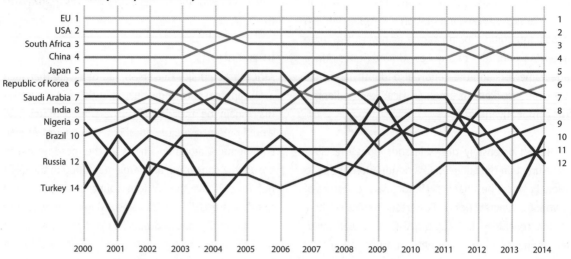

Source: ECA calculations using CEPII-BACI trade dataset.

important destination, was overtaken by China in 2012 and India in 2014. Japan, which was Africa's third-most important export destination in 2000, has been superseded not only by China and India, but also Brazil, South Africa and Switzerland (to which the value of gold exports has risen substantially) (Rank of Africa's export partners by value). Turkey, which was Africa's eighth most important export destination in 2000, rose to seventh in 2003–05, before falling behind Switzerland and the Republic of Korea to 10th place by 2014.

The story of Africa's most important import partners bears similarities (Figure 9.4). While the EU remains the most important source of Africa's imports, the United States was moved out of second place by China in 2005 and South Africa in 2012, before recovering to third above South Africa in 2013. South Africa fell one place, from third to fourth, as a result of China. India, which was Africa's eighth most important source of imports in 2000, climbed above Japan, the Republic of Korea, and Saudi Arabia to fifth place in 2014, while Japan fell from fifth to ninth. Also notable is the increasing importance of Turkey, from 14th position in 2000 to 10th in 2014, and Russia from 12th to eighth. Brazil comes 12th, after Nigeria in 11th, after being pushed down by Russia and Turkey.

The cumulative impact of the rise of emerging market economies has been an increase in Africa's exports to these markets from $18 billion to $130 billion over 2000–14, for an increase in the share of Africa's exports from 9 per cent to 15 per cent (Evolution of African exports and imports). Similarly, imports have risen

from $13 billion to $145 billion over the same period—equivalent to an increase in the share of Africa's imports from 8 per cent to 25 per cent.

This dramatic shift in the pattern of Africa's imports and exports reduces Africa's dependence on traditional trading markets such as the EU. The critical juncture posed by this better enables African countries to pursue alternative trade policy objectives that might otherwise be required. For instance, less reliant on the EU, African countries are better able to delay and turn down proposed EPAs.

The composition of Africa's trade with emerging markets is also important. As Africa's extractive industry exports and world commodity prices shows, the bulk of Africa's impressive almost three-fold increase in exports, from $194 billion in 2000 to $544 billion in 2014, is largely due to the expansion of extractive exports and the commodity price boom.[5]

A key driver of this trend has been the growth of extractive exports to emerging market economies, which accounted for 37 per cent of Africa's growth in extractive exports over this period (Composition of extractive industry exports to destination markets). By 2014, 88 per cent of products imported by China, India, Brazil and Turkey from Africa were extractive industry exports. In contrast, the impressive growth in intra-African exports has comprised a far larger share of non-extractive exports. Intra-African trade accounted for 32 per cent of Africa's total growth in non-extractive industry exports over 2000–14.

Figure 9.5

Evolution of African exports and imports

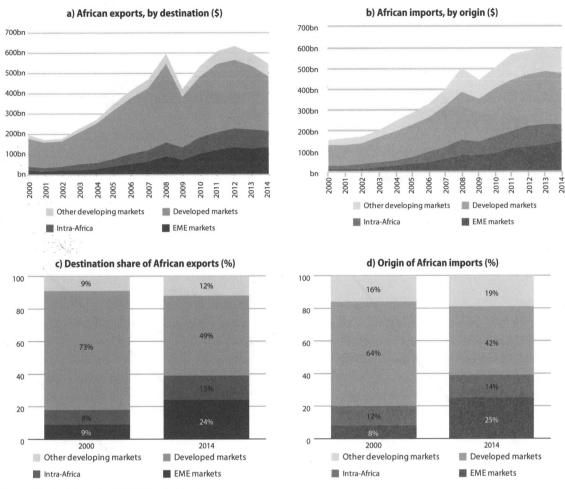

a) African exports, by destination ($)

b) African imports, by origin ($)

c) Destination share of African exports (%)

d) Origin of African imports (%)

Source: ECA calculations using CEPII-BACI trade dataset.

Figure 9.6

Africa's extractive industry exports and world commodity prices

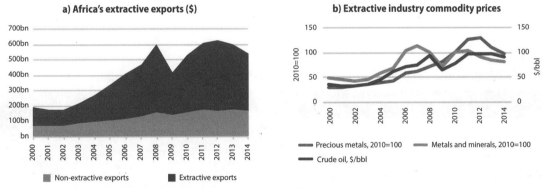

a) Africa's extractive exports ($)

b) Extractive industry commodity prices

Source: ECA calculations using CEPII-BACI trade dataset and World Bank Commodities Market Data.

Drilling down into these non-extractive exports, we see that intra-African trade experienced rapid growth in most categories of non-traditional exports, and notably more than other markets for consumer goods, capital goods, transport equipment, processed industrial supplies and processed food and beverages (Share of Africa's export growth in non-extractive export categories, by destination market), demonstrating the considerable importance of the intra-African market in boosting Africa's value-added industrial exports.

Figure 9.7

Composition of extractive industry exports to destination markets

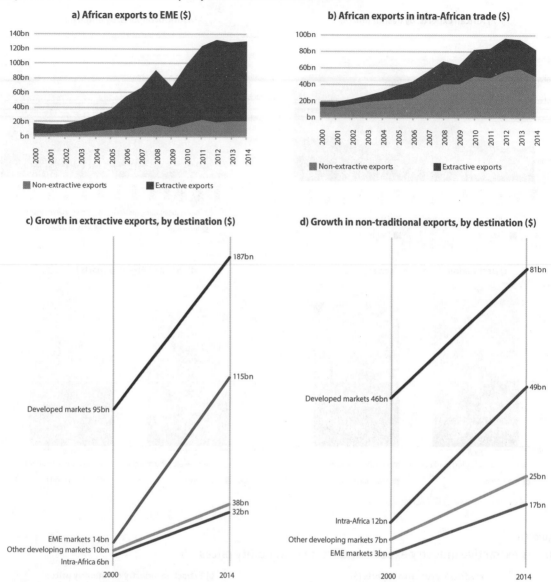

a) African exports to EME ($)

■ Non-extractive exports   ■ Extractive exports

b) African exports in intra-African trade ($)

■ Non-extractive exports   ■ Extractive exports

c) Growth in extractive exports, by destination ($)

187bn
115bn

Developed markets 95bn

38bn
32bn

EME markets 14bn
Other developing markets 10bn
Intra-Africa 6bn

2000   2014

d) Growth in non-traditional exports, by destination ($)

81bn
49bn

Developed markets 46bn

25bn
17bn

Intra-Africa 12bn
Other developing markets 7bn
EME markets 3bn

2000   2014

Source: ECA calculations using CEPII-BACI trade dataset.

Table 9.2

Share of Africa's export growth in non-extractive export categories, by destination market

Export category		EMEs	Intra-Africa	Developed markets	Other developing markets
Food and beverages	Primary	14	18	31	36
	Processed	3	51	30	15
Industrial supplies	Primary	43	15	6	36
	Processed	15	44	27	13
	Capital goods	3	57	28	12
	Transport equipment	5	45	45	6
	Consumer goods	5	46	30	19

Note: Values compare the export growth between three-year averages of 1998/2000 and 2012/14, and calculate the proportion of export growth attributable to each market such that $Share\ Attributable_{i,j} = (Exp_{i,j,t} - Exp_{i,j,t-1})/(Total_{i,t} - Total_{i,t-1})$, where i is the export category, j is the buying market, and t is the period. Exp is the value of exports of category i to market j while Total is the total value of exports from Africa of product j.

Source: CEPII's BACI dataset.

Implications

The dramatic rise in trade between Africa and emerging market economies reduces Africa's dependency on traditional EU trading partners, potentially giving the continent greater independence and flexibility in pursuing its trade objectives. However, Africa's exports to emerging markets have been concentrated in extractive industry exports, including products such as petroleum oils, gold and precious metals, and other metals and minerals. Current trade flows are unlikely to prove a panacea for African industrialization.

Intra-African exports, in contrast, tend to comprise an especially large share of industrial and value-added products that can be better used to support African industrialization. Moreover, the African market is expected to expand faster than any region in the world. African population growth is set to account for more than half the world's total by 2050 (UNDESA, 2015). Most African countries will more than double their populations in this period, and by the end, one in four people in the world will be African.

References

Aglionby, J., and H. Mance. 2016. "UK ready to shift focus of Africa aid to trade." *Financial Times*, 18 October.

Azmeh, S., and C. Foster. 2016. "The TPP and the digital trade agenda: Digital industrial policy and Silicon Valley's influence on new trade agreements." Working Paper Series No. 16-175. London: London School of Economics, Department of International Development.

Baldwin, R. 2014a. "The Impact of Mega-regionals: The Economic Impact." In World Economic Forum (WEF) (editor), *Mega-regional Trade Agreements: Game-Changers or Costly Distractions for the World Trading System?* Geneva: WEF.

———. 2014b. "The Impact of Mega-regionals: The Systemic Impact." In WEF (editor), *Mega-regional Trade Agreements: Game-Changers or Costly Distractions for the World Trading System?* Geneva: WEF.

Bauer, M., H. Lee-Makiyama, E. van der Marel and B. Verschelde. 2014. "The costs of data localisation: Friendly fire on economic recovery." Occasional Paper No. 3/2014. Brussels: European Centre for International Political Economy.

Bown, C. P., and H. L. Kee. 2011. "Developing Countries, New Trade Barriers, and the Global Economic Crisis." In M. Haddad and B. Shepherd (editors), *Managing Openness: Trade and Outward-Oriented Growth after the Crisis.* Washington, DC: World Bank.

Budree, A. 2017. *Policy considerations for e-commerce in South Africa and other African countries.* Policy Briefing. Johannesburg: Global Economic Governance Africa.

DfID (Department for International Development). 2017. *Economic development strategy: Prosperity, poverty and meeting global challenges.* London.

Draper, P., S. Lacey and Y. Ramkolowan. 2014. "Mega-regional trade agreements: Implications for the African, Caribbean, and Pacific countries." Occasional Paper No. 2/2014. Brussels: European Centre for International Political Economy.

Economist, The. 2017. "Donald Trump's presidency is about to hit Mexico: With a protectionist entering the White House, Mexico ponders its options." *The Economist*, 14 January.

European Parliament. 2015. *Protectionism in the G20.* Brussels: European Union. http://www.europarl.europa.eu/RegData/etudes/STUD/2015/549028/EXPO_STU(2015)549028_EN.pdf.

Financial Times. 2015. "The Doha round finally dies a merciful death." *Financial Times*, 21 December.

Harding, R., J. Smyth and M. Peel. 2017. "Asia looks to Beijing for new trade deals after Trump quits TPP." *Financial Times*, 24 January.

Inglehart, R., F. Ronald and P. Norris. 2016. "Trump, Brexit, and the Rise of Populism: Economic Have-Nots and Cultural Backlash." Faculty Research Working Paper Series RWP16-026. Cambridge, MA: Harvard Kennedy School.

Krugman, P. 2017. "Trump is Wimping Out on Trade." *New York Times*, 3 April.

Luke, D., and J. MacLeod. 2016. *Options for the UK's offer to developing countries on international trade: A perspective from Africa.* London: Overseas Development Institute. www.odi.org/publications/10480-brexit-and-developmenthow-will-developing-countries-be-affected.

Melendez-Ortiz, R. 2014. "The Impact of Mega-regionals: Discriminatory and Multilateralizing Potential of TPP and TTIP Provisions." In WEF (editor), *Mega-regional Trade Agreements: Game-Changers or Costly Distractions for the World Trading System?* Geneva: WEF.

Mendez-Parra, M., P. Papadavid and D. W. te Velde. 2016. "Brexit and development: How will developing countries be affected?" Briefing Paper. London: Overseas Development Institute. www.odi.org/publications/10480-brexit-and-developmenthow-will-developing-countries-be-affected.

Mold, A. 2017. "Much ado about nothing? The Impact of Brexit on the East African Community." Forthcoming.

Nguyen, M., and A. Ananthalakshmi. 2017. "TPP trade deal members seek to move ahead without U.S." *Reuters*, 19 May.

OECD (Organisation for Economic Co-operation and Development). 2011. *OECD Science, Technology and Industry Scoreboard 2011*. Paris. http://www.oecd-ilibrary.org/sites/sti_scoreboard-2011-en/06/10/index.html?contentType=&itemId=/content/chapter/sti_scoreboard-2011-64-en&containerItemId=/content/serial/20725345&accessItemIds=/content/book/sti_scoreboard-2011-en&mimeType=text/html. Accessed 3 October 2016.

Simon, M., and M. Mathieu. 2016. "Emergence of Mega-Regional Trade Agreements and the Imperative for African Economies to Strategically Enhance Trade-Related South–South Cooperation." Paper presented at the 19th Annual Conference on Global Economic Analysis, Washington, DC, 15–17 June.

Sommer, L., L. Calabrese, M. Mendez-Parra and D. Luke. 2017. *Smart Industrialization through trade in the context of Africa's transformation*. Policy briefing. London: Overseas Development Institute.

Stevens, C., and J. Kennan. 2016. "Brexit: a catalyst for EPA exit?" In M. Mendez-Parra, D. W. te Velde and L. A. Winters (editors), *The impact of the UK's post-Brexit trade policy on development: An essay series*. London: Overseas Development Institute. www.odi.org/publications/10480-brexit-and-developmenthow-will-developing-countries-be-affected.

te Velde, D. W. 2016. "Scenarios for UK trade policy towards developing countries after the vote to leave the EU." In M. Mendez-Parra, D. W. te Velde and L. A. Winters (editors), *The impact of the UK's post-Brexit trade policy on development: An essay series*. London: Overseas Development Institute. www.odi.org/publications/10480-brexit-and-developmenthow-will-developing-countries-be-affected.

Ueno, A. 2013. "Multilateralising Regionalism on Government Procurement." OECD Trade Policy Paper No. 151. Paris: OECD.

UNDESA (United Nations Department of Economic and Social Affairs). 2015. "World population projected to reach 9.7 billion by 2050." http://www.un.org/en/development/desa/news/population/2015-report.html. Accessed 7 April 2017.

USTR (Office of the US Trade Representative). 2016. *Beyond AGOA: Looking to the future of US-Africa trade and investment*. Washington. https://ustr.gov/sites/default/files/2016-AGOA-Report.pdf.

Endnotes

1   ECA modelling shows that effective and timely implementation of the CFTA would offset the negative outcomes of the three MRTAs on Africa. Instead of reducing them, Africa's total exports would increase by $27.5 billion. Intra-African trade would expand by $40.6 billion and the majority of this increase would be in industrial products such as electronics; machinery and transport equipment; chemical, textile and metal products; and processed food. This would help to support industrialization and structural transformation (Mevel and Mathieu, 2016).

2   Possible examples are fertilizers, machines, spare parts and packaged materials.

3   See, for example, the proposed WTO rules in the US paper (JOB/GC/94).

4   JOB/SERV/239/Rev.1 31 October 2016 Australia et al. "Domestic Regulation – Administration of Measures."

5   Extractive exports here include petroleum oils (SITC 33), gas (SITC 34), non-ferrous metals (SITC 68), metalliferous ores and metal scrap (SITC 28), crude fertilizers and minerals (SITC 27), coal, coke and briquettes (SITC 32), and the remaining precious metals in HS 71, uranium (HS 2844), and the basic iron products of HS7201–HS7206.

Chapter 10

Phase 2 Negotiations—Competition, Intellectual Property Rights and E-commerce

The scope of the Continental Free Trade Area (CFTA) includes disciplines on competition policy and intellectual property rights. Negotiations on these two areas are expected to be launched after the conclusion of the negotiations on goods and services. These disciplines are not usually included in a classic free trade agreement but would create a level playing field for all economic operators and facilitate policy convergence through common regimes in areas that affect liberalization of goods and services.

This chapter outlines the main issues that negotiators will face during phase 2 of the CFTA negotiations: that of competition policy and intellectual property rights. It also recommends phase 2 negotiations on e-commerce and the digital economy, for the CFTA to provide a platform to harmonize an African digital industrialization strategy.

Competition

In a free market, business should play a competitive game, and consumers should be the ultimate beneficiaries. Competition and consumer protection laws and policies therefore should promote competition, protect consumers' rights, make markets work better (including through the participation of informed consumers), improve efficiency in individual markets and enhance competition among businesses in any sector. Competition puts businesses under constant pressure to offer the best possible range of goods and services at the best possible prices. Consumer protection provides information and rights awareness to consumers, enforces rules against unfair and misleading commercial practices, promotes product safety and integrates consumers' interests across all economic sectors. It aims to balance the existing asymmetry between traders and consumers.

Dealing with anti-competitive practices in Africa

Developing countries have been one of the groups most affected by anti-competitive practices. For instance, data published in 2004 by the American Bar Association indicated that the total value of the potentially "cartel-affected" imports to developing countries was $51.1 billion, largely because developing countries account for a large proportion of consumers of products from international cartels. It affects them as producers as well; for example, by limiting access to technology, thus raising barriers to entry.

One example is the $200 million damage to vitamin consumers in six developing countries (India, Kenya, Pakistan, South Africa, Tanzania and Zambia) as documented by the Consumer Unity and Trust Society in 2003. While the cost and the harm of the anti-competitive practices are well known, it is surprisingly that there has been relatively little response by developing country governments or developing country consumers to these cartels.

In another example, a study by the University of Johannesburg in 2012[1] found that in Kwa Zulu Natal (South Africa), a cartel mark-up on the price of building materials was estimated at 51–57 per cent. Another study, under the auspices of UN Conference on Trade and Development (UNCTAD) Research Platform,[2] presented data from selected developing countries whereby 249 major "hard-core" cartels were prosecuted in more than 20 developing countries from 1995 to 2013. An original and relatively simple methodology has been developed to estimate cartels' economic harm, in price overcharges and consumers' welfare losses (Box 10.1).

Much has taken place on the African continent to address these challenges, including laws, regulations and institutions. Côte d'Ivoire, Egypt, Gambia, Kenya, Malawi, Namibia, South Africa, Tanzania, Tunisia and Zambia have all enacted laws. However, other countries do not have legislation in place (including the Democratic Republic of the Congo, Ghana and Nigeria). Moreover, a lack of implementation and enforcement of such laws presents a barrier for addressing competition at the continental level. The CFTA should design competition arrangements for a diversity of countries with varying institutional capacities for competition issues.

A regional approach is needed to deal with cartels, mergers and acquisitions and abuse

African competition authorities are increasingly dealing with anti-competitive practices that have a regional dimension, including cartels and abuse-of-dominance cases. A study by the African Competition Forum on Cement (covering Botswana, Kenya, Namibia, South Africa, Tanzania and Zambia) found anti-competitive practices in the cement sector. Cement is one product where a whole region can be cartelized, providing a powerful case study of how collusion can operate regionally. A bread cartel,[3] which was addressed in 2005 in South Africa, raised the price of bread in two other SACU countries (Lesotho and Swaziland).

These examples reveal the importance of regional integration in dealing with cross-border anti-competitive practices. Without safeguards to deal with anti-competitive practices, businesses and dominant firms—domestic (and especially) foreign—can abuse their market position. The abuse may take different forms, including predatory behaviour (eliminating local competition), price-fixing cartels and other market-sharing agreements. Such anti-competitive practices reduce choice, increase prices and thus deny consumers and other excluded producers the benefits of trade liberalization.

In the CFTA, member states have widely divergent territories, firm types, sizes and development levels. Dominance is therefore likely to be an issue in the continental market. At issue is that national competition laws operate on a "territorial" basis: They address the anti-competitive practices by foreign actors in their domestic market, but they do not address domestic actors using restrictive practices in other territories. Sectors where anti-competitive practices are suspected include agriculture (specifically fertilizers), communications (possible price fixing for telecoms), air transport, energy, retail and road freight.

The CFTA can draw on the experiences of a few regional economic communities (RECs): the East African Community (EAC) established a community Competition Act; the Southern African Development Community (SADC) Treaty prescribes an enforcement cooperation network; and the SACU Treaty advocates for cooperation in competition law and policy enforcement.

Resolving overlapping frameworks and harmonizing legal systems

In EAC, the newly established Competition Authority will have to evaluate what mechanisms can be used to implement its EAC Competition Act, given that only Kenya and Tanzania have operational national competition authorities. Burundi and Rwanda are at advanced stages of establishing national competition authorities, and Uganda is in the process of enacting a new competition law. The CFTA must decide at the continental level how to implement competition arrangements when countries are diverse in their competition institutions. Also diverse are Africa's various legal systems, notably on interpretation and harmonization, in order to put in place cooperation systems that "speak" to each other.

An article in the African Law and Business Journal,[4] which addressed the EAC Competition Authority, urged Burundi, Rwanda and Uganda to enact or implement competition laws. The article referred to the future interplay between EAC and the Common Market for Eastern and Southern Africa (COMESA) regarding the overlapping memberships of some countries and the lack of laws in others, plus how to deal with current cross-border anti-competitive practices.

COMESA has been active in dealing with cross-border mergers.[5] One benefit of having an institution like COMESA is that it closes the gap of absent extra-territorial application of national competition laws by addressing concerns spanning jurisdictions. Another is that it reduces the regulatory burden of merger notification for cases with a regional dimension, saving time and money. COMESA also promotes a sense of certainty and predictability because it removes the possibility of different outcomes and timings. A similar system should be designed for the CFTA.

Continental competition framework to support the CFTA

To implement any decision for developing competition law and policy in the CFTA negotiations, it will be necessary to design an effective competition framework. Existing competition policy and legislation at national and regional levels must be taken into account (for example, COMESA and EAC, the SADC competition enforcement cooperation arrangement and a SACU arrangement in draft stage). These can form a useful starting point for the various approaches in each region, as well as a reflection on practice for the CFTA.

There are some areas that the existing RECs do not deal with, such as rules governing private restraint on trade. The CFTA has the opportunity to close such gaps and strengthen existing competition law domestically and regionally; to build enforceable rules or secure member states' consensus to fix the gaps in the legislative and enforcement framework; and to allow for countries with no competition laws to enact some legislation in conformity with the agreed approach.

The following are the immediate priorities for CFTA member states:

- Agree on a common objective that the CFTA competition framework seeks to achieve.

- Identify and understand the provisions of the present competition laws, identify gaps in each of them and rationalize all systems in the framework of the CFTA competition law.

- Establish other parameters/areas of law that need to underpin the CFTA competition framework and formulate the key features of those laws, synchronizing them with the preferred approach that allows for seamless implementation. These may include rules on consumer protection, standard setting and customs law implementation, state aid and subsidies, procurement laws, adjudication and dispute resolution systems and rules.

- Secure the cooperation of the member states, their enforcement agencies, adjudicative bodies and the mirroring agencies at the regional level.

- Rationalize key issues of public international law, regional law and domestic law that may affect the legality of a CFTA competition framework that can be effectively ratified or incorporated in each member state. These could include the competition- and consumer protection–related rules under World Trade Organization (WTO) law and the bilateral trade and investment agreements that member states are already party to.

- Take into account existing ad hoc networks, such as the African Competition Forum (ACF), and examine its recent role in technical cooperation on competition law and enforcement, analysis, awareness raising and capacity building. ACF has 34 members, including 30 national competition agencies and four regional agencies. The ACF could be a good foundation to gauge which system—a cooperation network or a supra-national institution—would be most appropriate for the CFTA.

- Give attention to consumer protection issues, including how to distinguish them from competition issues and how to deal with diversity in legislative and institutional arrangements.

Proposal for a CFTA Enforcement Cooperation Protocol on Competition Law and Policy

A draft protocol should be developed after a careful analysis of every member state. It is recommended that such a protocol be enforced through a cooperation network (similar to the European Union [EU] Competition Network) operated by the CFTA Secretariat. Alternatively, member states could establish a supranational competition institution covering the work being done at regional and national levels. This second option would be more challenging to coordinate with existing frameworks, including the new ones. It would also be more costly.

A draft protocol on consumer protection is also needed. In line with the revision of the United Nations Guidelines on Consumer Protection in 2015,[6] to include electronic commerce and financial services, attention needs to be accorded to consumer protection issues. There is a need for in-depth analysis on consumer protection to design the appropriate instrument for the CFTA.

Intellectual property rights and innovation[7]

The CFTA provides Africa with an opportunity to progress along a new path for knowledge governance.[8] Such governance includes intellectual property (IP), and encompasses the range of formal or informal, legal, economic, social, cultural, political and technological structures that determine who can appropriate or access knowledge, and how (Open AIR, 2016). In the process, Africa can redefine the agenda for the negotiation of IP issues in trade agreements affecting the global North and South. To do so, African countries must first address their own fundamental priorities for IP, given the collaborative dynamics of innovation on the continent (de Beer et al., 2014).

The CFTA can provide a framework to address IP rights; there is, however, a backlash against the inclusion of IP in free trade agreements.

Intellectual property in trade agreements: Cautionary tales

Procedural and substantive failures around IP issues have contributed to a backlash against trade agreements. Concerns initially arose during the negotiation of the WTO's Agreement on Trade-related Aspects of Intellectual Property (TRIPS), which heavily favoured the interests of the most developed countries. IP issues were also among those that fostered aversion to the Trans-Pacific Partnership (TPP), especially those relating to digital and cultural policies and medicinal patents (Geist, 2016; Balsilie, 2016; IMF, 2016; Mui, 2017).

Agreements focused solely on IP issues have had an equally poor fate. The most notable misstep was when a group of countries tried to promote an ill-advised IP policy through an undemocratic process— which resulted in the Anti-Counterfeiting and Trade Agreement (ACTA). While Morocco was the only African country among the strange bedfellows involved in the ACTA,[9] its experience should be a warning for the rest of the continent. The procedural and substantive

problems with ACTA have been well documented in dozens of working papers,[10] a special journal issue,[11] and even a book (Roffe and Seuba, 2015). It has been called a "lesson in how not to negotiate an agreement on international cooperation in law enforcement" (Weatherall, 2011).

In each of these contexts, protectionist sentiments emerged to preserve national sovereignty over knowledge governance, put limits on the commodification of information, and safeguard the public domain. There is a common theme: Since the negotiation of TRIPS in the 1990s, countries at all stages of development, aided by an engaged civil society, have become more astute on IP issues. They have refused to stand idly by as inequitable IP provisions are folded into international trade agreements. It is clear to negotiators what will not work; what is not clear is how to update the previous century's outdated IP templates.

Closer to home, EAC's experience with anti-counterfeiting policy and regulation also raises a red flag. EAC prepared a draft policy on anti-counterfeiting, anti-piracy and other intellectual property rights violations and the EAC Anti-Counterfeit Bill, neither of which have been adopted (Ncube, 2016). The main criticism was that they espoused TRIPS-plus provisions, which were totally inappropriate for EAC's least-developed country (LDC) member states.[12] (The Kenyan High Court's struck down equivalent provisions in the Kenyan Anti-Counterfeit Act.)[13] EAC's mistake was to underestimate the complexity of IP issues, which led to inappropriate reliance on the rhetoric of lobbyists and inadequate consultation with local experts and civil society.

Despite the withdrawl of the US from the TPP and the demise of ACTA and similarly flawed agreements, regional trade integration involving IP remains possible. Canada and the EU overcame difficult odds to salvage the Comprehensive Economic and Trade Agreement (CETA).[14] Negotiations towards a Regional Comprehensive Economic Partnership between Australia, China, India, Japan, New Zealand, Republic of Korea and 10 ASEAN countries are ongoing.[15] And prospects for pan-African economic integration are good.

However, lessons must be learned from the experience of initiatives that failed: More must be done to ensure that negotiations are inclusive and consultative; that they regard implications for personal freedom of expression and privacy; and that they are respected as consistent with democratic legitimacy and development aspirations.

Africa's fragmented IP frameworks

As detailed in *ARIA VII*, Africa's IP regulatory framework is fragmented. An agreement regarding IP in the CFTA would need to overcome challenges on three levels: multiple subregional IP organizations, the proliferation of IP matters in RECs, and misalignment with the continent's overall development agenda.

Subregional IP organizations

The first challenge is that two subregional IP organizations exist: the African Regional Intellectual Property Organization (ARIPO) and the Organisation Africaine de la Propriété Intellectuelle (OAPI). And several African Union (AU) members do not belong to either of these two organizations, including regional powerhouses Egypt, Nigeria and South Africa.

Language is one issue dividing ARIPO and OAPI, with the former operating mostly in English-speaking countries, and the latter in French-speaking countries. Structural differences also exist. ARIPO member states have different IP frameworks, while OAPI member states subscribe to a unified IP legal system. *ARIA VII* identified the challenges of this prevailing model of two regional IP organizations that are independent from RECs and disengaged from the regional integration agenda.[16]

The following are four difficulties that flow from this bimodal issue:[17]

- Policy and institutional incoherence.

- Focus on the grant of patent rights at the exclusion of giving significant guidance on the exercise of those rights.[18]

- Harmonization efforts sometimes reducing the policy space available to member states.

- Lack of an IP cooperation framework for negotiating bilateral trade and investment agreements leading to the further degradation of policy space when Member States sign such agreements.

Negotiations surrounding Pan African Intellectual Property Organisation (PAIPO), conducted under the auspices of the AU, may help to address some of these difficulties, but a guiding framework will be necessary for any new organization. OAPI and ARIPO have recently concluded a third cooperation agreement with the intention to more closely align their work in 2017–21.[19] Previous agreements were signed in 1996 and 2005.

Regional economic communities

The second challenge is that there are multiple IP-related initiatives being led, or planned, by the RECs that do not include existing or proposed regional IP organizations. At least eight RECs have, to some extent, sought to address IP matters.

REC initiatives are necessary because of the independent disengagement of ARIPO and OAPI from regional integration efforts. One such REC initiative is the IP Agenda of the Tripartite Free Trade Area (TFTA). In 2016, to become more engaged in this area, ARIPO signed a memorandum of agreement with COMESA for COMESA's IP unit and programme to work closely with ARIPO.[20] This arrangement has implications because it indirectly feeds into the TFTA and ultimately the CFTA.

Misalignment with the continental agenda

The third challenge is the misalignment between the CFTA, PAIPO and Agenda 2063. The AU's adoption of Agenda 2063 includes the following aspiration: "An integrated continent, politically united, based on the ideals of Pan Africanism and the vision of Africa's Renaissance."

The Agenda 2063: First Ten-Year Implementation Plan 2014-2023[21] sets out implementation goals for the CFTA and PAIPO. The creation of the African Economic Community (AEC) and PAIPO are prioritized under the framework and Institutions for a United Africa.[22]

Alignment would secure the ultimate goal of protecting existing policy spaces from erosion by trade agreements; the national efforts to craft appropriate IP legislative and policy frameworks; and the management of regional cooperation.

Innovation in Africa is different: An IP Framework must reflect that

The innovation requirements of Africa differ fundamentally from those elsewhere in the world. Studies of African innovation have taught us that it occurs mainly in the informal sector and is not heavily reliant on conventional means of knowledge governance and appropriation (Kraemer-Mbula and Wunsch-Vincent, 2016; de Beer et al., 2013).

Even if formal IP protections were appropriate in such contexts, which they are not, research shows that such formal protection "cannot exist in the absence of strong institutions, including not just IP offices that register, disclose and education, but also a culture of respect and enforcement of IP rights" (de Beer et al., 2013). Such respect is impossible to build as long as the substantive provisions of IP law are far removed from the realities of everyday life in Africa.

For example, in an eight-country comparative study of copyright's impact on the access to education in Africa, researchers concluded that the challenge with copyright is not lack of legal protection, nor that countries' copyright laws do not comply with international standards. Rather it is the "lack of awareness, enforcement and exploitation of copyright." The study further concluded that even where there is awareness of copyright principles, people are unwilling to comply with principles that do not reflect their socio-economic reality (Armstrong, 2010). These observations must guide the procedural and substantive content of the CFTA IP framework.

A CFTA framework for solving IP issues

A CFTA IP agreement would primarily be an internal intra-African initiative in that it would serve as a binding statement of the signatory countries' position on IP matters. It would also serve as an important external guide for these countries when they negotiate free trade agreements (FTAs) with countries beyond the continent. In other words, these internal issues would guide signatory member states in their trade agreement negotiations with other countries or regional groupings.

Substantively, a CFTA IP agreement should emphasize flexibility, the importance of a transition period, and the preservation of policy space to create limitations and exceptions that suit countries at various stages of economic development.

Such an agreement should also recognize the particular IP challenges and opportunities of the African continent.

Box 10.1

Innovation in Nollywood

The Nigerian movie industry, also known as Nollywood, offers an excellent example of phenomenal growth not because of IP, but *despite* IP. The lax intellectual property regime in the industry has given rise to creative patterns of engagement between the industry and actors in the informal movie distribution networks in Nigeria. A formal approach to intellectual property would alienate and isolate members of such informal networks and criminalize them.

The industry instead continues to develop creative ways of leveraging the partnership and contractual potential of these informal distributors who are now critical stakeholders in the Nollywood value chain. Some members of the industry recognize that while intellectual property may be desirable, unbalanced implementation of IP policies often privileges few in the industry. It also comes at the expense of the cultural contexts that favour collaborative creativity and the enduring desires of individual artists and creators for exposure. The industry recognizes that such exposure holds greater opportunities and potential for creators.

Gradually, Nollywood continues to evolve, calling attention to the need for pragmatism and sensitivity in the making of intellectual property policy. Typical, formal IP regimes would be ill suited to this environment.

There are similar patterns with musicians in Egypt (Rizk, 2014). Africa's vibrant cultural industries provide an opportunity to explore how best to tailor intellectual property in the context of authentic African innovation and creativity. Piracy in emerging economies, including in Africa, is more a market failure than an IP problem (Karaganis, 2011).

A made-in-Africa approach to the agreement is possible because the negotiating parties have common Afro-centric values and priorities and are confronted by the same IP-related issues. The following two subsections provide suggestions for the appropriate principles to be included in the CFTA framework agreement on IP.

Procedural principles
Cognizant of the mistakes made with IP issues in other bilateral, plurilateral or multilateral trade agreements and treaties, a CFTA framework agreement on IP must be negotiated with a regard for democratic legitimacy. The root causes of illegitimacy include:

- The secrecy in which the negotiations were conducted and the associated lack of transparency of these negotiations.

- The lack of inclusive consultations with all relevant stakeholders—instead, negotiating parties appeared to follow a selective consultation process that typically excluded civil society.

- Negotiations taking place outside international bodies such as the World Intellectual Property Organization and WTO that have rules for public engagement and the sharing of information.

- Ignoring, concealing or downplaying the implications for personal freedoms, such as freedom of expression and privacy.

- Rushed processes that appear to propose simplistic solutions to complex problems

In 2012, similar procedural concerns were raised in Africa regarding the draft PAIPO statute. African IP experts then argued that "[t]he draft PAIPO statute is the result of a non-transparent process without open consultations with relevant stakeholders including civil society. No drafts of the statute have previously been issued let alone publicly discussed."[23] This (traditional) approach needs to be replaced by a more open, holistic and transparent process that includes all relevant stakeholders.

Thus in response to changed dynamics and heightened public expectations in the area of international law and policy making—and to minimize the risk of public push-back and failure—the CFTA negotiations must ensure fair, balanced and widely supported policy through democratic, open, transparent, inclusive and diligent processes. These include wide public consultations and debates. The processes and methods followed by international organizations, such as the World Intellectual Property Organization, and national lawmakers involve public access to draft documents as well as public hearings; these processes should be followed.

Substantive principles
The substantive issues that should be covered in an appropriate IP framework for Africa include the following.

Copyright. To encourage innovation and creativity, domestic frameworks should be established that are balanced, sound, coherent, practically relevant, context appropriate and responsive to digital technologies. This requires appropriate provisions pertaining to the scope of protection, including exceptions and limitations, and the terms of protection. With regard to exceptions and limitations, the inclusion of express provisions (these would cater to diabled persons; temporary copies; parallel importation; orphan works and text; and data mining) is imperative.

Patents. The agreement should not simply seek to secure the grant of patents for the sake of improving Africa's position in ranking systems. The continent needs better patents that are granted according to patent law that adequately address access to, for example, the need for medicines. This will require a more robust approach to using existing flexibilities and more aggressively leveraging policy space. (As noted, some of the RECs have provided leadership on this.) The CFTA Agreement ought to consolidate these efforts by incorporating them, instead of reinventing policies andr guidelines. National patent laws require substantive examination, and patent office capacity and processes need to be strengthened so that such examination is credible and effective.

Trademarks. Less conventional trademark-based strategies, such as communal trademarks, are better suited to translate the development vision of African producers into marketable inventions, because they combine elements of external protection with those of internal openness, inclusion and collaboration appropriate to the local conditions. However, such strategies are currently under-used in Africa; there is no domestic framework to aid their use and protection is lacking, and legal frameworks are tailored for the protection of conventional trademarks. The CFTA negotiations afford a platform to promote IP policies tailored to achieving some form of *sui generis* framework for the protection of the less conventional trademarks at the national level.

Traditional knowledge. In terms of IP and trade policy, traditional knowledge remains a key strength for Africa. It finds expression in major areas innovation and knowledge, including in medicine, agriculture, biotechnology and food. Not only has the continent been forceful at the global stage to galvanize support for global protection of traditional knowledge, there are also initiatives aimed at regional harmonization. The call is for negotiators to recognize the positions and policy statements in these protocols and guidelines when crafting an IP policy for the CFTA.

Competition. Competition policy and law can complement IP and trade rules to increase access to and reduction in the price of IP rights–protected knowledge and technology, if properly used. To be effective, IP rules and competition principles must be balanced. For this purpose, the provisions in the TRIPS Agreement (identified above) are indispensable and should be considered in the CFTA negotiations. The complex issue of the intersection between IP rights and human rights, which formed a challenge for some international trade agreements, should not be ignored in the CFTA negotiations. Key international human rights treaties contain provisions with links to IP rights. The focus of the CFTA negotiations should be how best to integrate human rights issues with IP law and policy, especially regarding questions of access to educational materials and health care in Africa. The CFTA negotiations should consider exploring the stipulations of maximum instead of minimum standards in the area of user-focused flexibilities, such as exceptions and limitations.

E-commerce

The global economy is experiencing rapid digitization, including shifts in traditional economic sectors and the emergence of new digital products and services. In Africa, e-commerce is expected to grow at 40 per cent annually over the next decade (KPMG, 2013). New

business models will continue to appear (Box 10.3), altering Africa's trade and industrialization pathway.

The raw material underpinning the digital economy is data. Data enables new business models to dominate markets through personally targeted advertisements across areas including logistics, agriculture, health, education and energy usage. As with all resources, there are considerable governance, political and security implications arising over its ownership and usage.

The growing size of the digital economy and the control of data has attracted proposals for international rules at the WTO. These would include measures to liberalize cross-border data flows and an open Internet, and to prohibit digital customs duties, data localization rules, local content requirements, and source code disclosure rules. They would also amount to TRIPS-Plus protections for certain parts of digital intellectual property. These rules could constrain the policy space that Africa needs to implement its own digital industrialization plans to harness the growing digital economy.

African countries face a digital divide with developed countries. Africa is the only region where mobile broadband penetration remains below 20 per cent, it has the fewest fixed-broadband subscriptions, at less than 1 per cent, and it faces among the highest prices for fixed broadband plans (many of which also have the slowest speeds) (ECA and South Centre, 2017). Africa also faces difficulties with international banking transactions as its domestic banks are not well linked to international banks; African small and medium-sized enterprises struggle to list on international e-market places or platforms; and delivery is constrained by poor transport infrastructure (ECA and South Centre, 2017).

Features of the digital economy, such as network effects, also foster the concentration of very large companies. This creates scope for anti-competitive practices, such as predatory pricing, which could challenge the development of domestic digital companies in African markets.

Another challenge accompanying the growth of the digital economy is the rise of automation. This runs the risk that tasks previously undertaken by manufacturers in developing countries will instead be automated in developed countries. A popular example is the case of Adidas relocating some of its manufacturing processes back to Germany to produce shoes with robots and 3D printers rather than with Asian labour (*The Economist*, 2017). Such new business models have clear implications for traditional manufacturing-based, export-oriented industrialization strategies. The evolution of such businesses models will affect the position at which developing countries can enter global value chains.

African industrialization will therefore require a rethinking of the continent's digital economy and the role of African data. An African digital industrial strategy is recommended to strategically address the opportunities and disruptive challenges offered by the digital economy. An active digital industrial strategy can include market creation for domestic firms, joint public–private ventures, government-engineered

venture capital markets, support for tech incubators and improved digital education.

It will be important to consider what kind of regional strategy can be put in place to process and gain value from Africa's own data (ECA and South Centre, 2017), to ensure that the small and fragmented African market does not prohibit Africa's successful start-ups from scaling up to competitive sizes. Here the CFTA can provide a platform for consolidating e-commerce rules and regulations, and establish an integrated market for Africa's own digital businesses. The rise of the digital economy will pose many challenges for African countries on the back of the digital divide, but with the right policies, it could be an opportunity to leap-frog development.

References

Adler, S. 2013. "Data – A Raw Material to be Mined." *IBM Big Data & Analytics Hub* (blog), 9 September. http://www.ibmbigdatahub.com/blog/data-raw-material-be-mined.

ARIPO (African Regional Intellectual Property Organization). 2016. *ARIPO Guidelines for the Domestication of the Marrakesh Treaty.* Harare. http://www.aripo.org/publications/copyright-publications/item/150-aripo-guidelines-for-the-domestication-of-the-marrakesh-treaty.

————. 2017. "OAPI and ARIPO Sign New Cooperation Agreement." http://www.aripo.org/news-events-publications/news/item/168-oapi-and-aripo-sign-new-cooperation-agreement.

Armstrong, C., J. de Beer, D. Kawooya, A. Prabhala and T. Schonwetter. 2010. *Access to knowledge in Africa: The role of copyright.* Claremont, South Africa: UCT Press.

Armstrong, C., and T. Schonwetter. 2016. "Conceptualising Knowledge Governance for Development." *The African Journal of Information and Communication* 19: 1–17 http://wiredspace.wits.ac.za/handle/10539/21749.

Atkinson, R. 2016. Testimony before the Committee of Ways and Means Trade Subcommittee hearing on "Expanding US Digital Trade and Eliminating Barriers to Digital Exports," Washington, DC, 13 July. http://waysandmeans.house.gov/event/hearing-expanding-u-s-digital-trade-eliminating-barriers-u-s-digital-exports/.

AUC (African Union Commission). 2015. *Agenda 2063: First Ten-Year Implementation Plan 2014–2023.* Addis Ababa: African Union. http://www.nepad.org/resource/agenda-2063-first-ten-year-implementation-plan-2014-2023.

Australian Government Department of Foreign Affairs and Trade. n.d. "Regional Comprehensive Economic Partnership." http://dfat.gov.au/trade/agreements/rcep/Pages/regional-comprehensive-economic-partnership.aspx.

Balsilie, J. 2016. Evidence to the Standing Committee on International Trade, 42nd Parliament of Canada, 1st Session, Number 15, Ottawa, 5 May. http://www.parl.gc.ca/HousePublications/Publication.aspx?Language=e&Mode=1&Parl=42&Ses=1&DocId=8245091.

COMESA (Common Market for Eastern and Southern Africa). 2017. "COMESA and ARIPO Sign MoU." http://www.comesa.int/comesa-and-aripo-sign-mou/.

Drache, D., and S. Trew. 2010. "The Pitfalls and promises of the Canada-European Union Comprehensive Economic and Trade Agreement." Working Paper. https://papers.ssrn.com/sol3/papers.cfm?abstract_id=1645429.

de Beer, J. 2013. "Applying best practice principles to international intellectual property lawmaking." *IIC-International Review of Intellectual Property and Competition Law* 44 (8): 884–901.

de Beer, J., C. Armstrong, C. Oguamanam and T. Schonwetter. 2014. *Innovation and intellectual property: Collaborative dynamics in Africa.* Claremont, South Africa: UCT Press.

de Beer, J., K. Fu and S. Wunsch-Vincent. 2013. "The informal economy, innovation and intellectual property – Concepts, metrics and policy considerations." Economic Research Working Paper No. 10. Geneva: World Intellectual Property Organization. http://www.wipo.int/edocs/pubdocs/en/wipo_pub_econstat_wp_10.pdf.

Drahos, P., and J. Braithwaite. 2002. *Information Feudalism: Who Owns the Knowledge Economy?* London: Earthscan Publications.

EC (European Commission). 2017. "EU-Canada Comprehensive Economic and Trade Agreement (CETA)." http://ec.europa.eu/trade/policy/in-focus/ceta/.

ECA (United Nations Economic Commission for Africa) and South Centre. 2017. *The WTO's Discussions on Electronic Commerce.* Analytical Note SC/AN/TDP/2017/2. Geneva: South Centre.

Economist, The. 2017. "Adidas's high-tech factory brings production back to Germany: Making trainers with robots and 3D printers." *The Economist,* 14 January. http://

www.economist.com/news/business/21714394-making-trainers-robots-and-3d-printers-adidass-high-tech-factory-brings-production-back.

Geist, M. 2016. Evidence to the Standing Committee on International Trade, 42nd Parliament of Canada, 1st Session, Number 15, Ottawa, 5 May. http://www.parl.gc.ca/HousePublications/Publication.aspx?Language=e&Mode=1&Parl=42&Ses=1&DocId=8245091.

IMF (International Monetary Fund). 2016. *World Economic Outlook Update*. Washington, DC. https://www.imf.org/external/pubs/ft/weo/2016/update/02/pdf/0716.pdf.

Karaganis, J. (editor). 2011. *Media piracy in emerging economies*. New York: Social Science Research Council. http://ssrc-cdn1.s3.amazonaws.com/crmuploads/new_publication_3/%7BC4A69B1C-8051-E011-9A1B-001CC477EC84%7D.pdf#page=15.

Kawooya, D. 2012. "A New Course for the Pan African Intellectual Property Organization is Urgently Needed." Letter to the 5th African Union Ministerial Conference on Science & Technology. *Change.org*, 18 October. https://www.change.org/p/a-new-course-for-the-pan-african-intellectual-property-organization-is-urgently-needed.

KPMG. 2013. *Africa's Consumer Story*.

Kraemer-Mbula, E., and S. Wunsch-Vincent (editors.) 2016. *The Informal Economy in Developing Nations: Hidden Engine of Innovation?* Cambridge, UK: Cambridge University Press.

Miles, J. 2016. "The EU-Canada Comprehensive Economic and Trade Agreement (CETA), Backroom Ministrations and Secret Negotiations." *Global Research*, 3 November. http://www.globalresearch.ca/the-eu-canada-comprehensive-economic-and-trade-agreement-ceta-backroom-ministrations-and-secret-negotiations/5554419.

Mui, Y. 2017. "Withdrawal from Trans-Pacific Partnership Shifts U.S. Role in World Economy." *Washington Post*, 23 January.

Ncube, C. B. 2015. *Intellectual Property Policy, Law and Administration in Africa: Exploring Continental and Sub-regional Co-operation*. London: Routledge.

Ncube, C. B., T. Schonwetter, J. de Beer and J. Oguamanam. 2017. *Intellectual Property Rights and Innovation: Assessing Regional Integration in Africa (ARIA VIII)*. Cape Town: Open African Innovation Research. http://www.openair.org.za/publications/intellectual-property-rights-and-innovation-assessing-regional-integration-in-africa-aria-viii/.

Open AIR (Open African Innovation Research). 2016. *Annual Report 2016: From Project to Partnerships*. http://www.openair.org.za/open-air-annual-report-2016.

Rizk, N. 2014. "From De Facto Commons to Digital Commons? The Case of Egypt's Independent Music Industry." In J. de Beer, C. Armstrong, C. Oguamanam and T. Schonwetter (editors), *Innovation & Intellectual Property*. Claremont, South Africa: UCT Press.

Roffe, P., and X. Seuba (editors). 2015. *The ACTA and the Plurilateral Enforcement Agenda: Genesis and Aftermath*. Cambridge, UK: Cambridge University Press.

UNCTAD (United Nations Conference on Trade and Development). 2014. *RPP Report: Measuring the Economic Effects of Cartels in Developing Countries*.

Weatherall, K. 2011. "Politics, Compromise, Text and the Failures of the Anti-Counterfeiting Trade Agreement." *Sydney Law Review* 33 (2): 229–262.

Endnotes

1   See https://ryan-hawthorne.squarespace.com.

2   http://unctad.org/en/PublicationsLibrary/ditc-clpmisc2014d2_en.pdf.

3   http://www.saflii.org/za/cases/ZACT/2010/9.html.

4   http://www.africanlawbusiness.com/news/6944-competition-law-developments-in-africa-i.

5   Covering sectors such as agriculture, electronics, pharmaceuticals, energy, automobiles, construction, mining, insurance, logistics, information technology, aviation, hospitality, telecommunications, packaging, payment systems, water treatment, retail, beverages, commodity trading and textiles.

6   http://unctad.org/en/Pages/DITC/Competition-Law/UN-Guidelines-on-Consumer-Protection.aspx.

7   This section is derived from a Background paper authored by Ncube et al. (2017).

8   For a conceptualization of "knowledge governance," see Armstrong and Schonwetter (2016).

9   The parties to ACTA were Australia, the United States of America, Japan, the 27 nations of the European Union, Switzerland, Canada, Singapore, South Korea, New Zealand, Morocco and Mexico.

10   Available at http://digitalcommons.wcl.american.edu/research/.

11   Focus Issue: Intellectual Property Law Enforcement and the Anti-Counterfeiting Trade Agreement (ACTA) (2011) 26 (13) American University International Law Review available at http://digitalcommons.wcl.american.edu/auilr/vol26/iss3/.

12   Ibid.

13   Act No. 13 of 2008, in *Patricia Asero Ochieng, Maurine Atieno and Joseph Munyi v The Attorney General*, HCCC Petition No. 409 of 2009.

14   CETA was signed on 30 October 2016. See EC (2017) available at http://ec.europa.eu/trade/policy/in-focus/ceta/. For some major controversies around the negotiation of CETA, see generally de Beer (2013), Drache and Trew (2010) and Miles (2016).

15   Negotiations for the Regional Comprehensive Economic Partnership were launched in Cambodia on 20 November 2012. See Australian Government Department of Foreign Affairs and Trade (n.d.).

16   Note 2, 72.

17   Ibid, 73.

18   On copyright, ARIPO has given guidance through issuing a guide on the Marrakesh Treaty that is broad enough in its scope to encompass the exercise of user rights. See ARIPO (2016).

19   ARIPO (2017).

20   COMESA (2017).

21   AUC (2015).

22   Ibid, 65–66.

23   See Kawooya (2012).

24   See Atkinson (2016).

25   For a more detailed explanation, see Adler (2013).